patch!

Cath Kidston

patch!

Cath Kidston

PHOTOGRAPHY BY PIA TRYDE

Quadrille
PUBLISHING

Introduction

Patch! is the most recent of my craft books, and this time I've taken the title very literally. As anyone who's visited my stores will recognise, all my designs are about reinterpreting the past and taking a more contemporary, colourful approach to tradition. Once I started to explore the fascinating theme of patching and pieced work, I became inspired by the possibilities. I discovered a huge wealth of historic ideas, and I've come up with over thirty projects which bring a new twist to these versatile techniques.

Patchwork evolved as a thrift craft in an era when new fabrics were scarce and expensive, so it is right on trend with today's ethos of sustainability and recycling. It simply involves sewing together pieces of fabric to create a larger design, a technique which encompasses everything from meticulously hand-stitching dozens of tiny silk diamonds to running up an over-sized tablecloth from a bundle of vintage tea towels. I've enjoyed playing with these changes in scale and speed, and like the idea that whilst some of the projects will take many relaxing hours to stitch, others can be completed in an afternoon.

Appliqué is patchwork's sister craft, and instead of sewing the fabric together, cut-out shapes are sewn, or patched, on to a background. I've always felt like a virtuous homemaker when doing any domestic repairs, so I've even included some proper patching – a simple square on a worn-out knee. There are more involved techniques too, like the beautiful 'Hidden Circles' pattern used for the hand-appliquéd laundry bag on pages 58–61 and the intricate embroidered jigsaw of 'Crazy Patchwork' used on the cushion on pages 80–83.

I wanted to include something for everybody, so whatever your level of expertise, I hope you'll find a project that you'll enjoy making. My own first patchwork project was worked with paper templates, in English style, so maybe the Child's Pentagon Ball on pages 96–99 or the Hexagon Pincushion on pages 130–131 would make a good starting point for hand stitching. Moving on to machined patchwork, there's a range of pretty and practical bags, embellished garments and home accessories. You'll find cushions of all shapes and sizes, two full-size bedcovers, a curtain panel and a comfortable beanbag made out of plaid blankets.

The thrill of searching for vintage fabrics at boot sales and flea markets has long been one of my greatest pleasures, and I've always loved collecting textile scraps. Patchwork is the ideal way to use these: shirtings, silk scarves, dress prints, fine cotton, ticking and embroidered linen all appear alongside my own prints, and the more eclectic and unexpected the combination of fabrics, the better the result.

My intention in this book has been to broaden the boundaries of traditional patchwork and to take it back to its early roots by re-using fabric in innovative ways. Search through your ragbag for hoarded scraps, look through the following pages, and be inspired.

Cath Kidston

Patch! Basics

This introduction includes all the stitchery skills you'll need to create the projects, along with hints and tips on choosing equipment, using a sewing machine and finding fabrics, as well as some background to the various patchwork and appliqué techniques involved.

Essential Equipment

One of the best things about patchwork and appliqué is that you don't need any specialist equipment to get started: don't forget that all those wonderful antique quilts were made with nothing more complicated than fabric, scissors, thread and a needle or basic sewing machine. Here's a quick guide to all the tools and equipment that you'll need to make the projects in this book – the 'sewing kit' that appears in each materials checklist.

PINNING AND STITCHING

Keep all your hand-sewing needles together in the felt pages of a needle book, where they are easily visible – they do tend to get lost in the filling of a pincushion. They come in various lengths and thicknesses, from a chunky '1' down to a delicate size '10', each intended for a particular purpose. A mixed starter pack will contain:

• long 'embroidery' or 'crewel' needles, with narrow eyes to accommodate stranded threads

• medium-length 'sharps' for general use, which have small round eyes for sewing thread

• short 'betweens' or 'quilting' needles, slender enough to slip easily through several layers of fabric. These are also good for joining English-style paper patches but may prove too small for some stitchers.

A large safety pin or bodkin is useful for threading cords through gathering channels. Smaller safety pins are always handy and are good for temporarily securing layers of fabric. Fine (0.6mm) steel dressmaker's pins are suitable for cotton and other fine fabrics as they won't leave any marks, but I prefer longer glass-headed pins, which show up well, especially on woollens and patterned cloth. Store them safely in a tin or pincushion, but have a small magnet to hand in case they go astray.

MEASURING AND MARKING

All stitchers need an accurate tape measure, and if you're going to make quilts or curtains, an extra long one is invaluable. Use a 15cm ruler for checking seam allowances and hems. A sharp HB pencil is all you need for transferring markings and outlines, but you may prefer a dressmaker's pen. Use tailor's chalk or a chalk pencil on textured and darker fabrics.

CUTTING OUT

Invest in the best steel-bladed scissors you can afford and they'll last you a lifetime. Dressmaking shears are useful for cutting out large items, but smaller scissors are preferable for patches. Keep a spare pair of household scissors for paper and don't ever use your fabric scissors for templates or they will quickly become blunt! Embroidery scissors with sharp points will snip seams and threads efficiently. Most patchworkers also have a rotary cutter, quilter's ruler and a cutting mat – you can learn more about these overleaf.

SEWING AND TACKING

Stock up with spools of white and mid-grey thread for piecing several different fabrics and a couple of bright colours for tacking, so stitches are easy to spot and unpick. All-purpose sewing thread is good for hand or machine piecing. It comes in a wide range of colours – pick a slightly darker shade if you can't find an exact match for your fabric. If you also buy a thread plait, made from many short interwoven lengths, you'll always have the right colour for small sewing tasks.

ODDS AND ENDS

A well-stocked work basket contains one or more thimbles – essential if you're to avoid punctures when hand sewing. Silicone versions mould to your finger tip and are easier to use than traditional metal. Seam rippers look frightening with their sharp points but are indispensible for unpicking stitches when things go wrong. A lint roller is handy for picking up threads and slivers of fabric. Finally, an old-fashioned block of beeswax for strengthening thread adds sweet scent to your sewing kit.

Cutting Out

Whether you are preparing the front and back panels of a cushion cover or a stack of patches ready for a quilt, accurate measurement and precise cutting are essential if your completed project is going to have a professional finish with the pieces joined correctly together.

PAPER PATTERNS

If you are making up a bag, cushion or pillowslip, you'll need rectangular panels of various sizes for the straps, gussets, lining and backings, as well as the elements needed for the patchwork or appliqué. The dimensions for each panel are given in the 'cutting out' list for the project. When two measurements are given for a rectangular piece of fabric, the width measurement is always given first, then the length. Transfer these measurements on to dressmaker's pattern paper, which is ruled with a grid of centimetre squares, then cut out along the printed lines. Pin the patterns to your fabric and cut out around the outside edge with your largest scissors. When measurements are given for individual patches, as for the curtain or washbag, draw your pattern up on 1mm grid graph paper in the same way.

If you are making a large backing for a finished quilt, it's easier to lay the fabric out flat and pin the quilt top to it, then cut the edge. This way you'll know the two fit together exactly and there's no measuring up to do.

TEMPLATES

On pages 156–160 you'll find the templates required for many of the patchwork and appliqué projects, including several geometric shapes alongside the 'Dresden Plate' petals used in the bag and cushion. There is an appliqué Stanley and a couple of rabbits, plus the embroidery guide for the red work hens.

The geometric shapes are a pentagon for the child's toy ball on pages 96–99, a hexagon for the pincushion on pages 130–131 and a diamond for the Harlequin Bag on page 46–49. All of these are made using the English patchwork technique of stitching over paper templates. The best way to make the multiple templates needed is to photocopy the page on to thin card, then cut out the shape you need. Draw round this card shape on to scrap paper and old envelopes. You can make your own templates in other sizes by adjusting the size on your printer or by using a simple drawing programme on your computer, or with a bit of school day geometry, a ruler and a pair of compasses.

The outline template supplied for the Bunny Sweater on pages 140–141 is intended for iron-on appliqué, so all you have to do is to trace the reversed silhouette directly on to the paper side of the fusible bonding web. The motif for the Bunny Blanket on pages 104–105 and the Stanley appliqué for the Personalised Dog Bed on page 132–135 are stitched on to their backgrounds and so are the right way round. Trace them onto kitchen paper and cut out around the pencil line to make the templates.

GO WITH THE GRAIN

Press your fabric well before cutting out, to remove the creases. A light spray of starch or silicone fabric stiffener should get rid of any that are especially stubborn. Look at it hard and you'll see it's made up from two sets of interwoven threads which lie at right angles to each other. These are called the warp and weft, and the direction in which they lie is called the 'grain' of the fabric. You should always position your templates so that the straight edges lie parallel with one set of threads (along the grain), or the final patches will distort and pull when stitched together.

PLANNING YOUR PATCHES

If your fabric prints have an all-over, small-scale pattern the placement of the templates isn't important, because all the patches will be more or less the same. When working with stripes and checks, however, you should plan the positioning a little more carefully, so that one edges of the patch will be in line with the stripes or squares. You may also want the patches to be symmetrical or matching, which will require extra fabric.

Pick out individual motifs or flower sprays from other larger-scale or sprigged designs, centering them within the patch, as for the flowered silks for the Boudoir Cushion on pages 76–79 and the nursery prints on the Pentagon Ball on pages 96–99. If you make them all the same (known as 'fussy cutting') you can create some interesting effects. I did this with this Hexagon Pincushion and can just imagine how effective this would look repeated across the surface of a whole quilt!

Organise your prepared patches in zip-up sandwich bags, ready to be stitched, and if you're feeling really efficient, you can label them too.

ROTARY CUTTING

This relatively new innovation speeds the cutting out process, especially when making a large project like the Star Throw on pages 106–109 or the Curtain Panel on pages 114–117. It also enables you to cut several layers of fabric at once. Three separate tools are required:

• A rotary cutter, which acts like a very sharp pastry wheel. There are several types and sizes, but all have a round, rotating blade set in a handle. A 45mm diameter is best for patchwork. Check that it can be securely retracted to prevent accidents and always handle with care.

• A quilter's ruler, made from clear perspex and etched with a grid of centimetres or inches. The largest size, used for panels and extra large patches, is 15 x 60cm. Along with a 15cm square that is marked with 45 degree angle (for triangles), this should cover most of your needs. Glue small strips of fine sand paper to the back of the ruler to stop it slipping.

• A cutting mat, with a self-healing plastic surface. If you have space, get one to cover the table top. The extra expense is worth it in the long run.

There are two ways to rotary cut and it's a good idea to practise on some spare fabric first, to get the hang of the technique. For panels and larger patches, place the fabric on the mat and line up the ruler with the printed grid. Hold the cutter so that the blade is upright and lies against the ruler, then press down firmly and glide it away from you. Do the same, matching the ruler to the correct distance, on the other three sides.

You can also use the grid marked on the ruler to measure your patches. Line one corner up with the grain of the fabric and cut along these two edges. Turn the ruler the other way round, so that the lines that indicate your required size line up with the cut edges, then slice off the fabric from these two sides.

Machine Know-how

Only a few *Patch!* projects are stitched completely by hand. All the others involve an element of machine sewing, whether it's joining patches together, seaming a backing for a cushion or making an entire bag or pillowcase. Don't let this put you off if you're a novice stitcher. Nothing requires a great degree of technical knowledge and there's only one curved seam in the book... everything else consists of basic straight seams and hems and you'll learn how to do these on the following pages.

CHOOSING A MACHINE

Some patchworkers like to use antique hand-operated machines, preferring the accuracy and slow rhythmic pace produced by turning the handle. The basic straight stitch made by an old Singer is all you really need to join patches.

Modern machines, however, have a swing needle which moves from side to side to create zigzag and overlocking stitches. These are useful for neatening and strengthening raw seams and for edging appliqué patches. Any other functions are a bonus, so if you're buying your first machine don't be tempted to overspend on a digital model that links to your laptop. A solid entry-level machine (never the very cheapest, which often are not substantial enough to deal with heavier cloth) should get you started and you can always upgrade if you decide to do a lot of sewing.

THE TECHNICALITIES

All machines work in the same way by linking two threads – one on each side of the fabric – to produce an interlinked stitch. The upper reel is threaded under tension along the arm and down through the needle. The lower thread is wound onto a small bobbin housed in a case that is set into the flat bed. Take time to read through the manufacturer's manual to learn a bit more about how to use your individual machine and to get to know some technical terms.

These are the four main parts with which you should be familiar.

• The presser foot, as its name suggests, presses down on the fabric as it passes under the needle. It's operated by a small lever that lifts it up and down. It should always be lowered before you start stitching. You will need to change the pressure when sewing thicker fabrics, such as the blanket used for the dog bed, and the manual will tell you where to do this. Machines are supplied with several feet – you'll need just the basic one for all your seaming and the narrow zip foot when inserting a zip or sewing piping.

• The top end of the machine needle is attached to the arm and the upper thread passes through a hole in its tip. Like sewing needles, these come in different gauges and a 'universal' 70–80 should be fine when working with cotton fabrics. You'll need to adjust the needle's position when the zip foot is in place.

• The reverse stitch control is very useful. It enables you to work a few stitches in the opposite direction to the seam at both the beginning and end of the line. This stops the thread unravelling and strengthens the join.

• The flat throat plate has a small hole through which the needle passes to pick up the lower thread. It is engraved with a series of parallel lines: you can just see these on the photograph opposite. The adjacent figures indicate the distance between the needle and the line in millimetres, in other words, the width of the seam allowance.

LOOKING AFTER YOUR MACHINE

You'll need to do a bit of routine maintenance to keep your machine running smoothly. Always store it away in the carrying case or dust cover and oil occasionally as directed in the manual. Clear lint and dust from the bobbin case with the tiny brush supplied. It's a good idea to change the needle frequently as it will become blunt with use and cause the stitches to become irregular.

Sewing Basics

Any specialist patchwork and appliqué methods are explained in detail, with step-by-step illustrations, in the Patch! Projects section. Here's a quick tutorial covering the other basic sewing and finishing techniques you will need to complete the projects.

SEAMS

Whether you are joining two tiny square patches or the front and back of a pillowcase, the basic seaming method is the same. On larger panels you may be asked to neaten the edges with a zigzag or overlock stitch. Pin the two pieces with right sides facing and the raw edges and corners aligned. You can then tack larger panels if you wish, by joining with a row of long running stitches, removing the pins as you go.

STRAIGHT SEAM

Machine stitch along the specified seam allowance, using the side of the foot or the lines on the flat bed to gauge the distance between the needle and the edge. Press the seam allowance open, as shown, or press both sides to the left or right according to the instructions. This is particularly important when joining patches. Working a few stitches in the opposite direction at each end reinforces the seam.

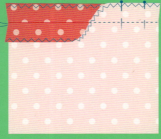

CORNER SEAM

When you come to a corner, keep the needle in the down position and lift the presser foot. Pivot the fabric and sew along the next edge. Trim the allowance to within 3mm of the stitches, then turn right side out and ease the corner into shape with a blunt pencil.

CURVED SEAM

There's only one curved seam used in all the projects, but as it's on Stanley's ear it's an important one! On an outside curve you need to reduce the amount of fabric in the allowance so that the seam will lie flat. Do this by snipping a series of evenly spaced little notches to within 2mm of the stitching, all round the curve.

CLOSING A GAP

When making a stuffed toy or the pincushion you'll need to leave a gap in a seam through which to add the filling. Press back the allowance on each side beforeturning through, add the filling, thenpin the two edges together and slip stitch, passing the needle through the folds for a neat finish.

HEMS

A raw edge can be finished by folding it over and stitching down the turning, as around the top of the Dresden Plate Tote Bag on pages 66–69, or by covering it with a narrow length of bias binding for a more decorative look, which I did for the Circles Laundry Bag on pages 58–61.

SINGLE HEM

Neaten the edge of the fabric, if directed, then with the wrong side facing, fold the edge back to the required depth.

Sometimes all you'll need to do at this stage is press it down, or you may have to machine stitch, just below the zigzag.

DOUBLE HEM

Fold and press the first turning to the given measurement, then make the second turning which may be the same or slightly deeper. Pin and tack, then machine stitch close to the inner fold or slip stitch by hand.

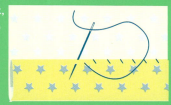

BOUND HEM

I bound the top edge of the Circles Laundry Bag on pages 58–61 by hand. Press the binding in half and slot it over the edge, tacking it down as you go. At the corners, mitre the surplus. Sew down with small stitches, catching down both folded edges at the same time.

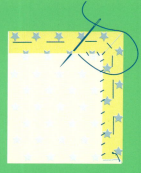

HANDLES

This method for making fabric handles could be used instead of webbing for the Tweed Messenger Bag on pages 38–41 and the Sugarbag Doorstop on pages 120–123. Cut a fabric strip twice the finished width, plus 2cm. Press under a 1cm turning along each long edge, then press in half. Tack edges together and machine stitch 3mm from the edge. Lastly, remove the tacking.

MITRED CORNER

To mitre the corner of a single hem, press both hems and unfold. Turn in the corner at 45 degrees and press. Trim off the corner to within 5mm of the diagonal crease, refold and stitch down.

REINFORCING STITCHING

When a handle is sewn to a bag the join has to be reinforced, so that it can bear weight. Tack one end of the handle (slightly more than its width), behind the bag.

Starting at the top right corner, sew a square or rectangle of machine stitches over the top. Now sew diagonally across to bottom left, back along the bottom edge and up to the top left corner.

Traditional Techniques

Even if it's just replacing a lost button, sewing by hand is so enjoyable! English Patchwork was the first 'proper' sewing technique that I learnt, and I will always remember the process of joining together scraps of fabrics to make something new. There are four other classic hand techniques which have been adapted for the projects in this book.

ENGLISH PATCHWORK

Also known as Paper or Mosaic Patchwork, this centuries-old method is used primarily to piece accurate geometric shapes. The iconic hexagon quilt, so popular in the 1970s, is made in this way. Each patch is tacked over a paper template and the folded edges then sewn together. The aim at one time was to work eight or nine stitches per centimetre but we are all a little more forgiving today! A traditional way of preventing the thread from fraying as it passes repeatedly through the fabric is to draw it firmly over a block of pure beeswax.

CRAZY PATCHWORK

The Victorians invented this extravagant patchwork style, indulging their love of ornament and decoration to the full. They made fantastic confections of brocade, velvet and satin in deep colours and with rich textures, then encrusted them still further with intricate embroidery stitches. It's a combination of appliqué and patchwork, in which fragments of cloth are laid out on a plain background and fitted together like a jigsaw to create a fragmented, crazed surface. The fabric is then stitched down and the seams embellished. I've reinterpreted this technique in a fresher, lighter way with my Crazy Patchwork Cushion on pages 80–83 and for the vase that forms the basis of the Flower Picture on pages 136–139.

CATHEDRAL WINDOW

A relatively recent development, dating from the 1920s, the 'windows' are usually worked with a frame of white cotton and patterned diamond-shaped 'panes'. For the Boudoir Cushion on pages 76–79 I chose a vintage cream sateen as the background for a collection of pastel lingerie silk. Like the Suffolk Puff, this is a technique that's always explored further by innovative stitchers, and it works well with a darker background. There is a variation called Secret Garden, where an extra layer of fabric is placed within the folded square, just before the points are stitched down. This is revealed when the edges are turned back and adds extra colour to the inside of the petals.

SUFFOLK PUFFS

You won't fail to notice that this is my favourite technique at the moment and, as you'll see, I've actually managed to incorporate puffs into five of the projects. In the following pages they are used to make a cushion cover, to embellish a cardigan and to create a necklace... see if you can spot the other two. Sometimes called yo-yos or pom-poms, they are undergoing something of a revival at the moment. They are very versatile and quick to make. All you have to do is cut out a circle of fabric, sew down a turning all around the edge and draw up your thread to gather up the fabric. To speed up this process you can even buy clever little gadgets that help you create puffs in a range of different sizes.

HAND APPLIQUÉ

Folded edge appliqué is another technique with a long history. It involves cutting out fabric shapes, tacking a narrow hem around the edge, then sewing the patch to a background. In mid-nineteenth century America it was used to create wonderfully colourful and ornate quilts, especially around the seaport of Baltimore. Folding narrow hems can prove fiddly, so for the Circles Laundry Bag shown opposite and the Dresden Plate Tote Bag and Cushion on pages 66–71, you'll learn you how to tack the fabric over a template first to create perfect curves.

Hand Appliqué

This term derives directly from the French verb 'appliquer' which translates as 'to put on', consequently the technique involves cutting out small pieces of fabric and literally putting them on to a background. The traditional way of doing this by hand is explained on the previous page, but you can also attach the shapes with iron-on fusible bonding web – a much quicker method. This type of appliqué was explored in my first sewing book *Make!*, where it was used to recreate designs from some of my most popular fabrics. This time simpler shapes and motifs are used as patches, to add decoration to bags, garments and cushions.

BONDING WEB

Fusible bonding web is a sheet of translucent paper with a backing of heat-activated adhesive. There are several types and weights sold under different trade names, but they are all do the same thing. Ensure you buy the correct one for your appliqué fabric: if you use heavyweight web on silk or lawn the adhesive will show through the fine weave.

All you have to do is trace the reversed outline of the motif directly on to the paper side of the web. Cut it out roughly and with the adhesive side downwards, iron the paper to the wrong side of the appliqué fabric (following the manufacturer's guidelines). Now trim precisely around the pencil line. Peel away the paper, place the motif on the background in its final position, and press with a hot iron to fuse the adhesive. Broderie Perse shapes (see below) can also be fixed down with bonding web. Cut a piece that is slightly larger than your chosen part of the fabric, iron it to the wrong side, then cut around the printed outline.

EDGING YOUR MOTIFS

Your motifs are now in place but the edges are still raw, so you'll need to neaten them to stop them fraying. The functional way to do this is by machine, with a narrow, closely-spaced zigzag or with one of the more decorative stitches. Use a matching thread if you want an invisible border (like that on the Hounds Bag on pages 54–57). A hand-embroidered finish would always be my first choice however, and on pages 28 and 29 you'll find instructions for some of my favourite stitches.

BRODERIE PERSE

If you've ever snipped out images from a magazine and glued them into a scrapbook (a rainy-day pastime for most kids at some stage), you'll be familiar with the idea behind Broderie Perse. This is another French term, meaning Persian Embroidery, although it's not from Persia and it isn't really embroidery! The earliest surviving examples date from the 1600s when exotic floral chintz was first imported into England by the East India Company. Individual flowers, leaves, birds and butterflies were cut from this highly-prized fabric and then sewn on to a plain background to form new pictorial designs.

Any printed fabric can be used for Broderie Perse and you can really let your imagination run riot when it comes to collaging the motifs. I found some fabulous full-blown roses on a furnishing remnant to fill the vase in the Flower Picture, shown at almost full-size on pages 138–139. This project also incorporates vintage buttons and some hand embroidery to draw in the stems and embellish the flowers. A more random interpretation can be found on the linen Appliqué Tea Towel in the country kitchen on pages 128–129. These nostalgic designs came from a length of homemaker-style barkcloth curtaining and are edged with an unobtrusive buttonhole stitch, worked in thread to match the fabric background. The third Broderie Perse project is the Hounds Bag on pages 54–57, which recycles motifs from a much more delicate fabric – a twill silk headscarf.

Embroidery &
Embellishments

Both patchwork and appliqué are so decorative in themselves that they scarcely need any more surface decoration, but sometimes an extra detail can provide the finishing touch that makes a piece really stand out. Embellishment can be understated – a line of simple stitches around a tweed patch for example – or an integral part of the overall design, like the feather stitch around the patches on the Crazy Patch Cushion.

BUTTONS
Buttons of all shapes and sizes can be used for practical purposes – fastening a pillowcase or securing a bag handle – or as pure ornament. I picked out a varied selection from my tin of vintage buttons to add highlights of colour and texture to the Flower Picture on pages 138–141. Keep an eye out for old cloth laundry buttons and those made from early plastics, wood or pressed glass. Mother-of-pearl buttons have a neutral, natural finish that goes well with any fabric and you can add extra colour by sewing them on with bright embroidery thread.

However carefully you stitch, there may be times when your seams don't line up perfectly at the corners. Joins that are not quite precise can be concealed with the careful placing of a few buttons... this secret cheat worked especially well on the Boudoir Cushion and it's also good for misaligned square patches.

LACE, RIBBON AND CORD
I'm not usually keen on a lot of frilly lace, but used with discretion it can be very effective. The centre panel of the Rose Knitting Bag on pages 50–53 is frramed with a simple triangular edging, which proved the perfect counterpoint to the white rose and daisy print. In the same way the fine

pink piping around the Crazy Patch Cushion on pages 80–83 picks up the colour of the embroidery thread and outlines the patchwork square.

If you don't fancy making your own piping and setting it into the seam you can simply sew a length cord or other trimming around the edge of the finished cushion. Shiny or cotton cord also makes an attractive drawstring for large and small bags, and you can finish off the ends with a few beads or a fabric tab. Ricrac is a good alternative to lace, and can be used as a border or inserted in seams to give a discreet scalloped finish. Children's garments are an exception to minimalism and a ribbon bow gives character to the Bunny Sweater on pages 140–141.

STITCHERY
You can create some interesting embellishments with just a few hand embroidery stitches, all of which are shown on the next two pages. Edge appliqué patches with blanket or coral stitch and cover plain seams with feather and fly stitches. Personalise your projects with a monogram worked in back or chain stitch. I have just discovered figural red work embroidery which I chose for the embroidered Red Hens Bag on pages 42–45.

There are several ways to transfer the hen or any other photocopied outline on to fabric. The simplest is to use dressmaker's carbon paper. Sandwich together the fabric, the face-down carbon, then the photocopy, taping down each layer so they don't shift. Draw firmly over the outline with a ballpoint pen. Alternatively you can improvise a light box. Masking tape the outline to a bright window, tape the fabric to the paper and trace the outline with a sharp pencil.

Embroidery Stitches

All the stitching in this book is worked with a long-eyed needle and stranded embroidery cotton or tapestry yarn. Both threads come in a skein that is held together with one wide and one narrow paper band. Hold on to the narrow band and pull the loose end of the thread gently to withdraw it, then cut off a 45cm length. Stranded embroidery cotton is made up of six loosely twisted threads, which can easily be separated. Working with all six strands gives bold stitches and three a medium line whilst two create a much finer effect. The project steps will always tell you how many to use.

RUNNING STITCH

This basic stitch is used in English patchwork for tacking fabric to templates and on a smaller scale, for quilting. It provides the simple outline around each square on the Tweed Messenger Bag on pages 38–41. The stitches should all be the same length, as should the spaces between them.

BACK STITCH

I used this for the wool CK cipher on the Tweed Messenger Bag on pages 38–41 and to 'draw' the red work hens on the embroidered Red Hens Bag on pages 42–45. Bring the needle up one stitch length from the beginning of the line, then take it back to the start point. Come up again one stitch length ahead of this first stitch and continue, keeping the stitches regular.

STRAIGHT STITCH

Tiny upright or angled straight stitches can be used to anchor appliqué patches or to add details, like the Blanket Bunny's whiskers on pages 104–105. Simply come up at A and down again at B to make a short straight line.

SATIN STITCH

So called because of its smooth, shiny finish, this is consists of a series of straight stitches worked alongside each other in the same direction, from A to B. Vary the lengths to fill the shape being worked.

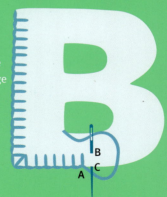

BLANKET STITCH

This classic edging stitch appears on the Appliqué Tea Towel on pages 128–29 where it was used to neaten the edge of the motifs. Come up at A, then take the needle up to B, through the fabric and out directly below at C. Loop the thread under the needle and pull it through. Repeat this sequence to the end.

TAILOR'S BUTTONHOLE STITCH

A reinforced version of blanket stitch, this was used on the Bunny Sweater on pages 142–143. Starting at A, take the needle down at B, in front of the thread and bring the point through at C. Loop the thread from left to right and pull through, lifting the needle so that the thread forms a small knot at the edge of the motif.

CHAIN STITCH

Use this for flexible wide outlines like the stems on the Flower Picture on pages 138–139 and for monograms or other lettering. Bring the needle out at A, then reinsert it the same place. Bring the point out at B and loop the thread from left to right under the needle. Hold the loop down and pull the needle through gently to draw up the thread. Finish off with straight stitch over the last loop.

LAZY DAISY STITCH

Single chain stitches make good petals but I worked a few long thin ones to make the tuft at the top of the Blanket Bunny's carrot! Work as for chain stitch, anchoring each loop with a short straight stitch.

SINGLE FEATER STITCH

This variation on blanket stitch appears on the Flower Picture on pages 138–139 where it's used to edge the circular patches. Come up at A and insert the needle at B. Bring the point out at C, below B and in line with A. Loop the thread under the needle and pull through.

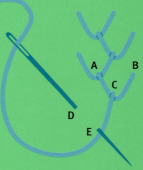

FEATHER STITCH

Look out for this pretty stitch on the embroidered Crazy Patch Cushion on pages 80–83 and the Red Hens Bag on pages 42–45. Keep all the stitches the same length and at the same angle on either side for a neat appearance. Come up at A and take it down at B forming a loose stitch. Bring the point out at C, over the thread and pull through. Work the next angled stitch from D to E over the looped thread. Repeat these two stitches to the end.

FLY STITCH

This is another good stitch to work over seams and I used it as an alternative to feather stitch on the Flower Picture vase on pages 138–139. Come up at A and take the needle back down at B, then back up at an angle, at C. Pull through over the thread and go down again, directly below at D. Repeat this stitch to form a continuous row.

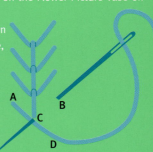

Choosing Fabrics

When it comes to selecting fabrics for patchwork and appliqué, you'll find the choice is limitless! Specialist quilt shops and department stores are piled high with rolls of new cloth and are a good source of remnants and fat quarters (the quilter's term for a 55 x 50cm rectangle). Don't forget, however, to search charity shops, flea markets and even the back of your own wardrobe for old fabrics to recycle in true patchwork tradition. For the items in this book I've used everything from silk scarves and tablecloths to hand-woven tweed and antique curtain material. The following guidelines will help you pick the right fabric for your own projects.

VINTAGE TEXTILES

Almost any vintage fabric can be used to make patchwork, as long as it is in good condition. Check carefully for stains, rust-marks or signs of wear cut away these areas. Holding the fabric up to the light will enable you to see where the threads have worn thin. Even if it appears to be in good condition, I always like to launder old cotton or linen first – the fabric often needs freshening up and if it can stand up to a gentle machine wash, it will be strong enough to sew.

COTTON AND LINEN

There is a wealth of wonderful domestic linen out there that's just waiting for you to come along: look out for hand-embroidered napkins, runners, pillowcases and dressing table mats. Fine quality sheets make good backings for projects like the Circles Laundry Bag on pages 58–61 or the Star Throw on pages 106–109 and even humble stripey tea towels come into their own when patched together to make a tablecloth. Printed versions are a good alternative to buying wider and more expensive fabrics – I was especially pleased with the Floral and Spot Tote Bag on pages 34–37, which is made from co-ordinating floral and spotty tea towels.

SILKS AND WOOLLENS

The rich textures of velvet, satin and silk add another dimension to patchwork, but these fabrics aren't always easy to work with. Delicate silk patches need to be backed with interfacing to hold their shape – as with the colourful Harlequin Bag on pages 46–49 – or combined with firmer fabrics. The 'Cathedral Window' technique used for the Boudoir Cushion on pages 76–79 is a good example of how to do this. Projects like floor cushions, that will get a lot of hard use, need to be made from larger patches of thicker materials, so old blankets are ideal for these (especially if you've had moths in the house).

PRINTS AND PATTERNS

Small-scale floral dress fabrics are the classic choice for patchwork, and work best when a few plain colours are thrown into the blend. You can mix large and small prints with checks and ginghams, but try to keep within a limited colour palette as I did for the Child's Cushion on pages 92–95, or the overall effect can be a bit overwhelming. I particularly like working with printed or woven stripes, cutting them into square or rectangular patches, then reassembling them to make new geometric patterns. At first glance, you wouldn't think that all the fabric for Personalised Dog Bed on pages 132–135 was salvaged from a single blanket.

'Fussy cut' patches of patterned fabrics, like those I made for the Hexagon Pincushion on pages 130–131, create rhythmic repeating designs or you can select interesting individual motifs for appliqué patches – I couldn't resist the nostalgic racing cars used on the Patched Dungarees on pages 142–143. For the framed Flower Picture on pages 138–141 I cut out a series of large rose motifs from glazed chintz and stitched them to a length of plain damask – an old technique called Broderie Perse first used when new fabrics were scarce and costly.

Patch! Projects

Designing the projects for this book, selecting the perfect fabrics and deciding exactly which techniques to use, was a hugely enjoyable task. Whether you're a needlework novice or an experienced stitcher, I hope you'll enjoy them as much as I have done.

Floral & Spot Tote Bag

MATERIALS
140 x 70cm spot print fabric
140 x 40cm floral print fabric
stranded embroidery thread in red
matching sewing thread
sewing machine
sewing kit

CUTTING OUT
from spot print fabric
seventeen 12cm squares
two 52 x 32cm lining panels
one 42 x 12cm lining base
from floral print fabric
seventeen 12cm squares
one 22 x 12cm pocket
two 60 x 8cm handle strips

SKILL LEVEL: 2

Here's a relaxed and roomy bag that's just the right size for a quick trip to your local shop, or for carrying books and a laptop. It's made from one of my all-time favourite fabric combinations – spots and flowers – and I love the contrast in scale between the bold denim-look polka dots and the delicate sprays of briar roses on their dark indigo background.

The seam allowance throughout is 1cm.

1 Lay out the thirty squares that make up the main bag in a chequerboard pattern, in three horizontal rows of ten. Sew them together in vertical rows of three, with right sides facing. You'll find detailed instructions for this in the Patch! Basics section, on page 20.

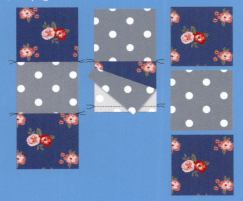

2 Press the seam allowances in opposite directions so that they will lie flat when the rows are joined. For each row with a spot square at the top and bottom, press the seams downwards and for each row with a floral square at the top and bottom, press the seams upwards.

3 Join the rows together to make a long rectangle. With right sides facing, match the long edges so that the seams butt up against each other. Insert a pin at each seam line and at the top and bottom corners, then machine stitch.

4 Press all the vertical seams open. Seam and press the two side edges to make a cylinder of patchwork. Press.

5 Sew the remaining four squares together to make the base, alternating the spot and floral prints. Press the seams open.

top tip I'LL LET YOU INTO A SECRET… THIS BAG IS ACTUALLY MADE FROM FOUR COTTON TEA TOWELS, ALWAYS A GREAT SOURCE OF NEW FABRIC IN SMALLER QUANTITIES!

Floral & Spot Tote Bag

6 With right sides facing inwards, pin one long edge of the bag base to four squares along the bottom edge of the main bag, matching the open seams. Pin the other long edge to the opposite side of the bag, leaving the short edges open. Make a 5mm snip into the bottom of each corner seam to open out the allowance. Machine stitch these two seams, starting and finishing each line of stitching 1cm from the short edge and working a few backwards stitches to strengthen.

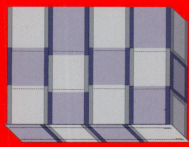

7 Pin the short edges of the base to the bag and machine stitch. Work two more rounds of stitching over the first lines to reinforce the seam.

8 Using a thick crewel needle and three strands of red embroidery thread, work a line of running stitch, 5mm in from each side seam.

9 Neaten the top edge of the pocket with a narrow double hem. Press under a 1cm turning along the other three sides. Pin the pocket to one lining panel, 6cm down from the top edge and 11cm in from the left side edge. Machine down in place, working a few extra stitches at the beginning and end of the seam.

10 With right sides facing, join the two edges of the lining panels to make a cylinder. Press the seams open, then press back a 15mm turning around the top edge. Make a 6mm snip into the seam allowance on the bag at each corner as for the main bag. With right sides facing, pin on the lining base, lining up two opposite corners to the two seams. Sew in place with two rounds of stitching.

11 Slip the lining inside the bag, matching up the base and two side edge seams. Pin together around the opening – the lining should sit about 5mm down from the top edge of the bag. Machine stitch 3mm from the top edge of the lining.

12 Press each handle strip in half widthways and unfold. Press a 1cm turning each of the four edges, then re-press the centre crease. Machine stitch 3mm from each long edge. Tack the ends of the handles to the sides of the bag so that they lie 5cm down from the top edge and overlap the side patchwork seams. Sew down with rectangles of reinforcing stitch (see page 21).

top tip LINES OF TOP STITCHING ALONG EACH SIDE SEAM DEFINE THE SHAPE OF THE BAG. TO MAKE THEM STAND OUT, MATCH THE COLOUR OF THE THREAD TO THE FABRIC: I CHOSE A WARM RED THAT HIGHLIGHTS THE ROSE DETAIL.

Tweed Messenger Bag

SKILL LEVEL: 1

Both practical and roomy, there's plenty of space in this over-shoulder messenger bag for all your daily essentials. It's quick to make from simple squares of tweed. I used a mixture of both old and new fabrics, and the soft, natural colours of the wool blend together really well. Each patch is outlined with a round of running stitches worked in tapestry yarn and the one in the centre is monogrammed.

MATERIALS

eighteen 14cm squares tweed fabric
tapestry yarn in shades to match
large crewel needle
75 x 38cm cotton fabric for lining
125cm of 5cm-wide webbing for
    bag handle
matching sewing thread
quilter's ruler
chalk pencil
sewing machine
sewing kit

1 Using a quilter's ruler and chalk pencil, mark a guideline on each tweed square, 2cm in from the edge. Thread the crewel needle with tapestry yarn to match each colour in turn, and sew a line of small running stitches around every chalk outline.

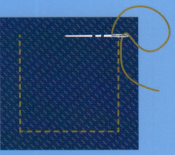

2 Arrange the first nine squares in three horizontal rows of three, moving them about until you have a balanced arrangement of colour and pattern.

3 Draw your initials on the centre square using the chalk pencil. Embroider over the lines with small back stitches (see page 30).

4 Join the squares in horizontal rows, starting at the bottom left corner. Pin the right edge of the first square to the left edge of the second square and machine stitch with a 12mm seam allowance. Pin and sew the third square in the same way. Press the two seams towards the left.

top tip I MADE MY BAG WITH A PATCHWORK PANEL AT BOTH FRONT AND BACK, BUT YOU COULD USE A SINGLE LARGE SQUARE OF TWEED TO MAKE A PLAIN REVERSE SIDE. A SMALL MONOGRAM IN THE CORNER WOULD PROVIDE EXTRA VISUAL INTEREST.

Tweed Messenger Bag

5 Join the three centre squares and press the seams to the right, then sew the top three squares together and press the seam towards the left.

6 With right sides facing, pin the bottom edge of the top row to the top edge of the centre row so that the seams match up. Insert a pin at both points where the seams meet and at each corner. Machine stitch leaving a 12mm allowance. Add the bottom row in the same way and press all the horizontal seams upwards.

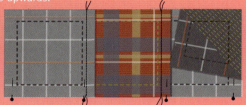

7 Sew the nine remaining squares together in the same way to make the back of the bag. Press the horizontal seams upwards. Pin the side and bottom edges of the front and back together with right sides facing, once again matching the corners and seams.

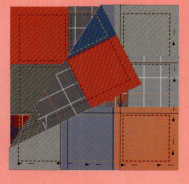

8 Machine stitch 12mm from the edge, then stitch over the line once again to reinforce. Clip a small triangle from each bottom corner so that they will lie flat (see page 20). Turn the bag right side out, ease out the corners and press lightly.

9 Neaten the top edge by turning back and tacking down a 12mm turning. You will need to open out the seams as you go, so that the opening doesn't become too lumpy.

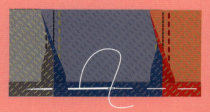

10 Pin the ends of the handle to the inside top corners of the bag, overlapping them by 5cm. The seams should lie halfway across the webbing. Tack in place, then machine stitch a rectangle of reinforcing stitches (see page 21).

11 Fold the lining in half with right sides facing. Pin and machine stitch the two side edges with a 1cm seam, then press back a 3cm turning all around the opening. Slip the lining inside the bag, matching up the side seams. Pin the folded edge 5mm below the top of the bag, then slip stitch it in place.

top tip IF YOU CAN'T FIND COTTON WEBBING IN THE RIGHT WIDTH OR SHADE, STITCH YOUR OWN WOOLLEN HANDLE FROM A 125 X 12CM LENGTH OF TWEED, FOLLOWING THE INSTRUCTIONS FOR MAKING STRAPS ON PAGE 21.

Red Hens Bag

MATERIALS

1m x 50cm red cotton fabric
50 x 15cm white linen fabric
1m x 50cm striped cotton fabric
2m of 2.5cm-wide white bias binding
off-white and red stranded cotton
  embroidery thread
four 2.5cm buttons
matching sewing thread
sewing machine
sewing kit

CUTTING OUT

from red cotton fabric
two 10 x 41cm side gussets
one 10 x 38cm bottom gusset
one 38 x 41cm back panel
two 8 x 70cm straps
two 8 x 15cm tabs
from striped cotton fabric
two 38 x 41cm side panels
two 10 x 41cm side gussets
one 10 x 38cm bottom gusset

SKILL LEVEL: 3

Redwork embroidery – simple outline drawings stitched on to a plain white background – was hugely popular at the turn of the nineteenth century. Over a hundred years on, it's undergoing a well-deserved revival. The finished embroideries in this distinctive red have long been combined with crimson cloth to make striking, graphic patchwork. I've started with this simple country-style bag... but dream of making a whole quilt, with an entire flock of little red hens and roosters.

The seam allowance throughout is 1cm.

1 Using the full-sized template on page 156, trace two left-facing and two right-facing hens within their rectangles on to the white linen fabric (see how to do this on page 26). Leave at least 6cm between each image. Stitch over the hen outlines in small back stitches, using three strands of thread, and embroider the frames in feather stitch (see pages 30 and 31).

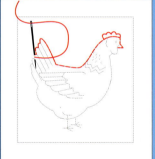

2 Trace the rectangle five times on to the red cotton fabric and work a round of off-white feather stitch around each outline, again with three strands of thread.

3 Trim each completed patch down to 14 x 15cm, making sure that there is an equal margin around the feather stitching.

4 Arrange the patches in three rows of three, alternating red and white, and with all the chickens facing inwards. With right sides facing, pin the side edges of the first two together and machine stitch.

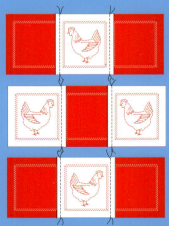

5 Add the third patch to the other side of the chicken, then join the other two rows. Press all the seams towards the red patches.

top tip FOR A FIXED, RATHER THAN AN ADJUSTABLE, HANDLE MAKE THE STRAP 10CM LONGER AND SEW

THE ENDS TO THE SIDE GUSSETS OF THE BAG. YOU COULD ALWAYS ADD THE BUTTONS AS A DECORATIVE FEATURE.

Red Hens Bag

6 Pin the bottom edge of the top row and the top edge of the centre row together, with right sides facing, so that the seam allowances all butt up against each other. Insert the pins along the seam lines and at both corners. Machine stitch. Add the bottom row in the same way. Press the seams open.

7 With right sides facing, pin the short ends of the side gussets to the bottom gusset to make a long strip. Machine stitch, starting and finishing 1cm from the end of each seam line.

8 With right sides together, pin one long edge of the completed gusset strip to the side and bottom edges of the back panel. Open out the unstitched ends of the seams so that the gusset fits neatly around the bottom corners. Tack in place then machine stitch, working an extra row at each corner to reinforce. Add the front panel in the same way, then turn the bag right side out and press the seams lightly. Press under a 1cm turning around the opening.

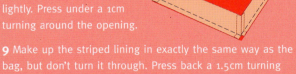

9 Make up the striped lining in exactly the same way as the bag, but don't turn it through. Press back a 1.5cm turning around the top edge.

10 Trim one end of each of the four strap and tab pieces into a shallow curve. Press under a 1cm turning around each piece. Press the bias binding in half widthways.

11 Tack the binding to the wrong side of the long and curved edges of one strap and one tab so 5mm overlaps to the right side. Tack the second strap and tab in place so the binding is sandwiched between them and machine stitch 3mm from the edge. Make two buttonholes, by hand or machine, 5cm and 10cm from the end of the strap. They should lie parallel to the long edges.

12 Pin and tack the completed strap to the left side gusset, so that 3cm lies inside the main bag. Attach the tab to the right side in the same way, then slip in the lining. Match up the seams and pin them together so that the top edge of the lining lies 5mm below the opening. Hand stitch the two together, making sure that the needle goes through the turned back hem around the main bag only, and the stitches don't show on the right side. Work extra stitches along the base of the strap and tab, or sew a rectangle of machine reinforcing stitches (see page 21) at the top of each side gusset.

13 Finish off by sewing two of the buttons to the tab 5cm apart, and the other pair to the side gusset, also 5cm apart.

top tip ADAPT THIS IDEA TO MAKE AN AUTOGRAPH BAG AS AN END-OF-TERM SOUVENIR: GET YOUR BEST FRIENDS TO SIGN FEATHER-STITCH TRIMMED PATCHES AND BACK STITCH OVER THEIR WRITING.

Harlequin Bag

MATERIALS
remnants of velvet and silk fabrics
   in a range of colours
lightweight iron-on interfacing
1.5m of 5mm cord
65 x 25cm toning velvet fabric
15cm circle of medium-weight card
matching sewing thread
glue stick
sewing machine
scrap paper

CUTTING OUT
from toning velvet fabric
two 15cm circles for bag and
   lining base
38 x 23cm rectangle for lining

SKILL LEVEL: 3

When I came across a collection of vivid antique silk and velvet scraps I was intrigued by the way the jewel-like colours – which range from ruby and topaz through to jade and amethyst – worked together, in true Harlequin style. I wanted to make them into something very special, and so came up with this velvet-lined drawstring bag design. It is made up of tiny diamond patches, hand-stitched over foundation papers... the perfect place to store your most treasured possessions.

1 Following the manufacturer's instructions, strengthen the finest silk fabrics by fusing lightweight iron-on interfacing to the wrong side.

2 You will need 139 diamond patches, 135 for the bag and four for the drawstring tabs. Cut out the backing papers using the template on page 156 as your guide and cover each one with fabric, mitring the corners neatly. You'll find detailed instructions for this on page 23.

3 Sew the patches together in fifteen diagonal rows of nine diamonds.

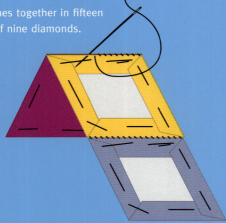

4 Join the completed rows to make a long rectangle.

5 With right sides facing, sew the two short edges of the rectangle together to make a cylinder.

6 Press lightly from the wrong side, then unpick all the tacking papers. Fold back and tack down the top halves of the diamonds at the top and bottom to give a straight edge around each opening.

top tip YOU CAN JOIN THE DIAMONDS RANDOMLY, OR LAY THEM ALL OUT FIRST, IN FIFTEEN
DIAGONAL ROWS OF NINE AND SHUFFLE THEM AROUND TO CREATE A MORE BALANCED ARRANGEMENT.

Harlequin Bag

7 Divide the bottom edge into four equal sections by inserting four pins into the fold, with three and a half patches between them. This will help you gather the edge evenly when you sew on the base.

8 Prepare the base by ruling two lines across the cardboard circle, dividing it into quarter sections. Sew a line of long running stitches 5mm from the edge of one velvet circle. Coat the back of the card lightly with a glue stick and place it centrally on the wrong side of the velvet. Gather up the thread so that the edge covers the card and fasten off securely. Insert four pins into the card, one at the end of each line.

9 Sew a line of running stitch 5mm from the bottom edge of the bag and draw it up until the opening is 1cm smaller in diameter than the velvet base. Line up the marker pins and pin the base centrally to the gathered opening – this is rather an awkward process, so you need to 'stab' the pins through the edge of the velvet and into the patchwork. Slip stitch the base to the bag with matching thread.

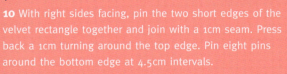

10 With right sides facing, pin the two short edges of the velvet rectangle together and join with a 1cm seam. Press back a 1cm turning around the top edge. Pin eight pins around the bottom edge at 4.5cm intervals.

11 Fold the remaining velvet circle in half, then quarters and position a pin at each fold. Now add another pin between each pair, to divide the circumference in eight equal section. With right sides facing, tack the base to the bag, matching the pins. Machine stitch 1cm from the edge and trim the seam allowance back to 3mm.

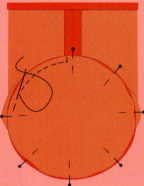

12 Sit the lining inside the bag and pin the two top edges together so that they line up exactly. Join together by hand, with a round of slip stitch.

13 To make the drawstring channel, machine two parallel rounds of straight stitch around the opening, 2.5 and 5cm down from the top edge. Unpick one of the diagonal lines of hand stitching between these two rows and secure the other ends of the seams with a few extra stitches. Make the other opening directly opposite, in the same way.

14 Cut the cord in half and secure one end to an elastic threader or small safety pin. Feed it through one opening, all the way around the drawstring channel, then back out of the opening. Thread the remaining half through the other opening.

15 Tie both cords together in an overhand knot, about 10m from the ends. Trim to 6cm. Fold one of the last diamonds in half lengthways and hold it over one cord so that the raw end is completely enclosed. Slip stitch the edges together, stab stitching through the cord. Unpick the tacking. Do the same on the other three ends.

top tip CHECK ANTIQUE FABRICS FOR ANY DAMAGED AREAS THAT MIGHT NOT BE STRONG ENOUGH FOR RE-USE. IF YOU HOLD THEM UP TO THE LIGHT YOU CAN EASILY DETECT ANY WORN PATCHES.

Rose Knitting Bag

MATERIALS
60 x 25cm red floral print fabric
120 x 50cm green spot print fabric
1m narrow lace
pair of bag handles
matching sewing thread
pencil and ruler
sewing machine
sewing kit

CUTTING OUT
from red floral print fabric
one 27 x 15cm centre flower panel
ten 7cm squares
from green spot print fabric
twelve 7cm squares
three 37 x 27cm side panels
two 7 x 58cm gussets
four 5 x 8 handle loops

SKILL LEVEL: 2

Vintage furnishing fabrics, like the classic rose curtain I found for this cheerful knitting bag, are idea for patchwork projects. The larger scale patterns make a change from small ditsy prints and are very versatile. I chose a complete rose motif for the octagon and then picked out a few of the smaller floral sprays to make the squares. The triangular lace trimming frames the centre panel perfectly, echoing the shape and colour of the petals.

The seam allowance throughout is 1cm.

1 Start off by joining the squares. With right sides facing, sew four spot and three floral patches together for the top and bottom strips, alternating the fabrics. Sew two floral patches to two spot squares for the side strips. Press all the seam allowances towards the floral squares.

2 Using a sharp pencil and a ruler, draw a diagonal line across the wrong side of the remaining four spot squares. Pin one to each corner of the flower panel with the line running from edge to edge. Machine stitch along the pencil lines, then trim the surplus fabric leaving a 1cm allowance on each seam. Press all the seams towards the centre panel.

3 Slip stitch the lace around the edge of the flower panel. Neaten the end by trimming it to 6mm, folding it back and stitching down.

4 With right sides facing, pin and stitch the two three-patch side strips to the side edges of the centre panel. Press the seams towards the centre. Pin on the top and bottom strips, matching the seams and corners. Machine stitch, then press the seams inwards.

top tip IF YOU ARE USING A PIECE OF OLD FABRIC, HOLD IT UP TO THE LIGHT TO CHECK FOR SMALL HOLES OR ANY PARTS THAT HAVE WORN TOO THIN FOR USE. MARK THESE WITH STICKY LABELS AND CUT YOUR PATCHES FROM THE SOUND AREAS.

Rose Knitting Bag

5 Draw a diagonal line across each bottom corner square and cut across these marks. Pin the finished front panel to one of the green spot side panels and snip a triangle from each bottom corner so that the two are the same size. Do the same with the other two side panels. Mark the 1cm seam allowance along the side and bottom edges of all four panels.

6 With right sides facing, pin one of the gusset strips to the side edge of a green spot panel. Machine stitch along the pencil line, as far as the corner. Sew a few reverse stitches to secure the end of the seam. Snip off the thread and remove the fabric from the machine. Make an 8mm snip into the seam allowance of the gusset, in line with the end of the seam.

7 Now swivel the gusset round so that the edge lies along the diagonal corner and pin the two layers together. Carry on machine stitching along the line, just as far as the next angle. Snip the allowance again, then sew the bottom edge and the second corner in the same way. Trim the end of the gusset in line with the top edge of the bag.

8 Sew on the front panel to complete the main bag. Turn right side out, ease out the corners and press the seams lightly. Press under and tack down a 1cm turning around the opening.

9 Press under a 1cm turning along each long edge of the four handle loops. Thread them through the holes in the handles, lining up the bottom edges.

10 Position a handle so that it lies centrally along the bag front. Pin, then tack the bottom edges of the handle loops to the wrong side of the opening, so that 2cm projects above the top edge. Tack the other handle to the back panel in the corresponding position.

11 Make up the lining and press the opening as for the main bag, but don't turn it through. Slip the lining into the bag. Match up the side seams and the top edges precisely. Tack the two together and machine stitch around the top edge, 3mm from the opening.

top tip I REALLY LIKED THESE TRANSPARENT BAG HANDLES, WHICH ARE UNDERSTATED AND DON'T DOMINATE THE PRETTY PRINTS.

INSTEAD OF INTRODUCING ANOTHER COLOUR, NATURAL BAMBOO WOULD MAKE A GOOD ALTERNATIVE IF YOU CAN'T FIND ANYTHING SIMILAR.

Hounds Bag

MATERIALS
70 x 90cm striped fabric
75 x 50cm floral print fabric for lining
old silk scarf or printed fabric
fusible bonding web
matching sewing thread
sewing machine
sewing kit

CUTTING OUT
from striped fabric
The stripes should run vertically on
each piece.
one 35 x 90cm rectangle for main bag
two 10 x 40cm side gussets
two 8 x 60cm straps
from floral print lining fabric
two 35 x 47cm rectangles

SKILL LEVEL: 2

Appliqué patches can be made from all kinds of unexpected fabrics, and I'm always on the look out for illustrative one-off prints. These four perky hounds started out on a vintage silk headscarf, of the kind worn by generations of countrywomen and dog-lovers. Such fine fabric needs reinforcement if it is to stand up to everyday wear and tear, so a fusible bonding web was used to fix them on to the deckchair striped canvas, and the raw edges were reinforced with machine stitch.

1 Decide which motifs from the patterned fabric you wish to use and plan their positions on the bag. Cut them out roughly and iron the fusible web onto the wrong side, following the manufacturer's instructions. Cut around the outlines and peel off the backing papers

2 Fold the bag in half lengthways and insert a pin at each side edge to mark the centre point.

3 Fold up the top 40cm – this will be the front of the bag. Arrange the motifs as you wish, remembering to leave at least 5cm at the top edge, then iron them in place. Work a round of 3mm wide machine blanket or zigzag stitches around the edge of each shape in matching thread.

4 Mark the centre bottom edge of the two side gussets with pins. With right sides facing, place one gusset across the bag, matching the pin to the centre point of the bag.

5 Make two 8mm snips into the seam allowance of the bag in line, 1cm in from each side edge of the gusset, so that it will fold around the corners. Pin the side edges of the bag to the sides of the gusset.

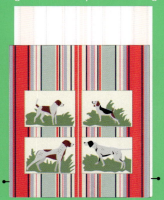

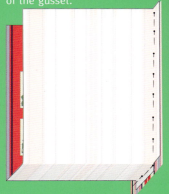

top tip YOU WILL NEED TO ALLOW MORE FABRIC TO MAKE A SYMMETRICALLY STRIPED BAG AND TO MATCH THE SIDE GUSSETS AND STRAPS. THIS EXTRA AMOUNT WILL DEPEND ON THE WIDTH OF THE REPEAT.

Hounds Bag

6 Machine stitch the bag to the gusset with a 1cm seam. Work three short diagonal lines of stitching across the corners to reinforce them, then trim the seam allowance at the corner back to 4mm (see page 20). Join the other gusset in the same way.

7 Press the seams open and then press back a 3mm turning around the opening. Turn the bag right side out and ease out the corners into right angles.

8 Pin the two lining pieces together with right sides facing and machine stitch around the side and bottom edges leaving a 1cm seam allowance. Press the seams open.

9 Now make a t-junction seam at each bottom corner to give depth to the lining. Fold it so that one side seam lies along the bottom seam. Draw an 8cm line across the corner, then machine stitch along this line. Trim the seam back to 4mm. Do the same at the other corner, then press back a 3.5mm turning around the top edge.

10 Slip the lining inside the bag, matching up the side seams. Pin the two together so that the lining lies 3mm below the top edge of the bag. Machine stitch 5mm from the top edge.

11 To make up the straps, press under a 1cm turning along each short, then each long edge of the two strips. Press them in half with wrong sides facing. Pin the folded edges together and machine stitch all round, 3mm from the edge.

12 Pin and tack the ends of the strap to the back and front of the bag and machine stitch down with a rectangle of reinforcing stitches (see page 21).

top tip ALTHOUGH YOU DON'T ALWAYS SEE THE LINING FABRIC, THAT DOESN'T MEAN IT HAS GO UNNOTICED.

I USED ONE OF MY FLORAL PRINTS INSIDE THIS BAG, IN A COLOURWAY TO MATCH THE CANVAS.

Circles Laundry Bag

MATERIALS
85 x 65cm white linen fabric
scraps of floral print fabric
2m pink bias binding
1.2m pink cord
matching sewing thread
sewing kit
dressmaker's pen or chalk pencil
long ruler or 60cm quilter's rule
thin card

CUTTING OUT
from white linen fabric
one 82 x 62cm rectangle
from floral print fabric
fifty petals; cut a thin card petal using
the template on page 156, then for
each petal trace the shape on to the
wrong side of the fabric and cut out
7mm from outline

SKILL LEVEL: 2

This laundry bag is hand appliquéd with a geometric arrangement of petal shapes, a traditional pattern known as 'Hidden Circles'. This is a wonderful way to repurpose tiny pieces of fabric, and the more prints you can find, the more interesting the finished bag will look. I chose a random mixture from my collection of old dress-making cottons and added a few vintage American feed sack fabrics – you'll see how a wide range of floral designs always sit happily together even though they vary in scale and colour.

1 Prepare each of the petals for appliqué. Pin a card template centrally on the wrong side of the fabric. Turn back the hem and sew it down through the card with long running stitches. Fold the corners into neat points. Press the turning with a hot iron and when cool, unpick the thread. After a while the card templates may become distorted, so change them regularly.

2 The petals have to be positioned accurately before they are stitched down. You can do this by eye, or by drawing a grid directly on to the fabric. Fold the fabric in half widthways. Press the fold lightly, then unfold.

3 Using a chalk pencil or a fading dressmaker's pen, lightly draw a 30 x 40cm rectangle on the right hand side, 6cm in from the fold and right edge, and 6cm up from the bottom edge. Mark three points on the top and bottom lines at 5cm, 15cm and 25cm from the left corners. Mark four points along the side lines at 5cm, 15cm, 25cm and 35cm down from the top corners. Join these dots to form a diamond grid.

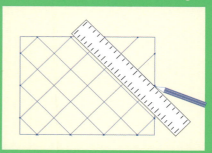

4 Lay 40 of the petals diagonally across the grid, rearranging them until you have a well-balanced layout of pattern and colour. Pin them in place, making sure they all touch at the tips.

top tip CUT OUT EACH OF THE PETALS TIP-TO-TIP ALONG THE DIAGONAL, BIAS GRAIN. THIS PART OF THE FABRIC HAS THE MOST 'GIVE' AND SO THE CURVED EDGES OF THE PETALS WILL LOOK SMOOTH AND CRISP.

Circles
Laundry Bag

5 Slip stitch the petals to the background using small diagonal stitches and a thread that matches the predominant colour of each fabric.

6 To mark the position of the drawstring channel, draw a pencil line 10cm down from the top edge, on the wrong side of the fabric. Bind the top edge and 12cm of each side edge – to just below the pencil line – with the pink bias binding.

7 Cut a 64cm length from the remaining binding and press under a 1cm turning at each end. Pin this along the pencil line, so that the neatened ends are aligned with the side edges. Using white sewing thread, machine stitch along the top and bottom edges of the binding, 2mm from the fold.

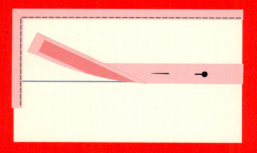

8 Refold the bag widthways and pin the side and bottom edges together. Machine stitch these two edges, leaving a 1cm seam allowance. Start at the bottom corner and end the seam by angling the stitches across the bias binding so that it ends just below the drawstring channel. Neaten the seam allowance with an overlock or zigzag stitch and turn right side out. Press lightly.

9 Fasten a safety pin to one end of the cord, or thread it through a large bodkin. Feed the cord all the way through the drawstring channel, in one opening and out of the other.

10 Tie the ends of the cord together in a loose knot and trim the ends to 10cm. Now it's time to use those two spare petals, to make the tabs. Tack each one over a card template, then leaving the card in place and fold them in half. Starting at the fold, stitch the sides securely together to 5mm from the point. Slip the tab over the end of the cord, securing the point to the cord with a few stitches, then sew the other sides together. Add the other tab in the same way.

---

top tip AS A FINISHING TOUCH, MY INITIALS WERE EMBROIDERED IN THE BOTTOM LEFT CORNER WITH FINE CHAIN STITCH, WORKED WITH THREE STRANDS OF THREAD. IF YOU ARE MAKING THIS AS A PRESENT YOU COULD ADD YOUR FRIEND'S MONOGRAM OR NAME.

Floral Washbag

MATERIALS
1m x 10cm green floral print fabric
1m x 10cm pink floral print fabric
30 x 60cm woven waterproof shower
   curtain fabric
25cm white nylon zip
matching sewing thread
sewing kit
sewing machine

CUTTING OUT
from green floral print fabric
twenty 8cm squares
from pink floral print fabric
twenty 8cm squares
two 3 x 4cm zip tabs

SKILL LEVEL: 2

One of the fascinating things about patchwork is the way that you can piece together printed fabrics to create a completely new design. To make this useful zip-up washbag squares were cut from two different colourways of my Lace Stripe cotton duck and then arranged alternately to make a chequerboard pattern, which looks as if it has been woven from lengths of floral braid.

1 Lay out the squares for the (identical) front and back of the bag, in four rows of five. Alternate the colours and the direction of the stripes to create the basketweave effect. With right sides facing, sew the patches together in horizontal rows, leaving a 1cm seam allowance.

2 Press the seam allowances to one side, alternating left and right, as you go down the rows.

3 Hold the top edge of the second row against the bottom edge of the first row together, with the seam matching and the allowances butting up next to each other. Insert a pin at each seam line and the corners, then machine stitch 1cm from the edge. Add the other two rows, then make up the second panel in the same way.

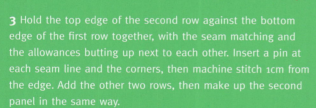

4 Press all the seam allowances open so that the patchwork will lie flat.

5 Rule a line 2.5cm up from the bottom edge of one panel, then trim along this line. Draw a 2.5cm square at each corner and cut them away. Do the same on the other panel.

top tip THIS VERSATILE DESIGN CAN BE ADAPTED BY ALTERING THE SIZE OF THE SQUARES:

MAKE THEM SMALLER FOR A MAKE-UP BAG OR LARGER FOR A CHANGING BAG (A GREAT BABY SHOWER GIFT!).

Floral Washbag

6 Pin the panels, wrong sides together, to the waterproof lining. Machine stitch the two layers together, sewing 3mm from the edge of the panels. Cut out neatly.

7 With right sides facing, stitch one of the zip tabs across the tapes at the top end of the zip. Press the seam towards the tab. Lay the zip along the top edge of a bag panel to check the size and sew the other tab to the bottom end, so that the outer edge of the tab lines up with the side of the bag. (You can stitch through the teeth without damaging the machine needle, as long as you are using a nylon zip, but avoid the tiny metal stopper at the bottom.)

8 Tack the top edge of one side panel to the zip and tabs with right sides facing. Fit a zip foot to the machine and stitch 6mm from the edge. Sew the other panel to the opposite side, then press the seams lightly and top stitch.

9 Open the zip and fold the bag so that the patchwork lies on the inside. Pin the side and bottom edges together, leaving the squared off corners open. Machine stitch the bottom edge with a 1cm seam, then sew the side edges, starting from the corners and sewing towards the zip. Secure both ends of the three seams with reverse stitches. Lightly press them open.

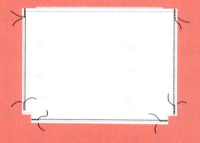

10 Now open out one of the open corners and refold it so that the side seams lines up with the bottom seam. Pin the two edges together and machine stitch with a 6mm seam. Do the same at the other corner, then turn right side out. Ease the corners out to make a flat base for the bag.

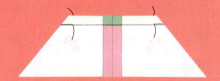

top tip IF YOU ARE A REAL PERFECTIONIST, YOU CAN NEATEN THE INSIDE SEAMS WITH AN OVERLOCKING STITCH OR BY BINDING THEM WITH BIAS BINDING, EITHER BY HAND OR MACHINE.

Dresden Plate Tote Bag

MATERIALS

13cm square each of four different floral print fabrics
13cm square each of red, pink and blue spot print fabrics
30 x 75cm calico
90cm of 2cm-wide cotton tape
scrap paper for template
matching sewing thread
sewing kit
sewing machine

CUTTING OUT

from floral and red and pink spot print fabrics
six pairs of matching outer petals
from blue spot print fabric
one 12cm circle
from paper
12 inner petals

TEMPLATES

Inner and outer petal shapes on page 156
12cm diameter circle

SKILL LEVEL: 1

This 'Dresden Plate' tote bag is suitable for beginners but it is also challenging enough for those who are more experienced stitchers. It is a combination of patchwork, appliqué and hand quilting, and so makes a good practical introduction to all three common techniques. This is a very clever way to use up old pieces of fabric as the design options are endless. Here I have used a selection of my signature floral, paisley and mini spot prints, but use whatever you have available at the time. If you like the look of this why not try the 'Dresden Plate' cushion on page 70.

1 Pin a paper template centrally to the wrong side of a petal and fold over the surplus fabric along the two side edges, sewing it down as you go. Don't worry about the raw ends at the point, as they will be concealed by the flower centre. When you come to the curved edge, make a series of little folds to gather in the turning. Tack the fabric down with small stitches and finish off with a double stitch. Cover all the templates in this way.

2 Lay the twelve petals out in a circle and decide on their arrangement – you could sew them together randomly, as shown here, or arrange them so that the matching petals lie opposite each other.

3 Hold the first two petals together with right sides facing. Starting at the right corner, join them with a row of small over stitches, picking up just a couple of threads from the folded fabric on each side. Fasten off at the end, then join the other petals to make the whole flower.

4 Press the flower lightly from the wrong side, then unpick the tacking stitches and remove the templates.

5 Fold the calico in half widthways. Place the finished flower centrally on the front, about 2cm up from the fold. Pin it in place, through the front layer only.

top tip WHEN YOU ARE TACKING THE FABRIC TO THE PAPER TEMPLATE, START OFF WITH THE KNOT ON THE RIGHT SIDE. THIS WILL MAKE UNPICKING THE THREADS A MUCH QUICKER PROCESS LATER ON.

Dresden Plate
Tote Bag

6 Slip stitch the folded, curved outside edge of the flower to the bag.

7 Now work the quilting that gives the flower its texture and secures it to the bag. Work a line of regularly spaced small stitches about 4mm inside the edge of each petal, starting and ending at the centre.

8 Fold back and tack down a 5mm turning around the edge of the blue spot circle, using a double length of thread. Draw it up tightly to make a Suffolk puff and fasten off the end securely.

9 Pin the puff to the centre of the flower to conceal the raw ends, and slip stitch it in place.

10 Fold the bag in half again, with the right side facing inwards. Pin the two sides together and machine stitch, leaving a 1cm allowance. Neaten the raw edges with an overlocking or zigzag stitch.

11 Press back a 5mm turning around the opening, then turn back and pin down a further 2cm to make a double hem. Machine stitch 3mm from the top edge and from the fold.

12 Turn the bag right side out and ease the corners into neat right angles with the point of your embroidery scissors. Press the seams lightly.

13 Cut the tape in half and press under a 5cm turning at each end. Pin the ends of one length to the front of the bag, 6cm in from the corners, so that the folds line up with the lower stitch line. Sew the ends in place with rectangles of machine stitches, reinforced with two diagonal lines worked from corner to corner (see page 21).

14 Make the second handle in the sames way and attach to the bag in the corresponding position at the back.

top tip VARIATIONS ON THIS PATTERN PRODUCED SOME OF THE MOST STUNNING PATCHWORK OF THE 1920S AND '30S. IF YOU'VE ENJOYED THIS, WHY NOT THINK ABOUT SEWING A WHOLE QUILT TOP?

Dresden Plate Cushion

MATERIALS

materials and equipment as for the bag
plus
35 x 75cm white cotton fabric
safety standard toy or cushion filling

CUTTING OUT

from calico fabric
one 30 x 35cm front panel
two 30 x 20cm back panels
from white cotton fabric
two 32 x 27 rectangles for cushion pad

SKILL LEVEL: 1

Here's a variation on a theme – a way to use the skills already learnt whilst making the tote bag. The calico is cut into three pieces to make the cover and the tape is turned into two ties to fasten as a bow at the back. The only extras you will need are the fabric and filling to make a small cushion pad.

1 Make up the patchwork flower as for steps 1–4 of the Dresden Plate Tote Bag on page 67. Pin it centrally to the front panel and hand sew it in place as for steps 6 and 7 on page 68. Make up the Suffolk puff and stitch it over the raw ends as for steps 8 and 9.

2 Press under a 5mm turning on one long edge of a back panel, then press under a second 1cm turning to make a double hem. Machine stitch down. Neaten one long edge of the other panel in the same way.

3 Lay out the front panel with the right side facing upwards. Place one back panel at side edge, with the right sides downwards and the raw edges matching. Pin together through all the layers and machine stitch all the way round, leaving a 1cm seam allowance.

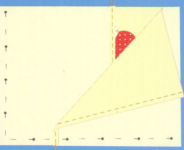

4 Turn the cover right side out and clip a small triangle from each corner, cutting to within 3mm of the stitching. Carefully ease out the corners with your embroidery scissors. Press the seams lightly.

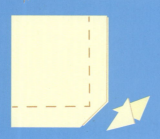

5 Cut the tape into four equal lengths and press under a 5mm turning at one end of each. Pin two of them to the top back panel, 8cm in from the corners, so that the fold lies along the stitched line. Hand stitch in place and snip a small triangle from each loose end.

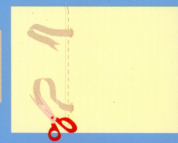

6 Pin the remaining ties to the other back panel, 5cm away from the first two. Hand sew them in place and trim the ends.

7 Pin the two cushion pad panels together. Machine stitch around the outside edge with a 1cm seam allowance, leaving a 10cm gap in one long edge.

8 Press back the seam allowance along the opening then turn right side out. Clip and ease out the corners as for the cover and press the seams. Stuff firmly with the cushion filling, then close the gap with slip stitch. Put the cushion inside the cover and tie two bows at the back.

top tip IF YOU DON'T WANT TO MAKE YOUR OWN CUSHION, USE A READY-MADE 30CM SQUARE FEATHER OR POLYESTER PAD, WHICH WILL SQUASH UP TO GIVE THE COVER A WELL-FILLED, UPHOLSTERED APPEARANCE.

Rose Linen Pillowcase

MATERIALS

old printed linen cloth
plain linen fabric for back
matching sewing thread
sewing kit
sewing machine

SKILL LEVEL: 1

As you may know, I have a passion for vintage textiles and have collected them for as long as I can remember. Old fabrics have a special quality that only comes from long use and will last for many more years – even if they show signs of wear, there are usually some areas that can be salvaged. When I came across a rose-bordered tablecloth that was in perfect condition apart from a torn centre, I knew it deserved a new lease of life, so here it is... transformed into a pretty pillowcase and backed with a linen cut from an old sheet.

CUTTING OUT

from printed linen fabric
six 28cm squares for front (see step 1)
from linen fabric
one flap: 53 x 20cm
one back panel: 78 x 53cm

I cut these two pieces so that the original hem-stitched edge of the sheet lies along the 53cm sides, which gave me ready-finished edges at the opening. This meant I had to adjust the width of the back panel to 76.5cm and the depth of the flap to 18.5cm.

1 Draw up a 28cm square template on dressmaker's pattern paper to use as your guide for cutting out the patches. Avoiding any damaged areas, cut one square from each corner of the cloth and two squares from the sides. You can mark guidelines on the template to make sure that the printed design will line up across all six squares.

2 Lay the patches out in their finished order. Starting at the bottom row, pin the side edges of the centre square and one of the corner squares together, with right sides facing. Machine stitch, leaving a 1.5cm seam allowance. Sew on the other corner square in the same way, then join the three top patches.

top tip THE FINISHED SIZE OF THIS CASE IS 50 X 75CM, SO YOU'LL NEED TO ADJUST THE SIZE OF THE SIX PATCHES TO FIT A LARGER OR A LONGER RECTANGULAR PILLOW. FOR A SQUARE PILLOW, CUT FOUR SQUARES, ONE FROM EACH CORNER OF THE ORIGINAL CLOTH.

Rose Linen
Pillowcase

3 With right sides facing, place the two pieces together so that the bottom edge of the top row lies against the top row of the bottom row. Line up the seams and pin them at right angles for a precise match. Pin the rest of the seam, and machine stitch 1.5cm from the edge. Press this long seam open.

4 If it isn't already neatened, make a narrow double hem along one long edge of the linen flap. Press under 5mm, then a further 1cm turning and top stitch the fold. Hem one short edge of the back panel as necessary.

5 Pin the long raw edge of the flap to one short edge of the finished front. Machine stitch together, leaving a 1.5cm seam allowance.

6 Lay the front panel out on your work surface with the right side upwards and open out the flap. Position the back panel over it so that the hemmed edge lies along the seam between the flap and the front panel. Turn the flap over the back panel and pin together along the top, bottom and left side edges.

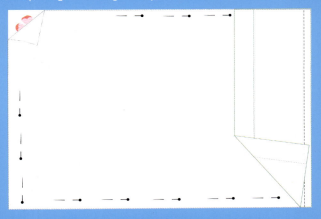

7 Machine stitch the pinned edges, then trim the seam allowance to 6mm. Neaten with a zigzag or overlocking stitch. Turn the pillow case right side out, ease out the corners and press the seams.

top tip IF YOU DON'T HAVE A SUITABLE TABLECLOTH TO UPCYCLE, A LARGE-SCALE PATCHWORK PILLOWCASE WOULD MAKE A GOOD FOCAL POINT ON YOUR BED: USE 28CM SQUARES CUT FROM SIX DIFFERENT STRIPES, SPOTS OR FLORALS, OR A MIXTURE OF FABRICS.

Boudoir Cushion

MATERIALS
120 x 60cm curtain lining fabric
scraps of floral print fabric
8 buttons
matching sewing thread
sewing kit
25 x 38cm cushion pad

CUTTING OUT
from lining fabric
six 26cm foundation squares
one 27 x 39.5cm back panel
from floral print fabrics
seventeen 7.5cm squares

SKILL LEVEL: 3

This sumptuous cushion is made from 'Cathedral Window' patchwork, the technique where sewing meets origami. It first evolved in the 1930s, when it was also known as 'Daisy Block' or 'Mock Orange Blossom'. The folded, petal-shaped frames provide a showcase for tiny fragments of fabric and some mid-twentieth-century charm quilts consist of dozens of cotton prints, all different. My version uses scraps of lingerie silk and rayon from that era, bordered with a soft sateen lining fabric, for a rather more glamorous look.

1 Start off by creasing the foundation squares into quarters wiht a cross, as a guideline to help you fold accurately. Fold the side edges together and lightly press the centre crease. Open out, then fold the top and bottom edges together and press the crease. Press a 5mm turning along each edge of the square.

2 With the turnings facing upwards, fold each corner to the centre, so that the edges of the square lie against the guidelines. Press the diagonal folds in turn.

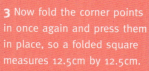

3 Now fold the corner points in once again and press them in place, so a folded square measures 12.5cm by 12.5cm.

4 Make a tiny cross stitch at the centre of the foundation square, through all the layers, to secure the folds and hold down the points.

5 Pin the first two foundation squares together with right sides facing and oversew the top edges together, as for paper-covered patchwork. Join on a third square, then sew the remaining three squares together. Pin both along one long edge, with right sides facing, and oversew. Press the completed piece lightly from the wrong side.

top tip SOME FABRICS I USED IN MY 'WINDOWS' ARE SHEER; I FOUND THE STITCHING BETWEEN THE BLOCKS SHOWED THROUGH.

TO CONCEAL THE JOINS, I POSITIONED 8CM SQUARES OF LEFTOVER LINING FABRIC BEHIND THE FINER SILKS BEFORE FOLDING BACK THE CURVES.

Boudoir Cushion

6 Pin one of the patches to each of the diamond spaces between the squares, making sure that the colours and patterns are balanced.

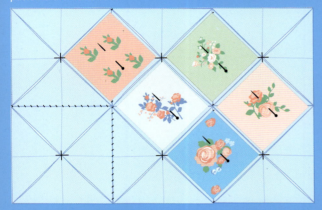

7 Turn back and pin down the foundation squares so that they conceal the edges of the flowered patches and create shallow curves.

8 Slip stitch down the folded edges through all the layers, using matching sewing thread.

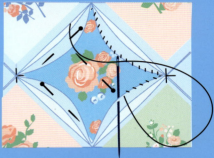

9 To fill in the triangular spaces around the edge, press the remaining patches diagonally in half. Pin them into the gaps and oversew the folds to the outside edges of the foundation squares. Turn back and stitch down the diagonal folds as before to conceal the other two edges.

10 Sew a button to the centre of each of the foundation squares. This not only looks decorative, but will conceal any imperfections in the stitching at the ends of the petals.

11 Make up the cushion by pressing under a 1cm turning all around the back panel. Check that it is the same size as the completed cushion front, adjusting the turnings if necessary, then pin the two together with wrong sides facing. Oversew two long and one short edges, insert the cushion pad, then pin and stitch the opening.

top tip IF YOU ENJOY THIS INTRIGUING TECHNIQUE, WHY NOT GO ON TO MAKE AN ENTIRE QUILT? YOU WON'T HAVE TO BACK OR LINE THE COMPLETED BLOCKS SO IT WILL BE QUICK TO DO, AND BECAUSE IT'S ALL HAND-STITCHED, YOUR WORK WILL BE VERY PORTABLE.

Crazy Patch Cushion

MATERIALS

selection of embroidered cloths
50cm square white linen fabric for
  cushion front
40cm square gingham fabric for
  cushion back
170cm pink bias binding
170cm fine piping cord
40cm square cushion pad
matching sewing thread
2 skeins pink stranded cotton
  embroidery thread
sewing kit

SKILL LEVEL: 3

Women of past generations spent hours patiently stitching household textiles – tray cloths, dressing table mats, napkins and runners – which we seldom use today. Rather than storing these away in a drawer, I wanted to show them off and give the fine embroidery a new lease of life. This crazy patchwork cushion, which uses sections salvaged from a collection of old linens, is my tribute to the work of our grandmothers.

1 Sort through your fabrics, picking out the most interesting areas of embroidery. Cut each patch into a multi-sided shape, with straight edges.

2 Draw a 40cm square in the centre of the white linen cushion front, ruling each line from side to side or top to bottom. Starting in the middle, arrange the patches on the white linen, in a crazy paving style. Overlap the edges to cover the square completely, then pin them in place.

3 Tuck under a 5mm turning along each of the uppermost edges and sew the patches to the linen, with small slip stitches worked in white sewing thread, as close to the folds as possible.

4 Redraw the 40cm square, going over the edges of the patches where they overlap the outline.

top tip WASH AND PRESS ALL THE CLOTHS AND DISCARD ANY WORN OR STAINED AREAS. YOU MAY FIND
THAT THE COLOUR OF THE FABRIC MAY VARY FROM SNOW WHITE TO CREAM BUT THIS ONLY ADDS TO ITS CHARM.

Crazy Patch Cushion

5 Thread a long-eyed needle with three strands of pink embroidery thread and stitch a row of feather stitch (see how to do this on page 29) over each folded edge. Make sure that the outer rows of stitching end 5mm from the pencilled outline.

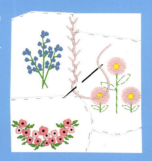

6 Cut the cushion front to size by trimming along the pencil lines. Press back a 1cm turning along each edge. Mitre the corners (see page 21) and then tack down the turning.

7 Prepare the piping by folding the bias binding over the cord and tacking the two sides together. Fit a zip foot to your sewing machine and sew a line of straight stitch close to the cord (this will keep the piping stable when you hand stitch the cover).

8 Starting close to one corner, pin the piping around the edge of the cover so that the cord peeps over the edge. Hand sew in place with white sewing cotton. Leave the first 3cm unstitched, and make small, closely spaces slip stitches all round the four edges. When you have completed the round, fold the two ends to the back so that they butt up closely against each other. Sew down on the wrong side and trim to 2cm.

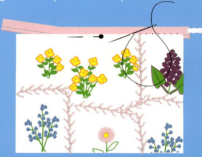

9 Press back 1cm around cushion back, mitring the corners as for the front.

10 Pin the back and front together and slip stitch the cushion back in place around three sides, sewing through the bias binding. Insert the cushion pad, then sew up the final side.

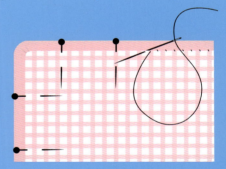

top tip SAVE YOUR TINIEST OFFCUTS OF PRINTED AND PLAIN FABRIC FROM YOUR OTHER PROJECTS AND USE THEM TO CREATE A MORE BRIGHTLY PATTERNED INTERPRETATION OF THIS THRIFTY TECHNIQUE.

Triangle Patch Pillowcase

MATERIALS

a selection of striped and gingham
   cotton fabrics in reds, blues
   and white
a cotton shirt with button front
red and white gingham for backing
matching sewing thread
quilter's ruler
rotary cutter and cutting mat
soft pencil and ruler
sewing kit
sewing machine

SKILL LEVEL: 2

The country-style colour scheme of red, blue and white has been reinterpreted many times over the years. To give this pillowslip a crisper, more contemporary look, I chose a repeating triangle design that was made up in cotton salvaged from check and striped clothing. To save a lot of fiddly stitching, I recycled a shirt front to make the buttoned opening.

1 Wash and press all the fabrics, then cut out eighteen dark and eighteen light 14cm squares. Using a ruler and a sharp, soft pencil, draw a diagonal line across each of the light squares, from corner to corner. With right sides facing, pin them together in pairs, one light and one dark. Machine stitch two parallel lines across the square, each one 6mm from the line. Cut the squares apart along the line.

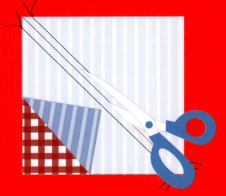

2 Trim the patches down to 11.5cm square, then press all the seam allowances towards the darker patches. Lay them out in five horizontal rows of seven squares, with all the dark triangles pointing towards the bottom right corner. Take time to rearrange them until the colours and patterns are evenly balanced.

3 Join the squares in vertical rows of five, starting at the top left corner. Pin the first two patches together with right sides facing, so that the bottom edge of the first square lies along the top edge of the second one. Machine stitch, leaving a seam allowance of 6mm, then join on the other three patches in the same way. Double check that all the dark triangles are facing in the same direction, as it's very easy to get them the wrong way round at this stage!

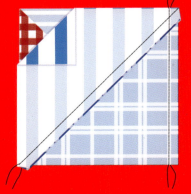

top tip THE PILLOWSLIP IS QUICKLY ASSEMBLED USING A ROTARY CUTTER AND QUILTER'S RULER
TO MAKE THE 'HALF SQUARE TRIANGLE' PATCHES. LEARN HOW TO USE A ROTARY CUTTER ON PAGE 17.

Triangle Patch Pillowcase

4 When the row is complete, press all the straight seam allowances towards the first square. Join the other six rows in the same way.

5 Now join the rows together. With right sides facing, hold the left edge of the first row against the right edge of the second row, matching the seams exactly. Insert a pin at each seam line and at both corners.

6 Machine stitch 6mm from the edge, then add the other five rows. Press all the seams in the same direction, towards the right.

7 Cut a rectangle of gingham to exactly the same width as the completed patchwork (approximately 53cm), but 5.5cm longer. This will be the back of the pillowslip.

8 Trim the buttonhole and button bands from one of the shirts. Each strip should be 6cm wide and as long as possible.

9 With right sides facing, pin the buttonhole strip to the left edge of the patchwork front and machine stitch with a 6mm seam allowance. Neaten the seam with a zigzag or overlocking stitch and press away from the buttonholes.

10 Pin the button band to the back, in the same way. Check that the buttons will line up exactly with the buttonholes, then sew in place and neaten the seam.

11 Fold the button band to the wrong side of the back along the seam line, then with right sides facing pin the top front and back together. Machine stitch 6mm from the edge around three sides and neaten the seam. Turn right side out, ease out the corners and press the side seams.

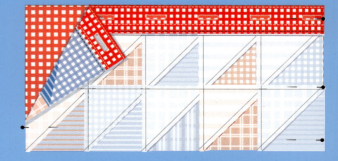

top tip TO MAKE THE BUTTON BAND LOOK A BIT MORE INTERESTING, I SNIPPED OFF THE ORIGINAL BUTTONS AND SEWED ON A MULTI-COLOURED SELECTION SAVED FROM THE OTHER SHIRTS I HAD COLLECTED.

Suffolk Puff Cushion

MATERIALS

120 x 40cm red spot print fabric
120 x 25cm blue spot print fabric
about 100 x 25cm in floral prints with
   a white background
94 x 42cm plain blue cotton fabric
tea bags
washing-up bowl
wooden spoon
matching sewing thread
sewing machine
sewing kit
40cm square cushion pad

CUTTING OUT

from red spot print fabric
45 circles
from blue spot print fabric
16 circles
from other print fabrics
20 circles

SKILL LEVEL: 3

When I discovered a square of Suffolk Puff patchwork amidst a bundle of vintage textiles I decided the pretty, softly faded fabrics needed a second chance. The panel was stitched to the front of a plain pink cushion and I was delighted with the way the unexpectedly bright colour peeped out through the spaces between the puffs. This inspired me to create a cushion cover from my own spot, star and floral haberdashery fabrics, but to keep the softness of the original piece I first dipped all the fabric in strong tea to tone down the colours.

1 Launder any new fabrics to remove the dressing used in the manufacturing process. Make up a dye bath by steeping five tea bags (traditional strong English breakfast tea rather anything fruity or herbal!) in a washing up bowl of very hot water. Remove them after about fifteen minutes.

2 Add the fabrics and leave them to soak for thirty minutes, stirring them with a wooden spoon now and again to ensure even coverage. Rinse, then leave to dry naturally and press well. Remember that the fabric will dry to a lighter shade, so if you would like it to be darker, just go through the whole process again.

3 Trace an 11cm diameter template on to paper and use this as a guide to cut out the fabric circles, as listed above.

4 Thread a long needle with a long length of thread and knot the ends together so that it is double.

5 To make a circle of fabric into a puff, fold back a 5mm turning around the circumference and stitch it down with a round of evenly spaced running stitches. The smaller the stitches, the finer your gathers will be: the ones used for the cushion shown here were 8mm long with equal gaps between them.

6 Gently draw up the thread to gather the circle, using the tip of your needle to push the raw edges inside if necessary. Take the needle down through the finished puff and fasten off the thread securely on the wrong side with a few short back stitches. Trim the thread close to the surface.

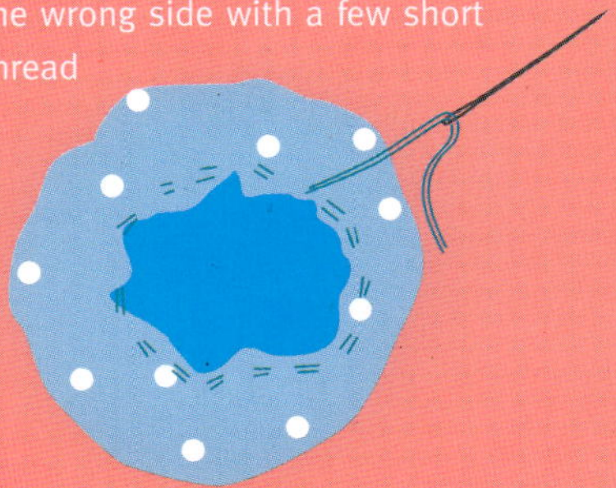

top tip SUFFOLK PUFFS CAN BE STITCHED TOGETHER IN MANY DIFFERENT WAYS: TRY ARRANGING THEM IN STRAIGHT ROWS, A CHEQUERBOARD PATTERN, DIAGONAL LINES OR JUST HAPHAZARDLY FOR A LESS FORMAL LOOK.

Suffolk Puff Cushion

7 Arrange the finished puffs in nine rows of nine, with the red spot ones around the outside edge and forming a central cross. Each corner then has five white and four blue spot puffs.

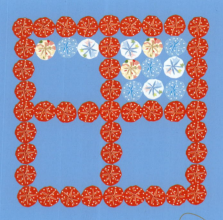

8 Sew together the top row of puffs. Hold the first two together with right sides facing and make several small, tight overstitches to join the edges together. Take the needle to the opposite side of the puff and sew on the next one in the same way. Do the same all the way along the row, making sure that the stitches all lie in a straight line, then fasten off securely. Join the other eight rows in the same way and lay them back out the the right order.

9 Now comes the tricky bit: joining the rows. Start by holding the top two rows together with right sides facing. Join the first puff of each row with a few stitches, then take the needle across to the bottom edge of the second row. Sew this point to the first puff of the third row, then repeat the process so that all the first puffs are stitched together.

10 Join all the second puffs, then the third, and continue until the cover is completed. Check it for any weak joins and re-stitch tightly.

11 Turn under and press a 1cm double hem at each short end of the blue fabric rectangle.

12 Place the fabric face upwards on your work surface and turn back 25cm at each edge. Pin the top and bottom edges together through all the layers and machine stitch, leaving a 1cm seam allowance.

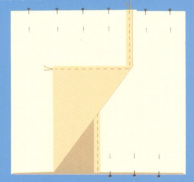

13 Turn the cover right side out and press. Place it face down on the finished puff cushion front, adjusting the position so that half a circle projects at each edge. Pin the cover to the cushion front and slip stitch the two together around the edge of the cover. Insert the cushion pad.

top tip IF YOU'RE NOT A TEA DRINKER, DON'T WORRY. STRONG, FRESHLY BREWED COFFEE CAN ALSO BE USED TO CHANGE THE COLOUR OF YOUR FABRIC, AND WILL GIVE IT A WARMER, BROWNER TONE.

Child's Cushion

SKILL LEVEL: 1

This simple cushion cover, made from nine bright squares, pays homage to one of the first sewing projects I did as a little girl. I can vividly remember sitting patiently as I completed each fabric-covered template in turn, and then the huge sense of achievement when I learnt how to stitch them together. It would still be a perfect starting point for beginners or for newcomers to English-style patchwork.

1 Thread your needle and keep it ready to hand. Pin a paper square centrally to the back of one of the fabric squares so that there is a 1cm margin all round.

2 Fold the top margin back over the template. Starting with the knot on the right side, sew the fabric to the paper with long running stitches. Fold over the next margin so that you have a neat right angle at the corner. Tack down this edge, then stitch down the other two edges. Work a double stitch to secure the thread and trim the end to 2cm. Cover all the papers in the same way.

3 Using the photograph opposite as your guide, lay the squares out in three rows of three, with the check patch in the centre surrounded by the eight flowery patches.

4 Pick up the first two squares on the top row. With the fabric sides facing, hold them together so that the left edge of the second square lies along the right edge of the first square. (Don't worry, this will make sense when you do it!)

5 Starting at the right hand corner, sew the two patches together with small over stitches.

6 Join the third square to complete the row, then make up the other two rows.

MATERIALS

a minimum of
  60 x 40cm check fabric
  40 x 10cm small-scale floral fabric
  40 x 10cm large-scale floral fabric
old envelopes and paper
matching sewing thread
sewing machine
sewing kit
25cm cushion pad

TEMPLATES

from check fabric
one 10cm square
two 16 x 26cm back panels
from small-scale floral print fabric
four 10cm squares
from large-scale floral print fabric
four 10cm squares
from paper
nine 8cm square templates

top tip MAKING UP THE CUSHION COVER BY MACHINE IS A REALLY JOB FOR TEENAGERS AND ADULTS, BUT IT WOULD BE A GOOD SEWING LESSON FOR OLDER CHILDREN WORKING UNDER CLOSE SUPERVISION, AS THE SEAMING IS VERY STRAIGHTFORWARD.

Child's Cushion

7 Now it's time to sew the three rows together in just the same way, making sure that the seam lines match up as you go. When you get to the end of the thread, make three stitches in the opposite direction to secure the end of the seam and trim the tail to 5mm.

8 Then you have finished sewing, unpick and remove all the papers, then open out the turnings around the outside edge. Press these so that they lie flat.

9 Press under a 1cm double turning along one long edge of each back panel. Sew this down by hand or machine.

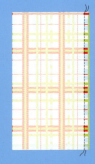

10 Place the cushion front on your work surface with the right side facing upwards. Position one back panel, face downwards, on the left of the cushion front so that the raw edges are matching. Lay the other panel on the right, then pin the layers together around all four sides.

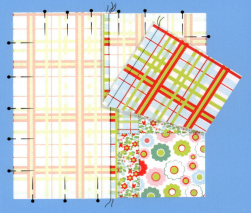

11 Machine stitch all the way around the edge of the cushion cover, leaving a 1cm seam allowance.

12 Snip a tiny triangle from each corner, 5mm from the stitching. Turn it right side out and ease out the corners into sharp angles with a pencil. Press the seams lightly then insert the cushion pad.

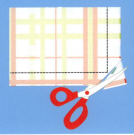

top tip MAKE THIS CUSHION INTO A SOUVENIR OF CHILDHOOD BY USING SCRAPS OF FABRIC FROM OUTGROWN SHIRTS, BLOUSES AND DRESSES. THEN SEW ON A FEW BUTTONS, BUTTONS OR EMBROIDERED MOTIFS FROM THE GARMENTS AS EXTRA DECORATION.

Child's Pentagon Ball

MATERIALS

twelve scraps of cotton, at least
 15cm square
used envelopes or old letters
tacking thread
matching sewing thread
250g polyester toy stuffing
sewing kit

SKILL LEVEL: 2

Every budding sports star has to start somewhere, so this soft patchwork ball is guaranteed to provide hours of goal practice for your favourite toddler. It's made from twelve hand-stitched pentagons – a variation on the usual honeycomb hexagon technique – and the pictorial fabrics are a blend of vintage nursery finds and my own prints for children.

1 Trace or photocopy the full-size pentagon template on page 156. Using this as your guide, cut out twelve pentagons from recycled paper.

2 Pin a paper pentagon to the wrong side of the first fabric scrap, centring it over either a motif or an interesting pattern area. Cut the fabric to the same pentagon shape but adding a margin, snipping approximately 1cm from the edges of the paper. Fold the fabric margin over each side of the paper pentagon in turn, stitching it to the paper as you go.

3 The ball is made in two separate halves. When you have covered all the papers, plan the layout for both parts. Choose the two strongest motifs and arrange five patches around each one, balancing the colours evenly on each side.

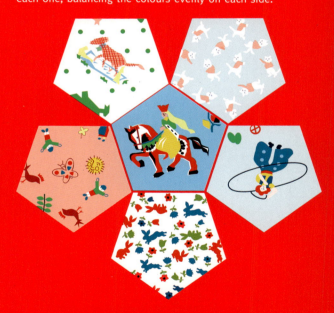

top tip THE FINISHED BALL MEASURES ABOUT 15CM IN DIAMETER, BUT YOU CAN CHANGE THE SIZE OF THE TEMPLATE TO MAKE IT LARGER OR SMALLER: 2.5CM PENTAGONS WOULD MAKE A TINY BALL THAT YOU COULD USE FOR A CHRISTMAS DECORATION.

Child's Pentagon Ball

4 Pick out the centre pentagon and one from the edge, and hold them together with right sides facing. Bring a threaded needle out through the right corner of the front patch, then oversew them along one edge. Work a few extra stitches at each end of the row to reinforce the seam.

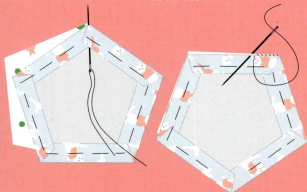

5 Sew the third patch to the next edge of the centre pentagon in the same way. To join the second and third patches, fold the centre patch in half so that the other two face each other and stitch the two adjacent edges together. Join on the remaining three patches in the same way, then make up the second half of the ball.

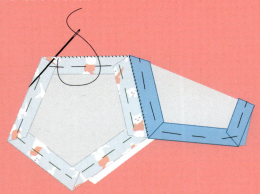

6 Seam the two halves together, remembering to reinforce all corners. At this stage the ball can be a bit awkward to hold, so fold it whichever way feels comfortable for you and adjust the two parts as you sew each pair of sides together. Leave the last two edges unstitched.

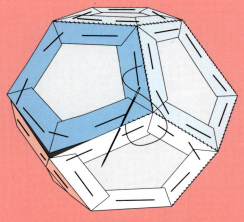

7 Unpick all the paper pentagons and remove. Turn the ball right side out through the gap and stuff with wadding. Carry on filling it until the ball has a good round shape, then over stitch the gap to close.

top tip CHOOSE A POLYESTER TOY FILLING THAT MEETS SAFETY STANDARDS AND USE THE HANDLE OF A WOODEN SPOON TO PACK IT DOWN. REMEMBER THAT TO MAKE A GOOD, SOLID BALL IT MAY TAKE MORE STUFFING THAN YOU EXPECT.

Stanley Toy

MATERIALS

dress-weight cotton in mixed prints
scrap of black felt or leather
7 litres of polyester toy filling
two 2cm black buttons
sewing machine
sewing kit

TEMPLATES

Trace off or photocopy the full size triangle, nose and ear templates on page 157.

CUTTING OUT

from mixed print fabrics
one hundred 7cm squares
ten triangles
five 7 x 10cm rectangles
from red spot fabric
four ears
from felt or leather
one nose

SKILL LEVEL: 3

As you may have already guessed, this one of my favourite projects of all… a patchwork version of my dog Stanley. I have to admit that he's almost as adorable as the original, but much better behaved! He's made from an eclectic mix of my lightweight haberdashery fabrics in reds and blues, including dots, flowers, cowboys and, of course, my pet's very own signature print – Mini Stanley.

The seam allowance throughout is 6mm.

1 Cuddly Stanley is made from two dog-shaped side panels (one the mirror image of the other) which are joined together with a gusset loop. Start by laying out 35 squares and five triangles as shown to make the left-facing side panel. With right sides, facing pin and stitch together the patches in each horizontal row.

2 Iron the seam allowances on the top row towards the left, then press the seams on the next row down towards the right. Press all the other rows, alternating the direction in which they lie. The muzzle seams go to the right, as do the top two leg rows. The bottom leg rows lie on the left.

3 To assemble the body, pin the bottom edge of the top head row to the top edge of the next row down, matching up the seams. Machine stitch. Press this and all the other horizontal seams downwards.

4 Now join the head to the top row of the body. Add the muzzle, the other two body rows, the two legs and the tail. Make up the right-facing body panel in exactly the same way, reversing the direction.

5 With right sides facing, pin the ears together in pairs and sew around the curved edges. Trim the seam back to 3mm at the tips. Turn right side out, and press. Tack in place at the top of the head.

top tip SAFETY FIRST: I'M SURE I DON'T HAVE TO REMIND YOU THAT ANY FILLING USED FOR SOFT TOYS SHOULD CONFORM TO RECOGNISED SAFETY STANDARDS, AND THAT THIS TOY IS FOR OLDER CHILDREN ONLY.

6 The gusset is a mixture of squares and rectangles. The rectangles lie next to the triangular patches at head and tail, and the squares next to the other body squares. Each of the 16 straight edges are assembled separately, then they are joined to make a loop.

7 Start at the tail and join six squares for Stan's back end. Seam two squares for the back paw, two squares for the inside leg, two squares for Stan's underbelly, and so on until you reach the tip of his nose. Seam two rectangles for his forehead, pick a single patch for the crown, two rectangles for the back of his head, three squares for his back and the final rectangle for his tail. Press the seams in one direction. Lay all the pieces in place around the left-facing body panel.

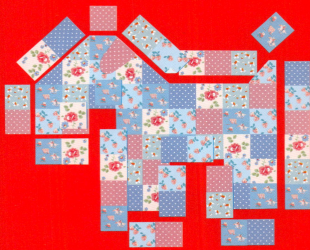

8 Insert a marker pin in the top patch of the first strip so you can find it again. With right sides facing, pin the top of the sole strip to the bottom end. Sew together, leaving 6mm unstitched at each end of the seam. Join the rest of the strips and single patches in the same way, then join to make a loop. Press the seams open.

9 Again starting at the tip of the tail, pin the loop to the body with right sides facing. Fold out the open ends of the seams so that the gusset will fit neatly at the corners. Sew all the way round, 6mm from the edge. Attach the right-facing body panel in the same way, leaving the underbelly unstitched.

10 Turn right side out and push out the corners. Pack the toy filling down into the paws, muzzle and tail, then into the head and body, using the handle of a wooden spoon to push it down firmly. Slip stitch the opening with a double length of thread.

11 Sew the two eyes very securely to sides of the head and stitch the nose in place with small over stitches.

12 Make a collar from a 35 x 10cm strip of red cotton fabric. Press in half widthways, then press under a 1cm turning at both long edges. Refold and top stitch 3mm from each edge. Fold under the edges and fit around Stan's neck. Trim the ends to fit snugly, then sew them together.

top tip AS A FINISHING TOUCH I HAD A BONE-SHAPED DOG TAG ENGRAVED WITH STAN'S NAME AND ATTACHED IT TO THE FABRIC COLLAR. YOUR LOCAL KEY-CUTTER SHOULD HAVE SOMETHING SIMILAR.

Bunny Blanket

MATERIALS

45cm square 10-count canvas
tapestry frame
fringed cream blanket
15 x 13cm blue felt
matching sewing thread
scrap of orange felt
small amount of polyester toy filling
stranded embroidery thread in green
   and black
tracing paper and pencil
sewing kit

TEMPLATES

Bunny, see page 158

SKILL LEVEL: 1

I like this adorable rabbit patch so much that I have used it twice, adapting it in two quite different ways. Here is its first appearance, cut from blue felted wool, gently padded and appliquéd to the corner of a vintage cream blanket. Have a look at the other version on page 141 – a flowery bunny (or two) would look equally good on the blanket and you could alter the size to make a whole rabbit family.

1 Trace or photocopy the full-sized bunny template on page 158 and cut out around the outside edge. Pin to the felt, then cut out as close to the paper as possible.

2 Pin the bunny to the corner of the blanket. Sew it down by hand with tiny over stitches, leaving 3cm open in the centre of the back.

3 Stuff small amounts of polyester filling through this space, using a pencil to push them right into the head, paws and tail end, then sew up the gap.

4 Embroider the eyes and nose in satin stitch (see page 28), using a single thread of black embroidery cotton. Add a few short black straight stitches for the bunny's whiskers.

5 Using blue thread, work curved rows of small running stitches at the front and back legs as indicated on the template. Cut out a little carrot from orange felt and sew it down around the edge with matching thread. Add a tuft of long, thin green chain stitches or several straight stitches to the top of the carrot (see page 29).

6 To make the tail, carefully snip off one strand of the fringe from the outside edge of the blanket (preferably on the opposite side to the bunny). Curl it up into an oval and stab stitch securely in place.

top tip THE RAISED TAIL AND WOOLLEN FRINGE MEAN THAT THIS TYPE OF DECORATED BLANKET SHOULD BE GIVEN ONLY TO OLDER CHILDREN (AS THERE MAY BE A CHOKING HAZARD FOR SMALL BABIES).

Star Throw

MATERIALS
for each block
45cm square of white cotton fabric
20 x 20cm each of four different
    print fabrics
10cm square darker fabric
10cm square fusible bonding web
printed fabric for binding
matching sewing thread
sewing kit
sewing machine

TEMPLATES
Photocopy the two templates on page
159 and transfer the outlines on to
thin cardboard

CUTTING OUT
for each star
eight star points, two from each fabric
for the binding
one 8cm wide strip, 10cm longer than
    the sum of all four sides (join strips
    to achieve the required length)

MEASURING UP
twenty blocks set in 4 rows of 5 =
178 x 221cm: adapt these proportions
to suit your own bed

SKILL LEVEL: 3

An ideal bedcover for sunny summer days, this throw is a
contemporary re-working of a classic design. It consists of
just a single layer of fabric, bound at the edge and decorated
with a repeating pattern of patchwork stars. These are a
variation on the 'Dresden Plate' pattern and because each star
is stitched to an individual square block the finished size can
be as as large or small as you wish.

1 Mark two dots at the two top corners on the seam line on
each of the star point patches.

2 Arrange eight patches in their
finished star shape. With right
sides facing, pin the first two
together along one long edge.
Machine stitch as far as the
dot, then work a few
backwards stitches to
secure the seam and trim
the thread. Add the other
six patches in this way, then
join the first and last together
to complete the star.

3 Press all the seams open and press back a 6mm turning
along each outer edge.

4 Neaten the edge of the white square with an overlocking
or zigzag stitch. Press it very lightly in half, then half again to
mark it into quarters.
Pin the finished star
to the square, lining
the points up with
the crease lines. Sew
in place, either by
hand or with a narrow
machine buttonhole
or zigzag stitch.

top tip THE STARS ON MY THROW ARE ALL IDENTICAL, BUT THIS DESIGN LOOKS EQUALLY

EFFECTIVE WHEN EACH SQUARE HAS A DIFFERENT STAR MADE FROM EIGHT RANDOMLY SELECTED PRINTS.

Star Throw

5 Trace the octagon outline from the template on page 159 on to the paper side of the bonding web. Iron it to the back of the dark fabric and cut out carefully around the outline. Peel off the backing paper and position the patch in the centre of the star. Press in place then machine stitch around the edge in a thread to match the fabric. Make up all the squares in this way.

6 Lay out all your finished squares. With right sides facing, join them in horizontal rows with a 1cm seam. Press all the seams open.

7 Again with right sides facing, pin the bottom edge of the top row to the top edge of the second row, matching the seams exactly. Machine stitch and press the seam open. Add the other rows in the same way.

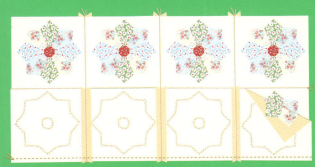

8 Press under a 1cm turning one long edge of the binding strip. With right sides facing, and raw edges matching pin it along the top edge of the throw, trimming the ends in line with the fabric. Machine stitch, then turn the folded edge over to the back. Pin it down so that the fold lies 3mm beyond the stitch line. Machine stitch in place from the front, sewing along the seam line between the throw and the binding. Bind the bottom edge in the same way.

9 When binding the side edges, fold under 1cm at each end of the fabric strip, and pin it down so that the folds project 1mm beyond the edges. Machine stitch and fold over as before, then stitch down from the front. Slip stitch the edges of the folds.

top tip USE AN OLD WHITE SHEET – COTTON OR LINEN – FOR THE BACKING SQUARES

AS AN ECO-ALTERNATIVE TO BUYING NEW FABRIC.

Hankie Bedcover

MATERIALS
printed hankies
flat sheet to fit finished cover
matching sewing thread
sewing machine
sewing kit

HOW MANY HANKIES?
The hankies are 50cm square. You will need 3 rows of 5 for a single bed, 4 rows of 5 for a double, 5 rows of 5 for a king size and as many as 6 rows of 5 for a super king. Measure up your bed first and decide how much of an overhang you would like at each side, then round off to the nearest 50cm.

SKILL LEVEL: 2

The Stone Roses hankie is far to pretty to be hidden away in a handbag or tucked away in a pocket. The design is an adaptation of one of my fabrics, with a deep curved border of blooms set around a central spray, and it is just one of a series of printed handkerchiefs. I love the way that new shapes are created when the pattern is repeated (see the picture on the previous pages), but the same technique would work equally well with an assortment of different designs.

1 Prepare the hankies by removing the labels, then laundering and pressing them. Wash and iron the backing sheet too if it's a new one, then there's no possibility of shrinkage in the future.

2 Join them first in short rows of three or more. Pin together with right sides facing and machine stitch 1cm from the hem. Press the seams open.

3 Lay the first two rows together along one long edge, again with right sides facing, and line up the seams. Insert a pin through each point where they meet, then pin the rest of the

edges together. Stitch and press as before, and continue until you have joined all the rows.

4 You'll need plenty of space for this step, so make sure you have a nice clean floor! Spread out and smooth the sheet. Place the hankies face down on top, lining the two up along one side and the bottom edge. Pin them together with the pins parallel to the hems, and trim the sheet to the same size as the hankies.

5 Machine stitch all the way round, leaving a 1cm seam allowance. Leave a 50cm gap along one edge and turn the cover right side out through this opening. Press back a 1cm turning along each side of the opening, pin the two layers together and slip stitch to close.

top tip I KNOW THAT IT'S NOT REALLY A PATCH PROJECT, BUT A SINGLE HANDKERCHIEF MAKES A GREAT CUSHION COVER! IMAGINE A WHOLE ROW OF THEM, EACH ONE IN A DIFFERENT FLORAL OR GREETINGS PRINT.

Curtain Panel

MATERIALS
floral fabric
striped fabric for the sashing, plus
   extra for the header and facing
plain fabric
10cm curtain header tape the same
   width as finished curtain
curtain hooks
matching sewing thread
sewing machine
sewing kit

SKILL LEVEL: 3

Like some of the best patchwork, this curtain is a combination of old and new fabrics. Large patches cut from the bouquets on my extravagant Blooms furnishing print are sashed with strips of vintage flannel shirting and offset with small squares of plain red cotton. The panel is unlined, so the various materials take on a wonderful stained glass-like quality when hung against a sunlit window.

HOW MUCH FABRIC?

First measure up to find the finished size of your curtain. The drop or length will be the distance between the bottom of your curtain pole and the window sill or floor. The width will be one and a half times the length of the pole for a single panel, or one and a half times half the width for each curtain of a pair.

For the curtain you'll need 12cm of 136cm wide plain, 35cm of 136cm wide striped and at least 50cm of 148cm wide floral fabric for each finished square metre (more if you want to include a lot of very flowery patches).

For the facings you'll need enough striped fabric to make two 8cm strips the same length as the curtain, one 8cm strip the same width and one 12cm strip the same width. You can join the fabric as necessary to create the right length.

CUTTING OUT

Cut the plain fabric into 8cm squares and the striped into eight 20cm rectangles with the stripe running lengthways. Cut the floral print into 20 cm squares, selecting different areas of the repeat for each one. Approximately 1 square metre of patchwork requires 16 large squares, 32 rectangular sashing strips and 16 small squares.

1 Lay all the large squares out and shuffle them around so that the more densely patterned ones are at the centre and there is a border of leaves and sprigs. Add in the squares and rectangles that make up the sashing. You will need sashing rows at the side and bottom edges to frame the panel, but not at the top edge.

2 Start by sewing together the horizontal rows of squares and rectangles in pairs. Pin the short ends of each patch together with right sides facing, then machine stitch leaving a 1cm seam allowance. You can speed up the process by chain piecing and then snipping them apart.

3 Join these pairs together, again with right sides facing and with a 1cm seam. Sew the final square of each row to the end of the last rectangle.

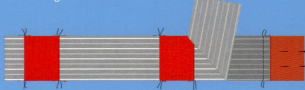

top tip IF YOU ARE MAKING A CURTAIN AS LARGE AS MINE, TRY TO PIECE IT ALL IN A SINGLE

SESSION, OR LEAVE THE PATCHES LAID OUT IN A PLACE WHERE THE LAYOUT WON'T BE DISTURBED.

114

4 Press all the seam allowances so that they lie towards the rectangles.

5 Now join the vertical rectangles to the large squares, in horizontal rows, again with a 1cm seam. Start at the left of each row and join on one patch at a time. Sew the last rectangle in each row to the right edge of the final square.

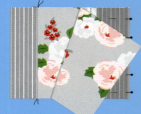

6 When each row is complete, press the seam allowances towards the rectangles.

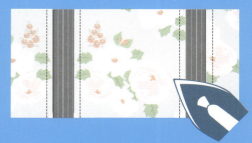

7 Starting at the bottom, sew the patches and sashing together. Place the first two rows together with right sides facing, so that the top edge of the sashing lies along the bottom edge of the patches. Insert a pin through both seams at the points where they meet. Pin the corners and the spaces between the pins, then machine stitch with a 1cm seam allowance. Press the seam towards the sashing. Join all the rows in this way.

Curtain Panel

8 Cut an 8cm strip of striped fabric to fit along the bottom edge to make the facing. Press under a 6mm turning along one long edge. Pin the raw edge to the curtain with right sides facing and machine stitch with a 1cm seam. Turn the facing to the wrong side, pin and tack down the turning and machine stitch from the right side, close to the long seam line. Press.

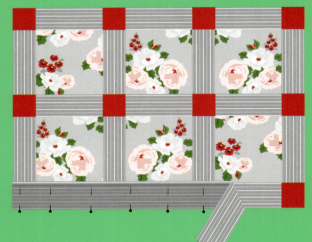

9 Neaten the two side edges in the same way. Cut the facings so that they are 2cm longer than the curtains and sew them on so that this extra fabric extends below the bottom edge. Press it under, in line with the hem, before folding back and sewing down the facings.

10 Cut a 12cm strip to go along the curtain header (or top edge), adding an extra 4cm. Press back a 3cm turning along one long edge. Pin the raw edge to the curtain with right sides facing, so that 2cm extends at each end. Machine stitch 1cm from the edge and press the seam up towards the facing.

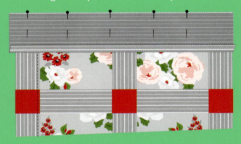

11 Press back the extra fabric in line with the side edges.

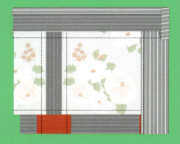

12 Press under 1cm at each end of the header tape. Draw out the three gathering cords at at both ends, then pin and stitch the tape to the top of the curtain, so that the top edge lies 2cm down from the fold and the bottom edge conceals the seam.

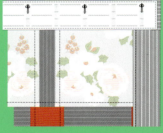

13 Gather the cords to the required width and knot. Insert the curtain hooks and hang in place.

top tip WHEN CUTTING OUT FABRIC WITH A WOVEN (NOT PRINTED) STRIPE, CUT IT FIRST INTO A LONG STRIP, FOLLOWING THE STRIPES, THEN USE A ROTARY CUTTER AND RULER TO TRIM IT INTO RECTANGLES.

Tea Towel Tablecloth

MATERIALS
linen and cotton tea towels
large reel of sewing thread
sewing kit
sewing machine

SKILL LEVEL: 1

When I had a look through my linen cupboard to find a suitable cloth for my new dining table I couldn't find anything that was the right size. However, the neatly folded stacks of linen tea towels, with their unexpected combinations of stripes and checks, gave me an idea... here are the biggest patches in the book!

MEASURING UP

An average tea towel is 40 x 60cm. Instead of getting into any complicated calculations, the best way to work out how many you will need is to gather together all your old tea towels and lay them over the tabletop, allowing a 50cm overhang at each edge!

1 Pick out the smallest tea towel and cut away the hemmed edges and any selvedges. You can do this by following the woven stripes or by drawing guidelines with a fabric marker and a large quilting rule.

2 Trim all the other towels down to the same size, using the small towel as a template. Pin it to each one in turn, centring it over the design, and cut away the margins.

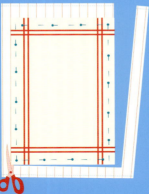

3 Neaten the edge of each towel by machine with a wide zigzag or an overlocking stitch. This will take a while, but it's worth it in the end!

4 Clear the floor and lay out the towels in rows. As with any other patchwork, you should aim for a good balance of colour and pattern, so take time to shuffle them about until you are pleased with the arrangement.

5 Join the horizontal rows along the long edges with a 1.5cm seam. Press all the seams open (this makes the cloth flatter than if they are pressed to one side).

6 Pin the first two rows together along one long edge, matching the seams and corners exactly. Join with a 1.5cm seam and press the seam open. Add the other rows in the same way.

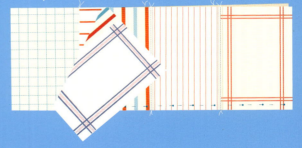

7 Press under a 1.5cm turning around the outside edge of the finished cloth. Mitre each of the corners (see page 21), then pin and machine down the hem 12mm from the fold.

top tip USE A MIXTURE OF OLD AND NEW TEA TOWELS, BUT WASH THEM ALL ON A HOT SETTING AND PRESS WELL BEFORE STITCHING: THEY MIGHT SHRINK AT DIFFERENT RATES WHICH MAY DISTORT YOUR FINISHED CLOTH.

Sugarbag Doorstop

MATERIALS

scraps of printed canvas or furnishing
   weight fabric
18cm of 2.5cm-wide webbing
20cm of 2cm-wide velcro
plastic beads or 2kg rice for filling
matching sewing thread
sewing kit
sewing machine

CUTTING OUT

from print fabric
twenty-seven 6 x 10cm rectangles
ten 6cm squares
from plain fabric
two 11 x 18cm rectangles for base

SKILL LEVEL: 2

A doorstop is one of those indispensable home accessories that is often overlooked, but there's no reason why it shouldn't be decorative. My patchwork version, in shades of dusky pink, olive and chocolate brown, combines extra large polka dots with furnishing size roses and a tiny floral sprig. It shows how just effective a mixture of fabric with different scale prints can look if you restrict yourself to a limited palette.

The seam allowance is 1cm throughout. Press each seam open after stitching.

1 All four side panels are made in the same way, from five rectangles and two squares. Lay out the patches for the first side as in the drawing. Starting at the bottom, join the two rectangles together. Next, go to the top left and sew the two squares to the adjacent horizontal rectangles. Join these two pieces together horizontally, then add the vertical rectangle to the right edge. Add the two joined ectangles to the bottom edge.

2 Draw a point 1cm in from the top and bottom edges at each corner, to mark the ends of the seam lines.

3 With right sides facing, pin two panels together along one side edge, making sure that they are both the same way up and the seams and corners are aligned. Machine stitch between the dots so that 1cm remains open at each end of the seam. Add the other two panels, then join the remaining sides.

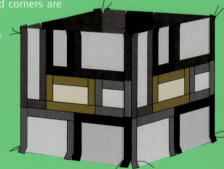

4 The top panel is made from the remaining two squares and seven rectangles, laid out as shown above. Firstly sew the two horizontal rectangles at the bottom together and add a vertical rectangle at each side. Join the two squares to the adjacent rectangles and then sew these two pieces together. Add the vertical rectangle to the right edge, then sew the two halves together.

top tip IF YOU ARE USING RICE AS A FILLING, LINE THE DOORSTOP WITH A LARGE PLASTIC BAG FIRST AND

SEAL THE IT WITH PARCEL TAPE. THIS WAY IT WILL STAY DRY AND THERE'S NO DANGER OF MOULD OR MILDEW.

Sugarbag Doorstop

5 Mark the ends of the seams on the wrong side, as for the side panels.

6 Pin the two ends of the webbing centrally to the sides of the top panel. Machine stitch 5cm from the edge, working two or three rows backwards and forwards to reinforce.

7 With the right side facing downwards pin one edge of the top panel to the top edge of one of the joined side panels. Machine stitch between the dots, working a few backwards stitches to reinforce both ends of the seam. Sew the other three edges in the same way.

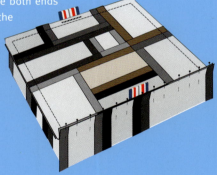

8 Press a 1cm turning over to the right side of one long edge of a base panel. Pin the fuzzy side of the velcro over the turning so that the right edge lies along the fold and machine stitch in place. Press the turning on the other panel to the wrong side and sew the hooked velcro over the turning in the same way.

9 Mark the ends of the seams on the outer corners as for the side panels. Stick the two pieces together, making sure that the top and bottom edges measure 18cm. Sew to the base of the doorstop in the same way as the top panel.

10 Trim a 5mm triangle from the end of each long seam to reduce bulk at the corners.

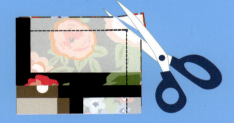

11 Open up the velcro and turn the door stop right side out. Ease out the seams and corners, then fill the with rice or beads (using a large serving spoon is the least messy way to do this) and close the velcro once again.

top tip I WAS LUCKY ENOUGH TO FIND AN ODD LENGTH OF STRIPED WEBBING FOR THE HANDLE, BUT YOU

CAN MAKE AN EQUALLY EFFECTIVE ONE FROM A STRIP OF FABRIC FOLLOWING THE INSTRUCTIONS ON PAGE 21.

Tartan Beanbag

MATERIALS
a minimum of 1m x 50cm each of
  three plaid fabrics
80 x 70cm plaid for base
0.5 sq m safety standard
  polystyrene beads in liner
54cm velcro
dressmaker's squared paper
matching sewing thread
sewing machine
sewing kit

SKILL LEVEL: 3

Patchwork isn't all about ditsy floral prints. Larger scale geometrics have a striking, bolder look and I really like the somewhat haphazard effect you get by juxtaposing plaids, tartans and checks. This comfortably squashy beanbag is covered in a combination of three woven fabrics, which started out as cotton picnic blankets. It would make versatile extra seating or a useful footstool, but it's so comfortable that it might just be commandeered by the family pet.

CUTTING OUT
from plaid fabrics
Cut the fabrics into 15cm strips, following the woven lines to keep the edges straight. Snip the strips into patches of different widths, ranging from 8 to 20cm wide.
from base plaid fabric
Fold the template along the marked line and use this as a guide to cut two base panels.

TEMPLATE
Make a circle template by drawing onto dressmaker's paper a circle with a 62cm diameter. Draw on a cutting line for the base panel.

The seam allowance is 1cm throughout. Press each seam open after stitching.

1 To make the side panel, join the patches into three rows, each 180cm long. Pin the side edges together and machine stitch with a 15mm seam. Press the seam allowance to the right and top stitch 3mm from the seam line.

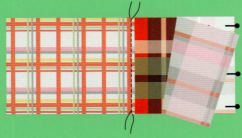

2 With right sides facing, pin the bottom edge of the first strip and the top edge of the second strip together. Machine stitch, again with a 15mm allowance. Join the third strip and press the seam allowances upwards. Top stitch as before.

top tip YOU COULD USE THIS ONE-OFF PLAID TO REVAMP AN OLD POUFFE OR OTTOMAN... BUT JUST

THINK HOW WONDERFUL A PATCHWORK UPHOLSTERED ARMCHAIR – OR EVEN A SOFA – WOULD LOOK.

Tartan Beanbag

3 Make a similar patchwork panel for the top, from six 75cm rows. Pin on the circle template, lining up the midpoint with the centre seam. Cut out carefully.

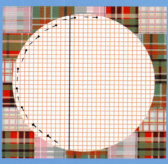

8 Press a 2cm turning back to the right side of the second base panel and sew the other part of the velcro to it in the same way.

4 Join the short edges of the side panel to make a cylinder, and top stitch the seam.

5 Position eight pins around the top edge of the cylinder at intervals of approximately 22cm. Insert eight pins in the outside edge of the circle, 24cm apart.

6 With right sides facing facing, pin the top to the sides, matching up the marker pins first so that they fit together without distortion. Machine stitch all the way round the top, 15mm from the edge.

9 Join the two halves of the base by pressing the velcro strips together, but at the same time, slip a sheet of paper between the two parts at the centre so that you can easily separate them later. Pin the slip of paper to the fabric.

10 Join the two halves of the base by pressing the velcro together, but slip a sheet of paper between the two parts at the centre, so that you can easily separate them later. Pin the paper to the fabric.

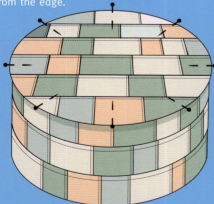

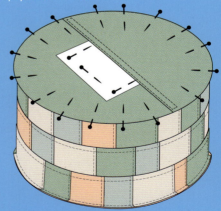

7 Press under a 2cm turning along the straight edge of one base panel. Pull apart the two part of the velcro. Pin the hooked part across the raw edge, 5cm from the fold and with an equal space at each end. Machine stitch around all four sides, 3mm from the edge.

11 Unpin the slip of paper and open out the velcro. Turn right side out and wrestle with the filler until it is inside the cover. You may need to remove some of the beads to make the finished footstool a bit squashier. Close the velcro.

top tip DON'T WORRY TOO MUCH ABOUT THE ORDER IN WHICH YOU ASSEMBLE THE STRIPS – THE COMPLETELY RANDOM ARRANGEMENT OF THE PATTERNS GIVES THIS TYPE OF PATCHWORK ITS INDIVIDUALITY.

Appliqué Tea Towel

MATERIALS
patterned fabric
plain tea towel
15cm spotty ribbon
fusible bonding web
stranded cotyon embroidery thread
sewing thread to match ribbon
sewing kit
iron

SKILL LEVEL: 1

Appliqué is a great way to repurpose some of the odd remnants that textile magpies just can't help hoarding, just like this length of fifties kitchen fabric with nostalgic homemaker imagery. I found the perfect background in a wide linen tea towel with a striped border… but somehow I feel that it might now be more for show than for everyday use.

1 Pick out your favourite prints from the appliqué fabric and cut them out roughly. Following the manufacturer's instructions, fuse them to the adhesive side of the bonding web. Use a sheet of paper towel to protect the iron.

2 Cut each motif out with a curved line, following the contour of the image and leaving a 6–10mm margin of plain fabric all round. Peel off the backing papers.

3 Lay the motifs out on the tea towel, starting with a balanced arrangement of the largest shapes and filling in the gaps with the smaller ones. Using a hot dry iron, press them in position.

4 Edge each motif with a round of blanket stitch, worked with three strands of embroidery thread in a colour to match the background.

5 Make the ribbon into a hanging loop by folding it in half, turning under the ends and stitching it to the top left corner of the tea towel.

top tip THE BLANKET STITCH EDGING GIVES THESE APPLIQUÉ PATCHES A WONDERFUL FINISH, BUT IF TIME AND PATIENCE ARE LIMITED, SIMPLY ANCHOR THEM DOWN WITH A MACHINED ZIGZAG IN CREAM SEWING THREAD.

Hexagon Pincushion

MATERIALS

minimum of 15 x 50cm floral cotton
   fabric
10 x 20cm pink cotton fabric
matching sewing thread
polyester wadding
sewing kit
thick paper for templates

SKILL LEVEL: 2

This simple pincushion design, made up of two hexagon
rosettes, has been a starter project for generations of hand
stitchers. I have given it a new twist by making the six floral
patches identical, so that a new repeating pattern is created
when they are joined together. Known to quilt makers as
'fussy cutting', this is a technique that opens up a whole new
way of working with fabric and has endless possibilities. Start
by making a different design for the front and back and you'll
see what I mean!

1 Cut out 14 paper hexagons for the lining papers following
the inner outline on page 159. You'll also need to make a
window template to help you choose the best floral motifs
and to cut accurate matching patches. Trace both outlines,
then cut out around them both to make a hexagonal frame.

2 Pick out your favourite self-contained flower motif and place
the window template over it. Draw around the outside of the
window, then cut out the hexagon.

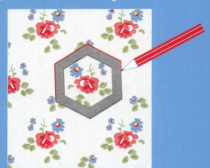

3 Now cut out eleven more matching floral patches. The
easiest way to do this is to pin the original patch precisely
over a similar motif then cut around the outside edge.

4 Following the outside edge of the
window, cut two large pink hexagons
for the centre of the rosettes. Pin
a template to the centre of a pink
hexagon. Working with the template
towards you, fold the surplus fabric
along one edge forwards and tack it to
the paper. Fold the other edges in turn,
stitching each one down as you go.

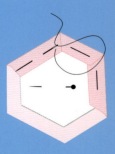

top tip 'FUSSY CUTTING' IS A FASCINATING METHOD, BUT IT CAN TAKE UP A LOT OF FABRIC. CHECK THAT
YOU HAVE ENOUGH TO MAKE SIX MATCHING HEXAGONS BEFORE YOU START TO CUT OUT THE PATCHES.

Hexagon Pincushion

5 Cover all the templates in this way then lay them out in the finished order, checking that the flowers within each rosette all face in the same direction.

6 Start by joining the centre to the bottom floral hexagon. Hold the two together with right sides facing, and double check that the innermost edge of the hexagon is at the top. Oversew this edge to the pink hexagon with small stitches, catching a few threads of the fold on each side with every stitch.

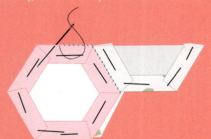

7 The next hexagon to the right fits into the angle between these two patches. Check that it is in the right position, then it to the first floral hexagon. Fold in half and sew the next edge to the pink centre. Sew on the other four floral patches in the same way, then make up the second rosette.

8 Pin the two completed rosettes together with the papers facing inwards and over stitch them together around the outside edge. Leave five hexagon sides unstitched at the bottom edge. Press these edges lightly to set the folds. Unpick all the tacking threads and then remove all the paper templates — this will involve a bit of fiddling about I'm afraid!

9 Stuff the cushion firmly with polyester filling using a pencil to make sure that it reaches right into the corners of the hexagons for a pleasingly plump appearance. Pin the opening and sew four of the edges together. Fill this last space, then slip stitch the final gap.

top tip HONEYCOMB PATCHWORK – A PATTERN MADE UP OF MANY INTERLOCKING HEXAGONS – HAS LONG BEEN A FAVOURITE TECHNIQUE FOR MAKING QUILTS, SO PERHAPS THIS PROJECT WILL INSPIRE YOU TO KEEP ON STITCHING.

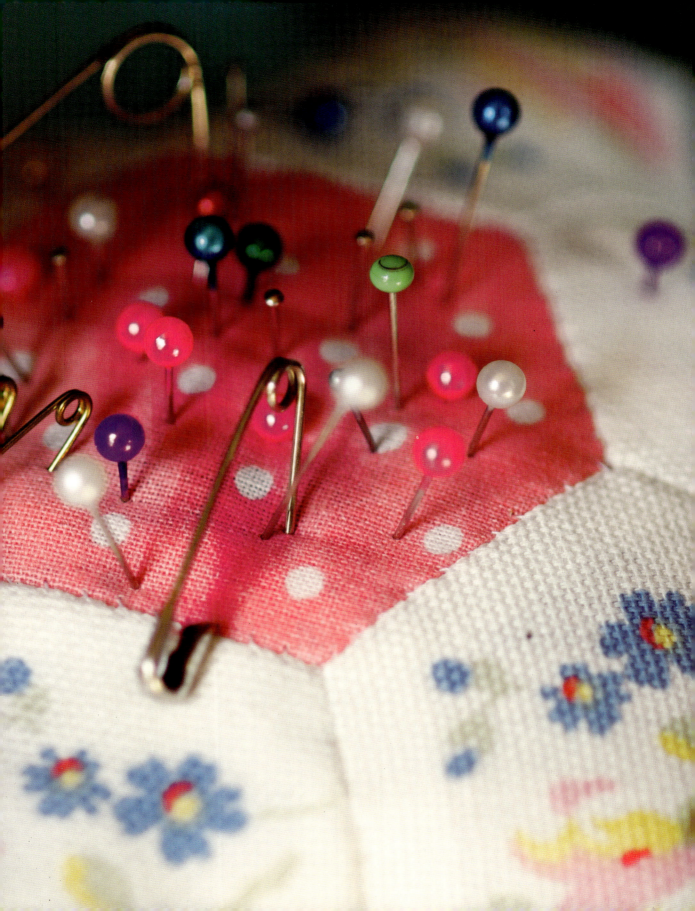

Personalised Dog Bed

MATERIALS

lightweight striped blanket
scraps of suede or felt in fawn, red and brown
red stranded cotton embroidery thread
pencil
90 x 60cm strong canvas
50cm heavy duty zip
matching sewing thread
sewing machine
sewing kit
81 x 56 x 15cm dog bed filler (http://www.onlineforpets.co.uk/water-resistant-rectangular-dog-cushion-navy-nylon.html)

CUTTING OUT

from blanket fabric
(A) twentyone 18cm squares
(B) three 14 x 18cm rectangles
(C) three 7 x 18cm rectangles
all of the above should have matching stripes
(D) twentyfour 13 x 18cm identical rectangles with a different stripe pattern
from canvas fabric
one 20 x 55cm rectangle
one 63 x 55cm rectangle

TEMPLATE

Stanley, see page 159

SKILL LEVEL: 3

None of my sewing books would be complete without a starring role for Stanley, my beloved Lakeland terrier. So far he has appeared in the guise of a hot water bottle cover, a beanbag and a needlepoint badge, and this time there's even a cuddly toy version of him on pages 100–103. This, however, is the one project that I know he'll really enjoy – a warm, woolly patchwork pet bed!

1 Lay out the five rows of patches, following the diagram. The top row starts with a B patch, then has four D patches alternating with three A squares and ends with a narrow C patch. The next row has four D patches alternating with four A squares. These two rows are repeated once, then the first row again.

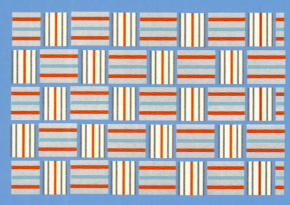

2 Join the patches in each horizontal row with a 1.5cm seam. Press all the seam allowances towards the D patches, then top stitch each seam to strengthen.

3 Seam the rows together, again with a 1.5cm allowance. Press each allowance downwards and top stitch. Trim a 1.5cm strip from one long edge so the piece measures 103cm by 76.5cm.

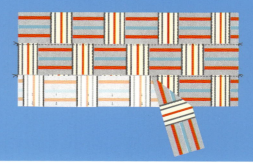

top tip START BY GENTLY LAUNDERING THE BLANKET AND BACKING CANVAS, SO THAT IF YOU EVER NEED TO WASH THE COVER IT WON'T SHRINK ANY FURTHER.

Personalised Dog Bed

4 The corners are stitched at right angles to give depth to the bed. At each corner in turn, fold and pin the two edges together to make a 45 degree angle. Mark a vertical line 12cm in from the corner. Starting 1.5cm up from the bottom edge, stitch along the marked line and trim away the excess fabric, 1cm from the seam.

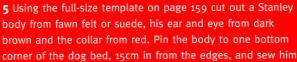

5 Using the full-size template on page 159 cut out a Stanley body from fawn felt or suede, his ear and eye from dark brown and the collar from red. Pin the body to one bottom corner of the dog bed, 15cm in from the edges, and sew him securely in place with small overcast stitches. Add the collar, eye and ear. Write your initials – or your dog's name – in the space above and stitch over the letters in chain stitch, using all six strands of the thread.

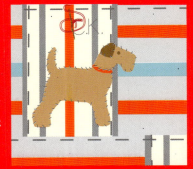

6 Press back a 1cm turning along one 55cm edge of each piece of canvas. Tack these folded edges to either side of the zip, leaving a 2.5cm gap at each end and 1cm between the folded edges. Fit a zip foot to your sewing machine and stitch the canvas to the tape, 5mm from the teeth. Tack together the bottom ends of the zip, then open it up.

7 With right sides facing, pin the patchwork to the base, opening out the unstitched seam allowance at the corners. The woollen fabric has more 'give' than the canvas, so you will have to ease the edges of the patchwork to fit the base exactly. Machine stitch twice around the outside edge with a 1.5cm seam.

8 Turn right side out, insert the filler pad and do up the zip. The filler is larger than the cover, to give the finished dog bed a well-stuffed, upholstered look.

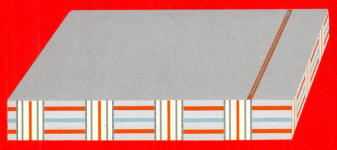

top tip | I USED A READY-MADE DOG BED FILLER FROM A SPECIALIST PET SUPPLIER TO GO INSIDE MY COVER, WHICH I CAN EASILY REPLACE WHEN IT BEGINS TO SHOW SIGNS OF WEAR.

Flower Picture

MATERIALS

large white damask napkin
striped tea towel
35 x 25 cm plain white cotton
30 x 20 quilt batting
scraps of floral, check and striped
    print fabric
floral furnishing fabric
plain green cotton fabric
fusible bonding web
buttons
stranded cotton embroidery thread in
    shades of green, red and cream
sewing kit
sewing machine

SKILL LEVEL: 2

One of the things that I like best about patchwork and appliqué is fact that you will eventually find the perfect use for every single scrap of fabric… even the very smallest fragments! If you are a hoarder (like me), you're bound to have a stash of offcuts, buttons, threads, beads and ribbons that have been left over from other projects, and this spectacular flower picture is a fantastic way to get creative with them. Look closely and you'll even spot the spare Suffolk puffs from the cashmere cardigan project on page 146.

1 Start by making the crazy patchwork vase. Enlarge the template on page 160 and pin it centrally to the white cotton fabric. Draw round the outside edge and unpin. Fill in the shape with scraps of dress weight prints and shirting, arranging them so the background is covered completely and the fabric overlaps the outline by 2cm all round. Pin down the pieces as you go.

2 Work a row of decorative embroidery over every join, using three strands of cream thread. I chose fly stitch as an alternative to the feather stitch on the Crazy Patch Cushion. You can see how to work both of these on page 29, along with the other stitches I used here straight stitch, chain stitch and single feather stitch

3 Using the template as your guide, cut a vase from batting. Pin this centrally to the back of the completed patchwork vase and trim the margin to 1mm all round. Snip into the curves, then turn back the margin around the top and side edges and tack it down.

4 Pin the vase centrally along one long edge of the napkin and slip stitch it in place. Cut a 15cm strip from one long edge of the striped towel, the same length as the napkin. With right sides facing, pin it along the edge of the napkin and over the bottom of the vase. Sew the two together with a 15mm seam, then press the seam towards the stripes.

top tip NO TWO APPLIQUÉ PICTURES WILL EVER BE THE SAME, SO USE MY DESIGN AS A SPRINGBOARD FOR YOUR OWN IDEAS. SEARCH THROUGH YOUR TEXTILE COLLECTION AND TAKE INSPIRATION FROM THE FABRICS YOU FIND THERE.

5 Select the prettiest flowers from the furnishing fabric and cut them out roughly. Following the manufacturer's instructions, iron the wrong side onto the bonding web and then cut out neatly around the outside edge of each motif.

6 Draw a few simple leaf shapes on to the paper side of the bonding web and fuse it to the back of the green fabric. Cut them out around the pencil lines. Make four or more Suffolk puffs, as shown on page 147 and using the bonding web, cut circles of fabric to go behind them.

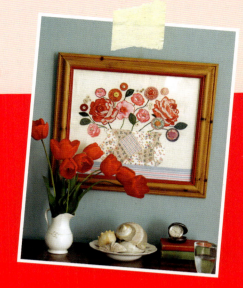

7 Now it's time for some flower arranging. Starting with the largest blooms, position the flowers, leaves, circles and puffs around the vase and shuffle them about until you're pleased with the design. Draw in the curving stems with a dressmaker's pen or chalk pencil, then remove the vase.

8 Peel off the backing papers and press down the flowers, circles and leaves. Slip stitch around the edge of the puffs.

9 Embroider over the stalk lines in green chain stitch and around the edge of the flowers using a variety of stitches to give texture to your picture.

10 Sew the matching buttons in groups of three to fill the spaces between the motifs and add others to the flower centres.

top tip TAKE THIS DESIGN FURTHER BY COMBINING IT WITH MACHINE PATCHWORK. YOU COULD ADD A

DEEP BORDER OF PATCHWORK SQUARES AND USE THE FLOWER BOWL AS THE CENTREPIECE FOR A SMALL QUILT.

Bunny Sweater

MATERIALS
floral print fabric
10cm of 2cm wide ribbon
black and red stranded cotton
  embroidery thread
fusible bonding web
pencil
sewing kit

SKILL LEVEL: 1

Hand knitted garments have a charm all of their own and are so much more appealing than machine made versions. I couldn't resist adding a flowered appliqué rabbit to this tiny v-necked sweater, along with a matching update of the classic elbow patch. The patches are purely decorative, but you could copy the idea if you ever need to cover up any moth holes or areas where the yarn has worn thin.

1 Trace the reversed rabbit template on page 158 and two circles on to the wrong side of the bondaweb and cut out around the outlines. Peel off the backing papers.

2 Position the rabbit centrally on the front of the sweater. Using a cloth to protect the wool from the heat, press it in place with a warm iron. Fuse the circles to the back of the sleeves.

3 Working with three strands of red thread, embroider a round of tailor's buttonhole stitch (see page 29) around the outside edge of each patch. Sew the bunny's eye in black satin stitch, then add three short straight stitches for the whiskers and a satin stitch nose.

4 To make the bow, cut a 7cm length from the ribbon. Fold it into a loop with the ends at the back. Stitching through all three layers, gather the centre of the ribbon. Fold the remaining piece in half width ways and wrap around the gathered part. Sew the ends securely to the wrong side, then sew the bow to the bunny.

top tip IF YOU PREFER TO USE TRADITIONAL SOFT LEATHER OR SUEDE FOR THE ELBOW PATCHES, YOU WILL NEED TO STITCH WITH A SPECIAL TRIANGULAR NEEDLE. THIS PIERCES THE LEATHER WITHOUT CAUSING IT TO SPLIT.

Patched Dungarees

MATERIALS

torn garment
scraps of cotton duck or denim
scraps of spot print cotton
small piece of quilt wadding
matching sewing thread
sewing machine

SKILL LEVEL: 1

Here is another example of functional patching, this time on the knees of a pair of toddler-sized dungarees. Once small children start crawling about it's always the knee areas that seem to get the most wear and tear, so these padded racing car patches will cover up the damage as well as providing extra protection. I added the two spot print patches – cut from old handkerchiefs – for a bit of extra pattern and colour.

1 Start by repairing the tear or hole. Undo the poppers at the inside legs and work several closely spaced lines of machine stitch to and fro across the gap. Use the reverse lever to stitch backwards.

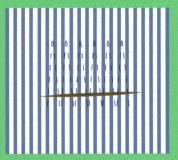

2 Cut two 6cm squares from the spotty fabrics and press under a 5mm turning around each edge of them both. Cut two 12cm squares from the heavier fabric: make them larger if you have a big rip to conceal. From the wadding cut two 11cm squares.

3 The large patches go centrally over the darns and the spotty squares peep out from behind them. Work out the positions, then machine stitch the spotty patches in place with a narrow zigzag in matching thread.

4 Place the wadding in position, then pin the large patches down over them. Rethread the sewing machine with a colour to match, then zigzag down.

top tip WHEN YOU ARE MAKING A REPAIR PATCH, MAKE SURE THAT IT IS A SIMILAR WEIGHT TO THE GARMENT.

I USED COTTON DUCK ON THESE CANVAS DUNGAREES, BUT DENIM WOULD HAVE WORKED JUST AS WELL.

Puff Collar Cardigan

MATERIALS

cardigan
selection of print fabrics – about 12cm
    square for each puff
pair of compasses and paper
self-cover buttons
matching sewing thread
sewing kit

SKILL LEVEL: 1

When I was planning the square cushion cover on page 88, all of the Suffolk Puffs were randomly strewn across my desk. I loved the mixture of fabrics and the way they overlapped, so started wondering whether there was another – slightly less formal – way in which I could use these pretty little patches. I came up with the idea of embellishing a cashmere cardigan with a 'collar' of puffs... great to wear over a summery floral tea dress. Turn to page 148 to see what I did next!

1 Cut an 11cm diameter disc of paper to use as your template. Using this as a guide, cut about 35 circles from the various fabrics and make them up into Suffolk Puffs, as shown on page 89.

2 Pin a row of puffs all the way around the neckline, at front and back, then arrange the rest on either side of the front to create a symmetrical collar shape. Overlap the edges of a few, then pin them all in place. Depending on the size and shape of your cardigan, you may find you need to make a couple more puffs to fill all the spaces.

3 Sew each puff down with a round of small straight stitches in matching thread. You'll need to stitch through all the layers where the puffs overlap.

4 It's the details that make things really special, so I as a finishing touch I replaced the basic buttons on this cardigan with small, round self-cover buttons, made from the foral fabric offcuts. The button kits provide all the instructions for how to do this.

top tip CHOOSE A NARROW COLOUR PALETTE TO COMPLEMENT YOUR CARDIGAN. I USED STRIPES, SPOTS AND GINGHAM IN SHADES OF PINK AND RED, THEN ADDED A SPRINKLING OF PUFFS IN A CO-ORDINATING FLOWERED DRESS FABRIC.

Puff Necklace

MATERIALS

scraps of plain and floral print
  dress-weight fabric
matching sewing thread
one long or two short chain necklaces
masking tape
sewing kit

CUTTING OUT

from floral print fabric
one 12cm circle
two 10cm circles
two 8cm circles
from plain fabric
two 12cm circles
two 8cm circles

TEMPLATES

8cm, 10cm and 12cm diameter circles

SKILL LEVEL: 1

Last but not least, is this sweet puff necklace – the ideal accessory to wear with your favourite floaty summer frock, or over a plain sweater. Offcuts of viscose crepe were used, which gives the puffs an especially three-dimensional aspect, but it would look just as good in any floral print with a toning plain fabric.

1 Make all the circles of fabric into puffs, as for the cushion cover on page 89. Lay them out in decreasing size to form a horseshoe shape, with the largest floral puff at the centre.

2 Pin the puffs to each other where they overlap, keeping them in the same formation. Sew them together with small stab stitches, sewing through all the layers of fabric.

3 Turn the puffs over and place the chain centrally across the back, following the curve. Secure it in place with short lengths of masking tape, then sew the chain to the back of the puffs.

top tip   INSTEAD OF SEWING THE PUFFS TO A CHAIN, YOU COULD STITCH A LENGTH OF NARROW RIBBON TO EACH END:

3MM-WIDE SATIN RIBBON WOULD BE SUITABLY DELICATE, OR TRY A WIDER DOUBLE-FACED VELVET FOR A LUXE LOOK.

Useful Addresses

Patchwork shops

The Bramble Patch
West Street
Weedon
Northamptonshire NN7 4QU
01327 342212
www.thebramblepatch.co.uk

Coast & Country Crafts & Quilts
Barras Moor Farm
Perranarworthal, Truro
Cornwall TR3 7PE
01872 870478
www.coastandcountrycrafts.co.uk

The Cotton Patch
1283–1285 Stratford Road
Hall Green
Birmingham B28 9AJ
0121 7022840
www.cottonpatch.net

Creative Quilting
32 Bridge Road
Hampton Court Village
East Molesey
Surrey KT8 9HA
020 8941 7075
www.creativequilting.co.uk

The Fat Quarters
5 Chopwell Road
Blackhall Mill
Newcastle Upon Tyne NE17 7TN
01207 565728
www.thefatquarters.co.uk

Patch – Fabric and Haberdashery
9 Bevan Street East
Lowestoft
Suffolk NR32 2AA
01502 588778
www.patchfabrics.co.uk

Patchwork Direct
Wesleyan House
Dale Road
Darley Dale
Derbyshire DE4 2HX
01629 734100
www.patchworkdirect.com

Patchwork Garden
630 Abbeydale Road
Sheffield
South Yorkshire S7 2BA
0114 258 3763
www.patchworkgarden-shop.co.uk

Pelenna Patchworks
5 Bevans Terrace
Pontrhydyfen
Port Talbot
West Glamorgan SA12 9TR
01639 898444
www.pelennapatchworks.co.uk

Quilter's Haven
68 High Street
Wickham Market
Woodbridge
Suffolk IP13 0QU
01728 746275
www.quilters-haven.co.uk

Tikki
293 Sandycombe Road
Kew
Surrey TW9 3LU
020 8948 8462
www.tikkilondon.com

Fabric and haberdashery shops

Bedecked
5 Castle Street
Hay-on-Wye
Hereford HR3 5DF
01497 822769
www.bedecked.co.uk

Cloth House
47 Berwick Street
London W1F 8SJ
020 7437 5155
www.clothhouse.net

Design-a-Cushions
74 Drum Brae South
Edinburgh EH12 8TH
0131 539 0080
www.design-a-cushions.co.uk

Harts of Hertford
113 Fore Street
Hertford SG14 1AS
01992 558106
www.hartsofhertford.com

John Lewis
300 Oxford Street
London W1A 1EX
and branches nationwide
08456 049049
www.johnlewis.com

MacCulloch & Wallis
25–26 Dering Street
London W1S 1AT
020 7629 0311
www.macculloch-wallis.co.uk

The Makery Emporium
16 Northumberland Place
Bath
Avon BA1 5AR
01225 487708
www.themakeryonline.co.uk

Mandors
134 Renfrew Street
Glasgow G3 6ST
0141 332 7716
www.mandors.co.uk

Merrick & Day
Redbourne Road
Redbourne
Gainsborough
Lincolnshire DN21 4TG
01652 648 814
www.merrick-day.com

Millie Moon
24–25 Catherine Hill
Frome
Somerset BA11 1BY
01373 464650
www.milliemoonshop.co.uk

Our Patterned Hand
49 Broadway Market
London E8 4PH
020 7812 9912
www.ourpatternedhand.co.uk

Rags
19 Chapel Walk
Crowngate Shopping Centre
Worcester WR1 3LD
01905 612330

Sew and So's
14 Upper Olland Street
Bungay
Suffolk NR35 1BG
01986 896147
www.sewsos.co.uk

Patchwork and sewing classes

Heatherlea Design
01332 661562
www.heatherleadesign.com

Just Between Friends
44 Station Way
Buckhurst Hill
Essex IG9 6LN
020 8502 9191
www.justbetweenfriends.co.uk

Liberty Sewing School
Regent Street
London W1B 5AH
www.liberty.co.uk

The Makery Workshop
146 Walcot Street
Bath
Avon BA1 5BL
01225 421175
www.themakeryonline.co.uk

Sew Over It
78 Landor Road
Clapham North
London SW9 9PH
020 7326 0376
www.sewoverit.co.uk

The Thrifty Stitcher
Unit 21
4–6 Shelford Place
Stoke Newington
London N16 9HS
07779 255087
www.thethriftystitcher.co.uk

Modern Approach Sewing School
Astra Business Centre
Roman Way
Ribbleton
Preston PR2 5AP
07910 740120
www.sewjanetmoville.co.uk

Sue Hazell Sewing Tuition
Southcombe House
Chipping Norton
Oxfordshire OX7 5QH
01608 644877
www.sewing-tuition.co.uk

The Studio London
Studio 1 & 5
Trinity Buoy Wharf
64 Orchard Place
London E14 0JW
020 7987 2421

Cath Kidston Stores

Aberdeen
Unit GS20, Union Square Centre,
Guild Square, Aberdeen AB11 5PN
01224 591 726

Bath
3 Broad Street, Milsom Place, Bath BA1 5LJ
01225 331 006

Belfast
24–26 Arthur Street, Belfast BT1 4GF
02890 231 581

Bicester Village Outlet Store
Unit 43a, Bicester Village,
Bicester OX26 6WD
01869 247 358

Birmingham – Selfridges
Upper Mall, East Bullring,
Birmingham B5 4BP
0121 600 6967

Bluewater
Unit L003, Rose Gallery,
Bluewater Shopping Centre DA9 9SH
01322 387 454

Bournemouth
5–6 The Arcade, Old Christchurch Road,
Bournemouth BH1 2AF
01202 553 848

Brighton
31a & 32 East Street, Brighton BN1 1HL
01273 227 420

Bristol
79 Park Street, Clifton, Bristol BS1 5PF
0117 930 4722

Cambridge
31–33 Market Hill, Cambridge CB2 3NU
01223 351 810

Canterbury
6 The Parade, Canterbury CT1 2JL
01227 455 639

Cardiff
45 The Hayes, St David's, Cardiff CF10 1GA
02920 225 627

Cheltenham
21 The Promenade, Cheltenham GL50 1LE
01242 245 912

Chichester
24 South Street, Chichester PO19 1EL
01243 850 100

Dublin
Unit CSD 1.3, Dundrum Shopping Centre,
Dublin 16
00 353 1 296 4430

Edinburgh
58 George Street, Edinburgh EH2 2LR
0131 220 1509

Exeter
6 Princesshay, Exeter EX1 1GE
01392 227 835

Glasgow
18 Gordon Street, Glasgow G1 3PB
0141 248 2773

Guildford
14–18 Chertsey Street, Guildford GU1 4HD
01483 564 798

Gunwharf Quays Outlet Store
Gunwharf Quays, Portsmouth PO1 3TU
02392 832 982

Harrogate
2–6 James Street, Harrogate HG1 1RF
01423 531 481

Heathrow Terminal 4
Departure Lounge,
Heathrow Airport TW6 3XA
020 8759 5578

Jersey
11 King Street, St Helier, Jersey JE2 4WF
01534 726 768

Kildare Village Outlet Store
Unit 21c, Kildare Village, Nurney Road,
Kildare Town
00 353 45 535 084

Kingston
10 Thames Street,
Kingston upon Thames KT1 1PE
020 8546 6760

Leeds
26 Lands Lane, Leeds LS1 6LB
0113 391 2692

Liverpool
Compton House, 18 School Lane,
Liverpool L1 3BT
0151 709 2747

London – Battersea
142 Northcote Road,
London SW11 6RD
020 7228 6571

London – Chiswick
125 Chiswick High Road, London W4 2ED
020 8995 8052

London – Covent Garden
28–32 Shelton Street, London WC2H 9JE
020 7836 4803

London – Fulham
668 Fulham Road, London SW6 5RX
020 7731 6531

London – Kings Road
322 Kings Road, London SW3 5UH
020 7351 7335

London – Marylebone
51 Marylebone High Street, London W1U 5HW
020 7935 6555

London – Notting Hill
158 Portobello Road, London W11 2BE
020 7727 0043

London – Selfridges
Oxford Street, London W1A 1AB
020 7318 3312

London – Sloane Square
27 Kings Road, London SW3 4RP
020 7259 9847

London – St Pancras
St Pancras International Station,
London NW1 2QP
020 7837 4125

London – Wimbledon Village
3 High Street, Wimbledon SW19 5DX
020 8944 1001

Manchester
62 King Street, Manchester M2 4ND
0161 834 7936

Manchester – Selfridges
1 Exchange Street, Manchester M3 1BD
0161 629 1184

Marlborough
142–142a High Street, Marlborough SN8 1HN
01672 512 514

Marlow
6 Market Square, Marlow SL7 1DA
01628 484 443

Newcastle – Fenwicks
Northumberland Street,
Newcastle Upon Tyne NE99 1AR
0191 232 5100

Oxford
6 Broad Street, Oxford OX1 3AJ
01865 791 576

Reading
96 Broad Street, Reading RG1 2AP
01189 588 530

St Albans
Unit 4, Christopher Place,
St Albans AL3 5DQ
01727 810 432

St Ives
67 Fore Street, St Ives TR26 1HE
01736 798 001

Tunbridge Wells
59–61 High Street, Tunbridge Wells TN1 1XU
01892 521 197

Winchester
46 High Street, Winchester SO23 9BT
01962 870 620

Windsor
24 High Street, Windsor SL4 1LH
01753 830 591

York
32 Stonegate, York YO1 8AS
01904 733 653

For up-to-date information on all Cath Kidston stores, please visit www.cathkidston.co.uk

Acknowledgements

My special thanks to everyone involved in the creation of this book: to Elaine Ashton and Jessica Pemberton, to Lucinda Ganderton and her assistant Lis Gunner for the making of the projects, to Pia Tryde for her inspiring photography, and to Anne Furniss, Helen Lewis, Lisa Pendreigh and Katherine Case at Quadrille Publishing.

Cath Kidston

Series Creative Coordinator: Elaine Ashton
Design Assistant to Cath Kidston: Jessica Pemberton
Patchwork Coordinator and Consultant: Lucinda Ganderton
Patchwork Assistant: Lis Gunner

Editorial Director: Anne Furniss
Art Director: Helen Lewis
Project Editor: Lisa Pendreigh
Designer: Katherine Case
Photographer: Pia Tryde
Illustrators: Bridget Bodoano and Joy FitzSimmons
Pattern Checker: Sally Harding
Production Director: Vincent Smith
Production Controller: Aysun Hughes

If you have any comments or queries regarding the instructions in this book, please contact us at enquiries@quadrille.co.uk.

This edition first published in 2012 by
Quadrille Publishing Limited
Alhambra House
27–31 Charing Cross Road
London WC2H 0LS
www.quadrille.co.uk

Projects, templates and text copyright © Cath Kidston 2011
Photography © Pia Tryde 2011
Design and layout copyright © Quadrille Publishing Limited 2011

Cataloguing-in-Publication Data: a catalogue record for this book is available from the British Library.

ISBN 978 184949 205 8

Printed in China

Templates

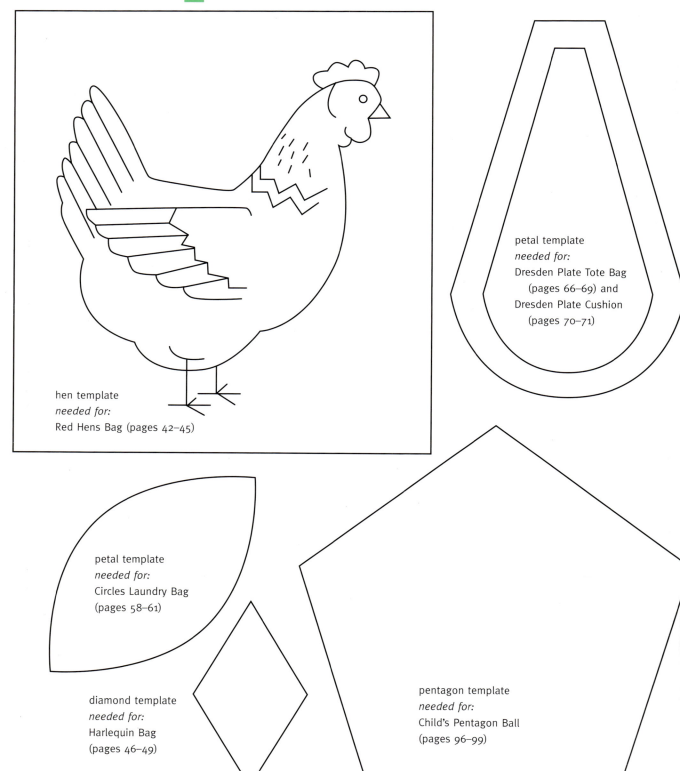

petal template
needed for:
Dresden Plate Tote Bag
(pages 66–69) and
Dresden Plate Cushion
(pages 70–71)

hen template
needed for:
Red Hens Bag (pages 42–45)

petal template
needed for:
Circles Laundry Bag
(pages 58–61)

diamond template
needed for:
Harlequin Bag
(pages 46–49)

pentagon template
needed for:
Child's Pentagon Ball
(pages 96–99)

Stanley's ear, nose, square, rectangle and triangle templates
needed for:
Stanley Toy (pages 100–103)

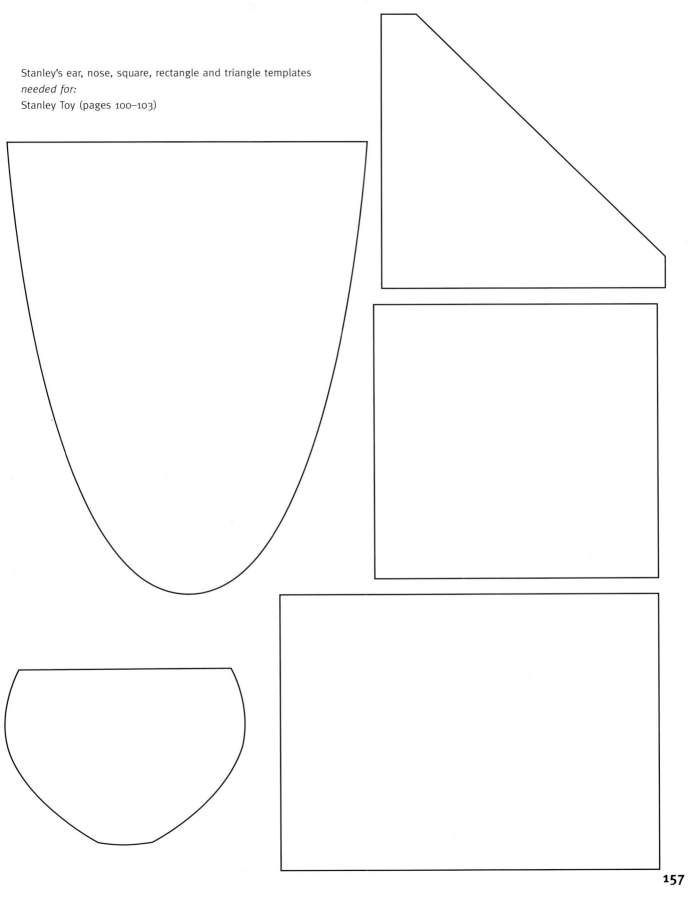

bunny and circle templates
needed for:
Bunny Sweater
(pages 142–143)

bunny template
needed for:
Bunny Blanket
(pages 104–105)

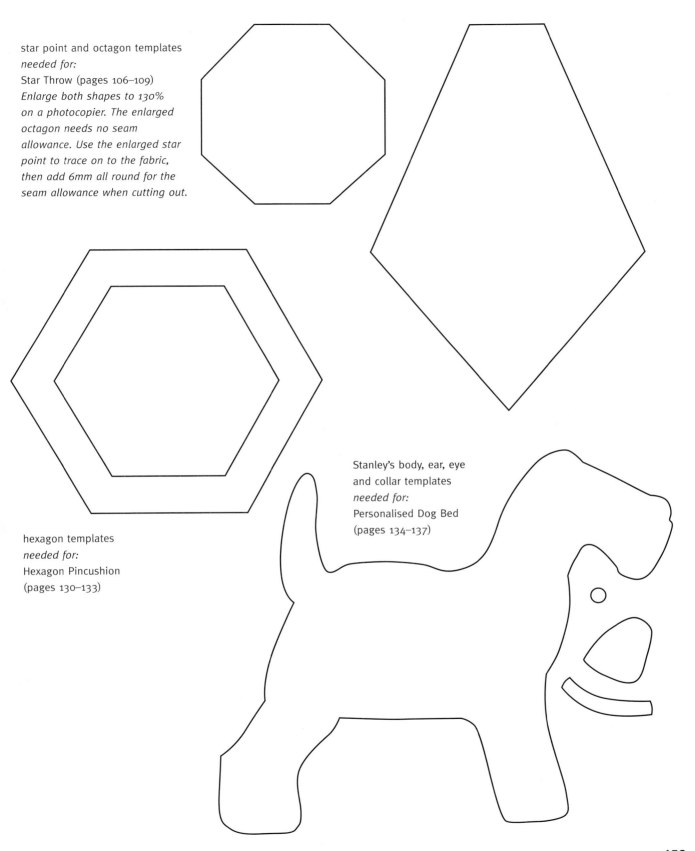

star point and octagon templates
needed for:
Star Throw (pages 106–109)
*Enlarge both shapes to 130%
on a photocopier. The enlarged
octagon needs no seam
allowance. Use the enlarged star
point to trace on to the fabric,
then add 6mm all round for the
seam allowance when cutting out.*

hexagon templates
needed for:
Hexagon Pincushion
(pages 130–133)

Stanley's body, ear, eye
and collar templates
needed for:
Personalised Dog Bed
(pages 134–137)

vase template
needed for:
Flower Picture (pages 138–141)

sew!

Cath Kidston

sew!

Cath Kidston

PHOTOGRAPHY BY PIA TRYDE

Quadrille
PUBLISHING

Contents

Introduction

I'm amazed at how many of my friends – of all generations – are now taking up needlework, whether they are sewing on a button, shortening the hems of their jeans or making their own cushion covers. Suddenly, sewing seems to be everywhere!

I was taught how to hand sew as a small child. I embroidered coasters and spectacle cases, which were proudly given away as presents, and I can clearly remember learning how to do blanket stitch. As a teenager I progressed to lessons on the school sewing machine and although it took a whole term to make a towelling dressing gown, my enthusiasm remained undiminished. But many of us don't have the first idea how to set about the rewarding process of creating something from scratch.

The idea for this book came about because I really felt that there was a gap in the market for a collection of inspiring and interesting sewing projects that would include something to suit everybody, whatever their previous experience. If you're an absolute beginner, an experienced stitcher or someone keen to renew rusty skills, Sew! will show you just how to make things yourself – with all the sense of achievement that brings.

If you are like me, you probably don't want to wade through a serious instruction manual but are looking for some practical and clear advice which you'll find in the Sew! Basics section. I also hope to encourage and inspire you at the same time. There are over forty projects in this book which range from old standbys like the covered coat hangers, that can be made in an hour

or so, to more long-term undertakings like the charming patchwork cot quilt. I hope you'll find something that appeals amongst the various napkins, lavender pillows, aprons, cushions and the many different bags, which include a cool iPod holder, a traditional duffel and my favourite new idea, the quirky inside-out tote.

Some of the best fun I had when planning the book was going through my textile archive, choosing precisely which prints and colourways to use for each project. As well as my own designs, there are old and new florals, stripes, ginghams, vintage linen and soft cotton sheeting. You'll see some of my tips on fabric choices as you read through the pages: mix and match patterns, go for detailed embellishments in clashing colours and always try out unexpected combinations. These are your starting points and you can develop and customise the basic designs as you wish. It's up to you how far you want to go and the journey is so rewarding.

All of the paper patterns are included, so there is no excuse not to start straightaway! Before long, you'll find you have a sewing project permanently on the go. I've always found getting started is easy: the hard bit is putting it down!

Cath Kidson

Sew! Basics

Essential Equipment

All the fabric and haberdashery needed for each project is detailed in the 'what you will need' lists. One of the last items is always 'sewing kit' – the basic tools required for all your needlework. You may already have many of them, but here's my guide to sewing box essentials.

NEEDLES

There are several types of needle, each designed for a particular task. They come in different lengths and diameters, from a thick '1' to a fine '10' for the most delicate work. Start off with a mixed packet, which will include:

• medium-length 'sharps' with small round eyes for sewing thread. These are for general stitching and tacking.

• 'crewel' needles which have longer eyes to accommodate thicker embroidery cotton. These are easier to thread and fine for hand-sewing too.

• short 'quilting' needles which go easily through several layers of fabric and wadding with a stabbing action.

• a large, blunt tapestry needle or larger bodkin will be useful for threading cords or elastic.

PINS

I always like to use long, slender glass-headed pins, which are not only pretty, but easy to spot against patterned fabric. Keep them in a pincushion or tin, with a magnet close to hand, just in case they spill.

SEWING THREADS

Lustrous No. 50 mercerized sewing cotton is an all-purpose thread for stitching on natural fibres, so it's good for these projects. Match thread to the main colour of your fabric; if this isn't possible, choose a shade darker. Use a contrasting shade for tacking so you can easily unpick the stitches. Use extra strong buttonhole thread for securing upholstered buttons, like those on the floor cushions. If you are going to do a lot of hand quilting, use special quilter's thread.

THIMBLE

Using a thimble for the first time can feel very awkward, but it's worth persevering if you want to avoid punctured fingertips! They come in various sizes, so choose one that fits snugly but not too tightly on your middle finger.

SCISSORS

You will need three basic pairs in three sizes:

• small embroidery scissors with narrow, pointed blades. Use these for snipping buttonholes, trimming threads and clipping curves and corners.

• a pair of medium-sized general purpose scissors for cutting out smaller items and your paper patterns.

• bent-handled dressmaker's shears for accurate fabric cutting. Invest in a good pair with steel blades and don't ever, ever use them for paper!

• pinking shears are also useful, but not essential. They produce a zigzagged edge that reduces fraying on un-neatened seams, and gives a decorative effect on felt.

MEASURING UP

A good tape measure is invaluable. Look out for a strong non-stretchy plastic one with metal tips. A clear ruler, marked with centimetre divisions is very useful when you are marking quilting lines, seams or buttonhole positions.

MARKING TOOLS

Water-soluble or fading ink pens are designed for transferring markings onto fabric, but traditional tailor's chalk or chalk pencils are just as good. Use a light colour on dark fabrics and vice versa. A sharp HB drawing pencil will give a fine, accurate line to guide your quilting.

top tip →

MORE USEFUL ITEMS WITH WHICH TO STOCK YOUR WORK BASKET INCLUDE: A NEEDLE-THREADER, A SEAM UNPICKER, A BIG REEL OF WHITE SEWING THREAD, SOME SPARE MACHINE NEEDLES, A CARD OF ELASTIC AND A TIN FOR SPARE BUTTONS, BUCKLES, SAFETY PINS AND OTHER ACCUMULATED BITS AND BOBS.

Sewing Machines

The range of sewing machines that is now on the market can seem a bit bewildering, whether you're a new enthusiast or an old hand who has been stitching for years! There is a huge choice available, from entry-level machines which have no extra gadgets, to highly technical electronic versions with pre-programmed stitches, alphabets and LCDs, that can be linked up to your own computer to create complex embroidery designs.

They may look different, but all have the same basic functions and all you need to make up any of my projects is a solid, functional machine that will give you a regular straight stitch with an even tension.

HOW THEY WORK

All sewing machines work by linking two threads, one above the fabric and one below it, to produce a lock stitch. The upper reel is threaded through the arm of the machine, and down to the needle whilst the lower thread is wound onto a small bobbin. For a straight stitch the needle stays in one central position, but for buttonholes and zigzags it moves from side to side. Original hand machines do not have this swing-needle function, but many are still in working order.

THE PARTS OF THE MACHINE

Take time to read through the manual that comes with your machine. This will have a useful diagram that labels all the various dials and switches: study this carefully and get familiar with the terminology. However complicated the computerised element may be, all machines have the same working parts and structure.

• The **spool pin** sits at the top right of the machine. Slip your reel of sewing cotton onto this and follow the manual's instructions to thread the end through to the needle.

• The **bobbin winder** is also on the top of the machine. This is used for winding thread from the main reel onto the small bobbins that carry the lower thread.

• The **tension adjuster** alters the amount of pressure on the upper thread.

• The **needle** screws into the arm of the machine, just in front of the presser foot. It has a hole at the tip, unlike a sewing needle. There are various sizes: you need a 'universal' or medium size 14/90 for these projects. Remember that the tip must always be sharp, so change needles regularly.

• The **presser foot** maintains pressure on the fabric as it passes under the needle. It lifts up and down with a lever. Your machine will come with several different feet, and many more are available for specialised stitching. Apart from the basic foot, you will need a zip foot which enables you to

sew close to piping cord or the teeth of a zip. Other feet are used for hemming, gathering or applying ready-made bias binding.

• The flat **throat plate** has a small hole through which the needle passes to pick up the lower thread. It is marked with a series of parallel lines. Align the edges of your fabric to these as you sew, for a regular seam allowance.

• The **feed dog** is a series of serrated ridges under the throat plate which move up and down to ease the fabric along, as it passes under the presser foot.

• The **bobbin case** is the one working part of the machine that you can't see immediately. It sits under the main bed and houses the bobbin with the lower thread. You can change the tension when necessary by adjusting the small grub screw.

• The **reverse stitch control** is very useful as it enables you to work a few stitches in the opposite direction at the beginning and end of each seam to prevent unravelling.

• The **foot pedal** plugs into the machine and is your speed control. Like a car's accelerator, the harder you press, the faster the machine will go, so take it easy at first.

TENSION

A line of machine stitching should look exactly the same on both sides. Do a sample row before starting work and if you can see a row of loops on one side, there is a problem with the tension. Check your manual and adjust the top or bottom thread as necessary.

ALWAYS USE THE SAME THREAD AT THE TOP AND BOTTOM OF THE MACHINE. IT'S A GOOD IDEA TO BUY SOME EXTRA BOBBINS AND FILL THEM BEFORE YOU START ON A NEW PROJECT — THIS WAY YOU CAN CHANGE OVER QUICKLY WHEN THE THREAD RUNS OUT.

Making The Patterns

THE PATTERN SHEET

Accompanying this book you will find a large, cleverly designed pattern sheet, which is printed on both sides with a series of coloured geometric shapes. At first glance this might seem to be a rather complicated underground map or a circuit diagram. Look closely and you'll see that each individual outline represents a clearly distinguishable pattern piece, which is marked with a letter from A through to Z and all the way up to PP.

Here are all the patterns that you will need to make the projects. Some of these shapes are one-offs – you'll easily spot 'W', the pattern for the quilted hottie cover and 'T', which is the specs case. Others are multipurpose and are used in two or more projects – for instance, the largest circle 'Y' is the pattern for the top and bottom of the beanie cushion but it also doubles up as a bath hat.

MAKING YOUR OWN PATTERNS

All of the outlines are actual size and include the seam allowance, so you can trace them off directly to make your own paper patterns. The quickest way to do this is to spread out the sheet and fix a length of ordinary greaseproof paper over your chosen shape, using lo-tack tape. Draw around the outside edge with a sharp pencil, using a ruler to help keep the lines straight if necessary.

Alternatively you can buy a pack of dressmaker's squared paper, which is marked with the same 1cm grid as the pattern sheet, and simply copy the pattern pieces onto this, transferring the measurements exactly.

PATTERN MARKINGS

As well as the letters, some of the pieces have an extra broken line drawn across them, which represents an alternative cutting line. The main shape of the oven glove, for instance, is 'U', and line '1u' marks the size of the mitts at each end.

Some of the squares and rectangles have additional broken inner lines, which will give you rounded corners. The instructions will always tell you when to follow these lines.

Other pattern shapes have one side indicated with a dotted line with a double-headed bent arrow pointing towards it. This indicates that the side of the pattern should be placed along folded fabric, to give you a double width or length.

CUTTING OUT GUIDES

Each of the projects has its own cutting out guide. Like the diagram on a dressmaking pattern, this shows you just which pattern pieces you will need and how best to lay them out on your fabric. The fabric quantities in the 'what you will need' shopping list always allow an extra 5cm all round from the minimum amount required, but if you want to match up prints or stripes you will need to buy extra fabric. These guides are shown on a grid, so that you can use them to scale up the shapes if the pattern sheet ever goes astray.

FABRIC GRAIN

You'll see that some of the pattern pieces on the cutting out guides are marked with a double-headed arrow, pointing from top to bottom of the page. This indicates the direction of the straight, lengthwise grain of the fabric, which runs parallel to the sides or selvedges. The cross grain – the bias – runs diagonally across the fabric and has a certain amount of 'give'. Some of the pieces, such as binding strips, have to be cut on the bias so that they will stretch.

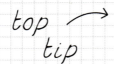
top tip

TRANSFER ALL THE MARKINGS, INCLUDING THE LETTERS, TO YOUR PATTERN PIECES BEFORE YOU CUT THEM OUT. KEEP THE PIECES FOR EACH PROJECT TOGETHER IN LARGE LABELLED ENVELOPES SO THAT YOU WILL BE ABLE TO REUSE THEM AT A FUTURE DATE.

Hems & Edges

A raw edge can be neatened in two ways: either by turning it back and stitching it down to make a hem, or by binding it with a narrow strip of fabric.

A single hem, with just one turning, is used for dressmaking and soft furnishings. Most of the projects require a double hem, which has two turnings. This gives a firmer edge, which is often top-stitched. The depth of the turnings will always be given in the step-by-step instructions.

A bound hem gives a very professional finish, especially if you use a contrasting fabric. You can buy bias binding – a narrow pre-folded strip of plain cotton – in a range of colours and two widths, or make your own from a co-ordinating print.

SINGLE HEM
Firstly, zigzag the edge of the fabric. With the wrong side facing, fold the edge up to the given measurement. You can use a ruler to make sure the hem is a consistent depth. Pin the turning, then tack it if you wish, and machine stitch, just below the neatened edge.

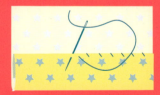

DOUBLE HEM
Fold and press the first turning to the required depth, then make the second turning, as directed. The first turning is usually shorter, but sometimes they are both equal. Pin and tack in place, then either machine stitch close to the inner fold or slip stitch by hand. Top stitch the outer fold on a pocket.

BOUND STRAIGHT EDGES
Open out one edge of the binding and, with right sides facing, pin it to the edge of the fabric. Machine stitch along the first fold. Turn the binding over to the wrong side and tack it down close to the fold. Finish by slip stitch as for the curved corner, or machine stitch on the right side, just inside the edge of the binding.

BOUND CURVES

A bound curve on a single layer of fabric needs to be reinforced with stay-stitch – a row of machine stitching worked about 4mm from the edge – to prevent it curling inwards. With right sides facing, tack the edge of the binding along the curve. Gather it in slightly so that the centre fold will fit comfortably around the outside edge without pulling.

Fold the rest of the binding to the back and sew down the edge by hand or machine. You may find that it helps to steam press the curve along the folded edge of the binding before you stitch.

MAKING YOUR OWN BINDING

For a straight edge, you can cut the fabric strips along the grain of the fabric, but for a curved edge they should be on the bias. Trim the ends diagonally, at 45 degrees. To join two strips, pin together with the right sides facing and the ends overlapping as shown. Seam between the points where they cross.

Press the seams open and trim off the projecting triangles. Fold the strip in half lengthways, with wrong sides together and press. Press each edge in turn towards the centre fold.

Seams

Joining two pieces of fabric is the most basic of all sewing techniques, and if you can do it neatly and accurately, you're ready to create any of the projects in this book!

Careful preparation pays off, and if you are new to sewing, it's worth tacking your seams together once they are pinned. This temporary stitch holds the fabric in place as you machine stitch, and is more stable than pins alone. Use a contrasting thread and sew with long running stitches, just inside the seam line.

When you're making an item that will be laundered or that will undergo heavy wear, it's a good idea to neaten the edges with a zigzag or binding, either before you join the seam or afterwards.

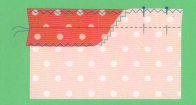

STRAIGHT SEAM

Pin the two pieces together with right sides facing and the edges aligned. Stitch along the given seam allowance, using the footplate lines as a width guide. Reinforce each end with a few extra stitches and press the allowance open or to one side, as directed.

CORNER SEAM

When you reach a corner, keep the needle down and lift the presser foot. Turn the fabric and continue along the next edge. Trim the allowance, to within 2mm of the stitch line. Turn right side out and gently ease the corner into shape with a blunt pencil.

T-JUNCTION SEAM

This seam is used to give width to bags. Join the side and bottom seams and press open. Refold the open corner so that the ends of the seams are aligned. Pin the two sides together and stitch. Trim the allowance and bind or zigzag to neaten.

CURVED SEAMS

Trim the allowance back to 6mm so that the seam will not be too bulky. For outside curves, like the top of a heart, cut out a series of regularly spaced little notches to within 2mm of the stitch line. For inside curves, make a series of snips at right angles to the stitching.

CLOSING A GAP

Sometimes you'll need to leave a gap in a seam through which to add the filling. Press back the seam allowance on each side before turning right side out. Pin the two edges together and slip stitch, passing the needle through the edges of the folds for an unobtrusive finish.

TOP STITCHING

Use this to secure folded edges or to reinforce a seam. On a fold, stitch 3mm in from the edge using the presser foot opening as a guide. For a straight or curved seam, press the allowance to one side, then stitch through all three layers from the right side, 3mm from the join.

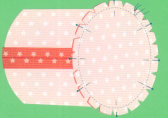

CIRCULAR SEAM

Cut 6mm notches around the circle and 1cm slits at the end of the fabric tube, spacing them 2cm apart. Fold the circle and tube four times so you have eight equal divisions and mark the ends of the folds. Pin together, right sides facing, matching the marks. Tack just inside the seam line, then machine with the circle on top.

PIPED SEAM

Piping – a tube of fabric–covered cord sewn between the two layers – defines a seam visually. Cut a narrow bias strip and fold it around a length of cord with wrong sides facing. Tack close to the cord and unpick any visible tacking once the seam is completed.

Fastenings

A visit to your local haberdashers or needlework supplier will show you just how many different types of fastenings exist. Some of these you may have already used when making clothes or soft furnishings: press-studs, hooks and eyes, fabric-covered buttons and zips, whilst others are designed specifically for homeware and accessories, such as magnetic bag fasteners and spring toggles.

I always love to add extra detail by using traditional hand-sewing techniques, and the buttonhole stitch loops used on the specs case and quilted purse are my current favourites. I used tailored rouleau loops for the hottie and shoulder bag. Handmade buttonholes, also worked in tailor's buttonhole stitch, give individual character to the shoulder bag strap and the large tote – and the effort and patience involved in creating them will pay off in the end!

BUTTONS

Although I've used them to fasten most of the bags and cases in this book, buttons have many other decorative purposes. Fabric-covered buttons are ideal for upholstering cushions, and I've used shirt buttons as the finishing touch on the lavender pillow, and as eyes for the various appliqué birds and the Stanley toy. Scour antique and charity shops for one-off examples, salvage them from old garments and sort through the family button tin to find vintage examples in pressed glass, painted plastic, metal, wood or lustrous mother-of-pearl.

HANDMADE BUTTONHOLE

Draw a line, the same size as your button, along the grain of the fabric. Reinforce it with two lines of back stitches. Carefully cut along the line. Using a long length of stranded cotton, sew a round of tailor's buttonhole stitch around the slit, curving each end. Stitch from right to left, inserting the needle upwards, then pulling it back towards you so that the looped thread forms a small knot at the base of each stitch.

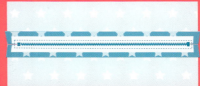

BUTTONHOLE STITCH LOOP

This is also worked in stranded thread. Fasten on at the edge of the fabric and make a foundation bar of three or four loose stitches. Starting from the right, work tailor's buttonhole stitch over the threads, looping the thread twice under the needle as shown. Fasten off at the left.

ROULEAU LOOP

A rouleau is a narrow flexible tube, made from a bias strip of fabric. Fold the strip in half and stitch about 3mm from the fold, slanting the end of the seam out to the corner. Trim back the seam allowance to 3mm. Thread a tapestry needle with strong thread, fasten it to the corner and tie the ends together. Pass the needle carefully through the tube so that the fabric is gradually turned right side out.

ZIPS

This is a quick method for inserting a zip into a seam. Press back a 2cm turning along each edge, then tack the two folds loosely together. Tack the closed zip securely to the wrong side, so that the teeth lie exactly along the join. Fit a zip foot and sew the zip in place 6mm from the outside edge of the teeth. Stitch three times across the top and bottom edges at right angles. Unpick the tacking.

Ties & Handles

Ties and handles can be viewed as purely functional aspects of a design – the means by which you carry a bag, for example – but in fact they provide a great opportunity to add extra detailing, such as a splash of contrasting colour or a new texture.

You can buy some interesting ready-made handles, like the cane loops bound with scarlet twine that I hunted down for the knitting bag, but you easily can make your own from folded and stitched strips of fabric. A similar construction technique is used for apron ties and these are particularly effective when a plain colour is used alongside a print: take a look at the cowboy apron on page 90.

TWO-PART HANDLE
The button-on strap for the shoulder bag has rounded ends, and so I made it from two pieces of fabric. These were sewn together with a gap left in the seam, then turned right side out and top stitched. A similar strap with square ends could be made by the folded handle method opposite, which is more straightforward.

REINFORCING STITCHING
Give additional strength to the ends of your handle with reinforcing stitching. Machine stitch a square or rectangle, then sew diagonal lines between the corners.

WEBBING
Webbing is a sturdy woven tape, which you can find in subtle natural cotton colours or more vivid nylon shades. It comes in widths from around 2cm to 8cm. I used a 4cm webbing to make the handle on the shopper bag, stitching the two edges together along the centre, so it is easier to grip.

FOLDED HANDLE OR TIE

Press the strip in half lengthways with right sides facing, then press the sides to the centre. Tack, then top stitch the two edges to make a strong, open-ended strap. You can sew the ends together to make a looped handle. To mitre the ends, fold and press each corner inwards at 45 degrees before pressing in the sides. Press the end triangles inwards.

NARROW TIES

The washbag's stylish ties are made from long rouleaux. Dressmakers use a thin latchet hook to turn these through, but you can use the method on page 25. Pull the needle slowly, so the fabric doesn't get jammed. The jewellery roll ties are a cheat's way of making a similar fabric tie: simply slip stitch together the folded edges of a length of bias binding.

CORD

I chose a soft woven cotton cord for the duffel bag. Piping cord, which would work equally well, is twisted and a little firmer. It comes in various thicknesses from around 4mm–12mm. The iPod case has a drawstring made from the narrow nylon cord used for Roman blinds. You'll find both this and piping cord at furnishing suppliers.

Appliqué & Quilting

Appliqué – creating designs from cut out fabric shapes – is a great way to use up all kinds of scraps and offcuts. I like to work with Bondaweb, the quickest way to trace and fix down the motifs, but tried out a more traditional technique for the bird cushion. The full-size trace-off templates are on pages 155–160. Remember that you may need to reverse these outlines, as iron-on appliqué always gives you a mirror image of the original template.

IRON-ON APPLIQUE

Read the manufacturer's instructions before starting work, and check the heat setting on your iron. Use a pressing cloth if you are working with felt.

1 Trace the outlines onto the paper side of the Bondaweb with a pencil. Cut them out roughly, leaving a small margin around each shape.

2 Place the motifs onto the wrong side of the fabric, with the paper upwards, fitting them together like a jigsaw. Press down with a dry iron.

3 Cut each shape out around the outline. Peel off the papers and position them on the background fabric, adhesive downwards. Press in place.

EDGING THE MOTIFS

Edging each element with a round of stitching is both practical and decorative: it prevents any fraying and adds extra definition to the shapes.

STRAIGHT STITCH

You can finish each motif by hand with small straight stitches worked at right angles to the edge in sewing cotton or stranded embroidery thread.

ZIGZAG

An open zigzag, machined in plain white, gives a hardwearing finish to items that will need to be laundered.

SATIN STITCH

A narrow satin stitch edging is the most functional of all. Match the sewing thread to the colours of the felt.

TURNED-EDGE APPLIQUE

Start off by tracing or photocopying the motif and cut out each separate element from paper. You can use the paper templates several times.

1 Pin the template to your fabric with wrong sides upwards. Cut out leaving a 4mm allowance, then fold this margin over and tack down.

2 Press to set the fold and unpick the papers. Pin the shape in position and slip stitch the folded edge to the background.

3 For a raised effect, gently push a small amount of polyester filling under the shape before stitching it down.

QUILTING

Quilting gives a raised, padded look to fabric and the technique can be as sophisticated as the padded purse on page 130 or as cosy as a hottie cover. Simply sandwich a piece of cotton batting or polyester wadding between your main fabric and a backing fabric, and stitch all three layers together.

For a diamond pattern, use a clear ruler, a set square and a sharp pencil to mark a grid across the surface of your fabric. Tack the three layers together securely and stitch along the pencil lines using a short quilting needle.

Decorative Details

If you love textiles as much as I do, you are sure to have your own hoard of trimmings, stored away and awaiting a new lease of life. Used with discretion, lace, braid or ricrac can provide the perfect detail that completes a project and adds a personal touch.

A narrow border of crisp white lace will enhance a sprigged floral print, and always looks great with its natural partner, vintage linen. Try an edging of primary coloured ricrac or a ribbon bow to bring out the brighter tones within a fabric design, and if you can't get a precise match, follow my example and go for a gloriously clashing contrast. You can add accents of colour with velvet bows, but sometimes a simple bias binding or cotton tape will work just as well. Good haberdashery departments and specialist stores have an enticing array of new trimmings, and you can easily find vintage lace and ribbons at flea markets, antique dealers and even charity shops if you persevere and if you enjoy a good rummage.

Embroidery is another effective way to add colour and fine detail, such as the cowboy lassos on the boy's apron or Stan's name on his dog tag. Hanks of stranded cotton threads come in a rainbow of colours. Use all six strands and a long-eyed needle for bold stitches, and a few threads and a finer needle for more delicate work.

HAND STITCHES

Most of the projects in the book are sewn by machine, but you'll find that they also involve a few hand and embroidery techniques. Most of these are explained in the step-by-step instructions, but here are a few other basic stitches, which you may find useful.

RUNNING STITCH

This is worked on a large scale when you are tacking or gathering, and on a smaller scale for hand quilting. The spaces and the stitches should always be a consistent length.

BACK STITCH

Use this for hand seaming on small projects and for 'writing'. Take the needle backwards and down through the fabric, then bring it back up one stitch length ahead of the first stitch.

CHAIN STITCH

This gives you a broad, flexible line. Loop the thread under the point of the needle from left to right before you pull it through, then take the needle back down through the loop of the last stitch.

RICRAC

There's something very appealing about ricrac braid – it always looks cheerful and comes in wonderful colours. If you set it into a seam or under a turned back hem, you get a little row of scallops peeping out. I used bright red ricrac to trim the rosebud egg cosies and a broader, more subtle yellow to edge the flap of the quilted purse.

LACE

Border lace has one straight and one curvy edge. Work a row of running stitches along the straight edge and pull up the thread if you want a gathered effect, or leave it flat for a plainer look. The torchon lace I used on the lavender pillow was a lucky find from my local sewing shop. For the bath hat I used a narrower and more practical broderie anglaise with a pre-gathered edge.

RIBBON

The double-face velvet ribbon used to embellish the pincushion was a bit of an extravagance, but as I only needed a short length it was worth splashing out for a luxurious finishing touch. Remember that there's more to ribbon than just bows however: the tablecloth is edged with red and white gingham ribbon that is an exact match for the appliqué fabric.

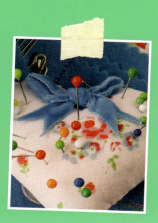

Sew! Projects

The challenge I set for myself with this book was to design projects that were practical as well as pretty. I selected a variety of items that cover all the basic sewing skills and added in some decorative details. Combing through my fabric archives to find the perfect print for each one was so much fun; the best possible inspiration to pick up a sewing needle and thread!

Square Cushion

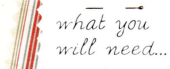

what you will need...

- 75 x 65cm ticking
- 30 x 50cm floral print in similar weight
- 2 large buttons
- matching sewing thread
- sewing kit
- sewing machine
- 45cm square cushion pad

SKILL LEVEL

Ticking stripes and pretty floral prints always complement each other, so mix and match the two fabrics to create this deceptively simple cushion. It's an ideal starter project and to make things really easy there's no need to stitch any buttonholes – simply snip off the buttons when the cover needs to be laundered.

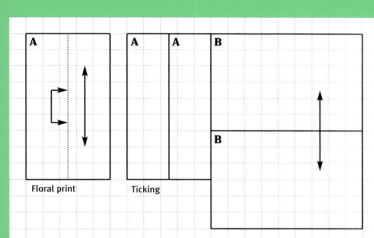

Floral print

Ticking

cutting out

Centre front: Cut 1 x A from floral print, on the fold
Side fronts: Cut 2 x A from striped fabric
Back panels: Cut 2 x B from striped fabric

The seam allowance throughout is 1.5cm

1 With right sides facing, sew the side fronts to the long edges of the centre front. Press the seams open.

2 Hem the top edge of the bottom back panel by pressing under 1cm, then a further 4cm. Pin and stitch down. Neaten the lower edge of the top back panel in the same way.

3 Position the cushion front and bottom back panel together, with right sides facing, lining up the raw edges. Lay the top panel in place, again matching the edges.

4 Pin the three pieces together, then sew around all four sides. Clip the corners (see page 22) and turn the cover right side out. Press lightly.

5 Insert the pad and fasten the cover by sewing the buttons securely through both panels, 2cm down from the edge and 12.5cm in from the corners.

top tip → DEPENDING ON THE WIDTH OF THE PATTERN REPEAT, YOU MAY NEED TO ALLOW EXTRA TICKING TO ENSURE THAT THE TWO SIDE FRONTS ARE SYMMETRICAL. LINE UP BOTH BACK PANELS CAREFULLY WHEN CUTTING OUT, SO THAT THE STRIPES WILL MATCH ACROSS THE OPENING.

Bolster Cushion

what you will need...

- 85 x 55cm floral print cotton
- 2 x 4cm self-cover buttons
- matching sewing thread
- buttonhole thread
- sewing kit
- sewing machine
- 50cm bolster cushion pad with 18cm diameter

SKILL LEVEL

There's something about a feather-filled bolster that adds a little boudoir luxury to any setting, and the cylindrical shape makes an impact whether on its own or piled alongside an assortment of other cushions. Don't be put off by the circular seams – you'll find clear instructions for this on page 23.

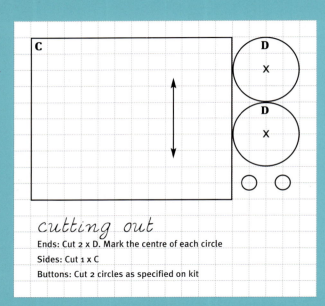

cutting out

Ends: Cut 2 x D. Mark the centre of each circle

Sides: Cut 1 x C

Buttons: Cut 2 circles as specified on kit

1 Press back a 1cm turning along each short edge of the main piece.

2 With right sides facing, pin these two edges at the corners. Slip stitch the front and back folds together for 5cm at each end, leaving a long opening between them.

3 Find the centre of each end piece by folding the circles into quarters and mark this point. Following the diagram and steps on page 23, sew one to each end of the main piece with a 1.5cm seam.

4 Turn the cover right side out and ease the circular seams into shape. Insert the cushion pad through the side opening.

5 Gather up the outside edge of each small circle and slip them over the domed tops of the self-cover buttons. Tighten the threads, then clip on the backings as directed by the manufacturer.

6 Pass a length of buttonhole thread through one of the button shanks and thread both ends through the eye of a large, long needle.

7 Plunge the needle through both the cover and the bolster at the marked centre point, then bring the needle out through the side of the bolster. Pull the thread up tightly and fasten off securely.

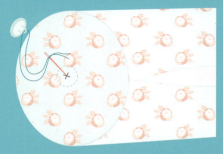

8 Pin the edges of the opening together and slip stitch the two folds to complete the cover.

top tip I CHOSE A VINTAGE FRENCH ROSE PRINT FOR MY CUSHION, BUT YOU CAN OPT FOR A MORE FORMAL LOOK BY USING TICKING, CUT SO THE STRIPES RUN EITHER LENGTHWAYS OR AROUND THE COVER. THE TRADITIONAL WAY TO FINISH A BOLSTER IS WITH A CONTRASTING ROUND OF PIPING AT EACH END.

Bird Cushion

SKILL LEVEL

You'll find these dear little birds popping up in different guises throughout the book! Here I've used the motif in both sizes to make a whole family in turned-edge appliqué, complete with padded wings. The combination of yellow ricrac, crisp spots and ditsy flowers gives a spring-like freshness to the design.

what you will need...

- 50 x 20cm white cotton fabric
- 50 x 60cm floral print cotton
- tracing paper and pencil
- 15cm square blue spotted fabric
- 15cm square pink spotted fabric
- polyester toy filling
- 2 small buttons
- 2 black seed beads
- green stranded embroidery cotton
- 1m 12mm-wide ricrac
- matching sewing thread
- sewing kit
- sewing machine
- 30 x 45cm cushion pad

cutting out

Centre front: Cut 1 x E from white cotton

Top and bottom front: Cut 2 x F from floral print

Back panels: Cut 2 x E from floral print

templates

Small bird and Mini bird, page 159

1 Following the steps on page 29, make up the body and wing pieces for the four birds, reversing two of them. Sew the bodies to the centre front. Add the beads to the small birds and the buttons to the large birds for eyes.

2 Stitch a length of ricrac to the top and bottom of the centre front, so that the curves just touch the edge of the fabric. Pin the top and bottom fronts in place, with right sides facing.

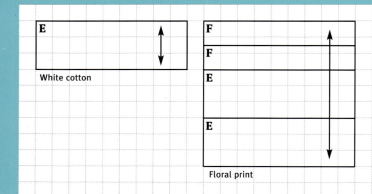

3 Machine stitch the seams 6mm from the edge. Carefully press so that the ricrac curves point outwards and the seam allowances lie inwards. Embroider the green grass with a few lines of straight stitch.

4 Hem one long edge of each back panel. Place the cushion front right side upwards, then position the back panels along the top and bottom, with raw edges aligned. Pin together and seam all four sides, 1cm from the edge.

5 Clip the corners and turn the cover right side out. Insert the cushion pad and slip stitch the opening to close.

 top tip

IF YOU CAN'T FIND THE RIGHT SIZE PAD, YOU CAN QUICKLY MAKE YOUR OWN BESPOKE FILLING FROM TWO RECTANGLES OF CALICO CUT 2CM LARGER ALL ROUND THAN THE FINISHED COVER. JOIN WITH A 1CM SEAM, TURN THROUGH, AND STUFF WITH POLYESTER WADDING. SLIP STITCH TO CLOSE.

Floor Cushions

SKILL LEVEL

Long summer days are just made for outdoor living and these thick, square cushions will ensure your creature comforts whether you're at a festival, picnicking, camping, or simply lounging about in the garden. You'll need a specially long and strong upholstery needle to secure the buttons that give them their special padded look.

what you will need...

- 140 x 90cm floral print cotton duck
- 50 x 50 x 10cm foam cushion pad
- 5 x 2.5cm self-cover buttons
- 5 x 2.5cm buttons
- buttonhole thread
- upholstery needle
- matching sewing thread
- sewing kit
- sewing machine

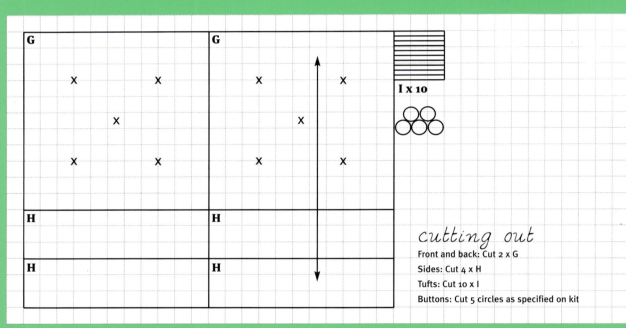

cutting out

Front and back: Cut 2 x G
Sides: Cut 4 x H
Tufts: Cut 10 x I
Buttons: Cut 5 circles as specified on kit

top tip → GETTING THE BUTTONS TO SINK RIGHT BACK INTO THE FOAM FILLING ACTUALLY TAKES QUITE A BIT OF EFFORT, SO BE PREPARED TO WORK HARD! SEE IF YOU CAN RECRUIT A FRIEND TO HELP PUSH THE PAD DOWN ON EITHER SIDE OF THE BUTTON POSITIONS AS YOU PULL THE THREAD.

Floor Cushions

1 Mark the 5 button positions on the front and back pieces, one at the centre and four points 20cm diagonally in from each corner.

2 Pin the long edge of the first side to one edge of the front piece. Starting and finishing the seam 1.5cm in from the raw edges, machine stitch together with a 1.5cm seam. Join the other three sides to the front in the same way.

3 Now pin and stitch the short edges of all four sides together to make a shallow box. Seam each edge from the point where it meets the front to 1.5cm from the corner.

4 Carefully trim a small triangle of fabric from all three pieces at each corner.

5 Pin and stitch three edges of the front panel to the 'box' in the same way and clip the corners.

6 Turn the cover right side out and press under a 1.5cm turning along the two open edges. Insert the cushion pad and pin the folded edges together. Slip stitch from corner to corner.

7 Cover the buttons as directed. Fold two tuft strips into loops, overlapping the ends by 2cm, then cross one over the other. Thread 50cm of buttonhole thread through a button and pass both ends through the upholstery needle. Plunge the needle into the front of the cushion at a marked point.

8 Push the needle right through the pad, bringing it out at the corresponding mark on the back. Pass the ends of the thread through the holes in a plain button. Pull up tightly so that the buttons sink into the pad. Knot and trim the ends. Add the other buttons in the same way.

top tip

HIGH DENSITY SEATING FOAM CAN BE ORDERED FROM SPECIALIST SUPPLIERS, WHO WILL CUT IT TO THE EXACT SIZE AND DEPTH REQUIRED. ASK FOR A STOCKINETTE WRAP, WHICH SOFTENS THE EDGES, PROTECTS THE FOAM AND MAKES IT EASIER TO GET THE PAD INSIDE YOUR COVER.

Flower Cushion

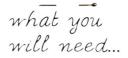

what you will need...

- 35 x 55cm white cotton fabric
- 50 x 80cm red cotton fabric
- selection of floral print scraps
- bondaweb
- pencil
- matching sewing threads
- sewing kit
- sewing machine
- 35 x 50cm cushion pad

SKILL LEVEL

All stitchers are magpies at heart and inevitably acquire an eclectic ragbag, bulging with remnants, offcuts and fabric salvaged from old garments. In a spirit of 'make do and mend' I chose some of my favourite vintage prints to appliqué this red, blue and white cushion: a great way to utilise even the tiniest scraps.

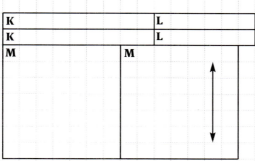

J — White cotton

K   L
K   L
M   M — Red cotton

cutting out

Front: Cut 1 x J from white cotton

Top and bottom borders: Cut 2 x K from red cotton

Side borders: Cut 2 x L from red cotton

Back panels: Cut 2 x M from red cotton, following the square corners

templates

Small flower, page 160

The seam allowance throughout is 1cm

1 Decide which two fabrics to use for each motif. I alternated contrasting red and blue flowers so that the outlines stand out clearly where they overlap.

2 Following the inner outlines, trace twenty ovals (two lots of six petals for the daisies, plus eight leaves), two small circles for the daisy centres, two flower heads and four stalks onto Bondaweb. Cut out and iron onto the prints.

3 Iron down each complete motif in turn, starting at the right and working towards the left. Edge each shape with straight stitch.

4 Trim 6cm from one short edge of J, so it measures 39cm.

5 Stitch a side border to each side edge of the front and press the seams outwards. Add the top and bottom borders, again pressing the seams outwards.

6 Make a 1cm double hem along one side edge of each back panel. Lay out the completed front with the right side facing upwards and place one panel, right side down, across each side, so that the hems overlap in the centre.

7 Pin the three pieces together and machine stitch around all four sides. Clip the corners, turn right side out and press.

8 Insert the pad through the opening. Instead of buying a pad, you can make one from two 37 x 52cm rectangles of calico: see the 'top tip' for the Bird Cushion on page 40.

top tip → TO MAKE SURE THAT THE MOTIFS ARE EVENLY SPACED, LAY ALL THE PIECES OUT ON THE CUSHION FRONT BEFORE YOU REMOVE THE BACKING PAPERS AND MARK THEIR POSITIONS WITH A FADING PEN. ALLOW A 2CM BORDER AT THE SIDES AND 4CM ALONG THE TOP AND BOTTOM EDGES.

Padded Placemats

what you will need...

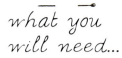

- 35 x 85cm laundered plaid cotton duck
- 30 x 40cm pre-shrunk cotton batting
- matching sewing thread
- sewing kit
- fading pen
- ruler
- sewing machine

SKILL LEVEL

Placemats are on the list of useful items that everybody needs at some time, whether it's to protect a polished wooden surface or to add colour to a table setting. Make your own from fabric that co-ordinates with your cutlery, crockery and glassware, and you'll find that every mealtime takes on a festive air.

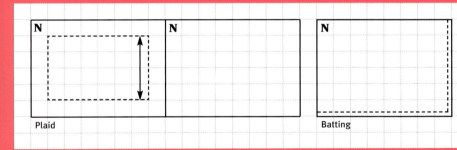

cutting out

Front and Back: Cut 2 x N from plaid cotton duck

Padding: Cut 1 x N from cotton batting. Trim 12mm from one long and one short side

1 Use a fading pen and a ruler to mark a rectangle, 5cm in from the edge, on the right side of the front panel. Pin the padding the wrong side of this panel, centring it so that there is a 5mm margin all round. Tack it in place.

2 Now pin the back panel to the front panel with right sides facing, so that the front panel is sandwiched between the padding and the back.

3 Machine stitch the three layers of fabric and padding together, leaving a 20cm gap along the centre of the bottom edge. Sew 5mm from the edge, so that the stitches run just outside the edge of the wadding.

4 Press back the seam allowance along each side of the opening, clip the corners and turn the placemat right sides out through the gap (see page 22). Tack the opening, making sure the seam allowances lie flat, and slip stitch to close.

5 Machine stitch along the marked line on the front using thread to match or contrast with the main fabric. Finish off with a round of top stitch, 3mm from the outside edge.

top tip → IF YOU USE A PLAID OR CHECK DESIGN AS I DID, SIMPLY FOLLOW THE GEOMETRIC GRID PATTERN TO CUT OUT YOUR MATS AND AS A GUIDE FOR THE RECTANGULAR STITCHING. REMEMBER TO ALLOW EXTRA FABRIC IF YOU WISH TO CENTRE THE PATTERN OR IF YOU ARE GOING TO MAKE A MATCHING SET.

Floral Napkins

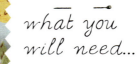

what you will need...

- 45cm square floral print
- 60 x 30cm toning plaid or check
- matching sewing thread
- sewing kit
- sewing machine

SKILL LEVEL

The final touch for your table setting has to be a set of napkins. Here I've picked the painterly 'Rose' print on a powder blue background and bordered it with 'Woven Check', the plaid design used for the mats, to show how two mismatched fabrics can look stunning together if they share a colour scheme.

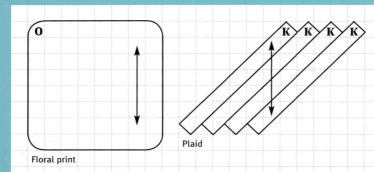

O

Floral print

Plaid

K K K K

cutting out

Napkin: Cut 1 x O from floral print, following the rounded corners

Binding: Cut 4 x K from plaid, on the bias

1 Join the four bias strips at the short ends, overlapping the points as shown on page 21. Press the seams open and trim the points in line with the straight edges. Trim the ends at right angles.

2 Press the binding in half widthways, along the entire length, then press under a 5mm turning at one long edge.

3 Stay stitch the corners of the napkin.

4 Starting in the centre of one side, pin and tack the unpressed binding edge around the napkin, right sides facing. Ease the binding around the corners as on page 21.

5 Trim the end of the binding at a right angle when you have completed the round, allowing a 2cm overlap. Press under 5mm at the loose end and tack in place.

6 Turn the other edge of the binding back to the wrong side of the napkin, so that the raw edge is enclosed, and tack down the fold. Finish off by slip stitching the fold in place.

top tip

OLD-FASHIONED ETIQUETTE DEMANDED NAPKINS IN A RANGE OF SIZES, FROM DAINTY 30CM SQUARES FOR AFTERNOON TEA UP TO ENORMOUS STARCHED DAMASK VERSIONS FOR FORMAL DINNERS. MAKE YOURS IN THE SIZE THAT SUITS YOU BEST, ENLARGING THE 45CM SQUARE IF NECESSARY.

Heart Teatowel

what you will need...

- 65 x 80cm white linen
- 25 x 65cm floral dress print
- 20cm squares of 6 floral prints
- bondaweb
- matching sewing thread
- sewing kit
- sewing machine

template

Large heart, page 157

SKILL LEVEL

Ditsy floral fabrics always muddle along, side by side, if you keep the patterns on the same scale. I cut six large hearts, each from a different print, to create the iron-on appliqué borders for this teatowel, and edged each one with a round of machine zigzag so that they'll stand up to the daily drying routine.

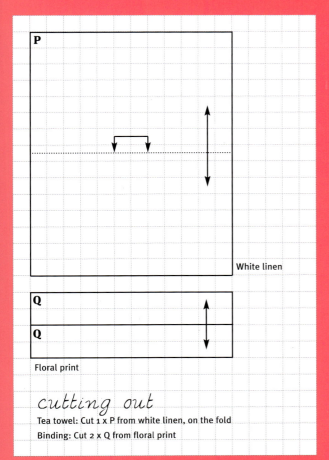

P

White linen

Q

Q

Floral print

cutting out

Tea towel: Cut 1 x P from white linen, on the fold
Binding: Cut 2 x Q from floral print

1 Pin one binding strip, right side down, to each short side of the linen. Machine stitch, 1cm from the edge and press the seam allowances outwards.

2 Press and pin a 1cm double hem along each long side. Top stitch, 3mm from the inside fold.

3 Press under 1cm along the raw edge of both bindings. Turn this to the wrong side and press so that the folds lie just beyond the stitch line. Pin and top stitch from the right side. Slip stitch the open side edges.

4 Trace six hearts onto Bondaweb. Following the technique on page 28, iron each one onto a different fabric. Cut them out and peel off the backing papers.

5 Fold the teatowel in half widthways to find the centre. Position one heart centrally at each end, with the points 1cm away from the binding strips.

6 Iron in place, then add another two hearts at each end, leaving a 2.5cm space on either side of the first motif. Press down. Using white thread, zigzag around each heart by machine.

top tip

OLD LINEN TABLECLOTHS AND SHEETS HAVE A WONDERFULLY SOFT QUALITY THAT ONLY COMES FROM DECADES OF USE AND LAUNDERING. NOT ALL OF THEM SURVIVE INTACT HOWEVER, SO MAKING ONE-OFF TEATOWELS IS A GOOD WAY TO RECYCLE THE BEST PARTS OF THE FABRIC.

Half Apron

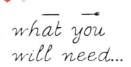

what you will need...

- 45 x 130cm cotton duck
- 2m 2cm-wide bias binding
- matching sewing thread
- sewing kit
- sewing machine

SKILL LEVEL

You can brighten up the most mundane household and gardening chores with this practical half-apron: its three pockets are just the right size for dusters or secateurs and twine. Select a vivid floral print for maximum cheerfulness and trim the edges with bias binding in an even stronger colour.

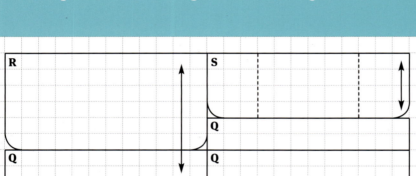

cutting out

Apron: Cut 1 x R
Pocket: Cut 1 x S. Mark a line 15cm from each short side
Ties: Cut 3 x Q

1 Following the directions on page 20, neaten the top edge of the pocket with bias binding. Mark the centre point of this edge. Pin the side and bottom edges to the main apron, matching the rounded corners, and machine stitch, leaving a seam allowance of 6mm.

2 To mark the pocket divisions, rule a line 15cm in from each side edge. Sew the two layers together along both lines.

3 Bind the side and bottom edges, referring to the technique for curved corners on page 21.

4 Join the short ends of the three ties to form one long strip and press the seams open. Press in half lengthways and unfold. Now fold both long edges to the centre crease and press in place. Mitre the short ends (see page 27). Open out the centre fold and fold the strip in half lengthways to find the centre point.

5 Matching up the two centre points, pin the apron to the strip so that the raw top edge lies along the crease. Pin and tack the top edge of the apron to the lower half of the strip.

6 Turn the upper half of the strip over the top edge of the apron and tack it down. Tack the top and bottom halves of the loose ends together to make the left and right ties. Top stitch 3mm all the way along the short and long edges of the strip.

top tip → APRON POCKETS ALWAYS GET THE MOST WEAR AT THE TOP CORNERS, SO WORK A FEW EXTRA REINFORCING STITCHES AT THE TOP END OF THE DIVIDING LINES AND AT THE POINTS WHERE THE TOP CORNERS OF THE POCKET PIECE MEETS THE MAIN APRON.

Egg Cosy

what you will need...

- 15 x 20cm floral print
- 15 x 20cm felt
- 20cm ricrac
- matching sewing thread
- sewing kit
- sewing machine

SKILL LEVEL

No breakfast tray is complete without a couple of boiled eggs and plate of 'soldiers'. These jolly cosies are made from a rose print and lined with green felt to keep the eggs toasty warm. The curved seams are machine stitched, but this project is also a good way for practising some basic hand stitching.

Floral print

Felt

drawing up the pattern

Cosy: Use piece T with line 1t as the bottom edge
Tab: Use piece I, with line 1i as the right edge

cutting out

Cosy: Cut 2 from floral print
Lining: Cut 2 from felt
Tab: Cut 1 from felt

1 Fold one cosy piece in half widthways to find the centre line. Fold the tab in half lengthways and tack it centrally along the crease, on the right side, so that the two ends line up with the top edge.

2 Pin the second cosy piece over the first, with right sides facing. Stitch the side and top edges together, with a 5mm seam. Clip a series of notches from the curved part of the seam allowance, spacing them 1cm apart (see page 23).

3 Turn the cosy right side out, ease the seam into position and press lightly.

4 Pin the two felt linings together, and stitch 5mm from the side and top edges. Trim the seam allowance back to 3mm.

5 Slip the lining inside the cosy and line up the open edges. Turn them both up together to make a 5mm hem around the opening. Tack in place.

6 Fold the hem up once again. Starting at the centre back, slip the ricrac behind the turning so that the scallops peep out over the top edge. Trim the ends and tuck them under the hem. Tack through all the layers, then stitch the top edge down.

top tip

WHEN YOU ARE CHOOSING TRIMMINGS AND BINDINGS, PICK OUT ONE OR MORE KEY COLOURS FROM THE PRINTED FABRIC. THIS BRIGHT GREEN FELT IS AN EXACT MATCH FOR THE ROSEBUD STEMS AND LEAVES WHILST THE RED RICRAC IS THE SAME COLOUR AS THE DARKEST PETALS.

Birdie Tablecloth

SKILL LEVEL

Long refectory tables require extra large tablecloths, which aren't always easy to find, so I created this one-off cover by giving a new lease of life to an antique linen sheet. I added an iron-on appliqué border of large hearts and birds cut from two colours of gingham and a toning floral print. The matching edging, made from gingham ribbon, is a speedy and effective way to finish off the cloth. You could use the small-scale versions of these motifs to embellish a set of napkins to go with the tablecloth.

what you will need...

- plain tablecloth or sheet
- for each heart and bird repeat:
  - 2 20cm gingham squares
  - 20 x 25cm floral print
  - 2 small buttons
- bondaweb
- matching sewing thread
- sewing kit
- gingham ribbon to fit around edge of cloth, plus 5cm
- sewing machine

templates

Large heart, page 157, and Large bird, page 159

1 Decide how many repeats of the heart and bird motif you would like. I spaced three at regular intervals along the sides and centred one at each end.

2 You'll find detailed instructions for iron-on appliqué on page 28. For each repeat you will need to trace two birds, two wings and a heart onto Bondaweb. Reverse one of the birds and its wing, so that they will face each other.

3 Fuse the wings and heart onto the floral print and iron one bird onto each of the ginghams. Varying the fabrics gives extra animation to the finished design, so mix and match the prints and checks for each pair of birds, their wings and the heart. I used three different ginghams in all: red, green and pink.

4 Fold the tablecloth into quarters and press the folds lightly to mark the centre of each side: use this crease as a guideline for ironing down the first motifs. You can then fold the long sides in half again, to mark the positions for the other two repeats.

5 Edge each individual piece, either with a round of short straight stitches or with a machine zigzag or satin stitch. Finish off by stitching the gingham ribbon around the edge of the cloth, mitring it at the corners and overlapping the ends with a neat hem.

top tip

IF YOUR SHEET HAS ANY INDELIBLE MARKS OR HOLES, YOU CAN CONCEAL THEM WITH CAREFULLY POSITIONED MOTIFS. WASH AND IRON THE APPLIQUE FABRICS FIRST, AS THE TABLECLOTH IS BOUND TO NEED LAUNDERING AT SOME STAGE AND ANY SHRINKAGE WILL DISTORT THE DESIGN.

Oven Glove

what you will need...

- 65 x 85cm cotton duck
- 45 x 80cm cotton batting
- 2.5m bias binding
- matching sewing thread
- sewing kit
- sewing machine

SKILL LEVEL

Here's another re-working of an everyday essential: even if you prefer heating up ready meals to baking wholemeal bread and trays of cupcakes, you'll need to have an oven glove! This project is very easy to put together and makes a good introduction to the techniques involved in binding edges.

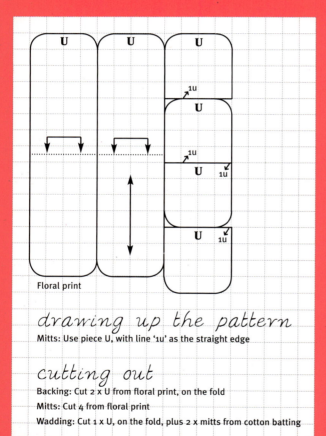

Floral print

drawing up the pattern

Mitts: Use piece U, with line '1u' as the straight edge

cutting out

Backing: Cut 2 x U from floral print, on the fold
Mitts: Cut 4 from floral print
Wadding: Cut 1 x U, on the fold, plus 2 x mitts from cotton batting

1 Start by stacking up the three pieces that make up the first mitt: a mitt with its right side down at the bottom, then a mitt padding in the middle and another mitt on top with its right side upwards.

2 Pin and tack all the layers together around the outside edge. Neaten the straight edge with bias binding, either by hand or machine, as shown in the steps on page 20. Do the same for the second mitt.

3 Sandwich the two backings and the remaining piece of padding together in the same way and tack close to the outside edge.

4 Pin a mitt at each end of the backing and tack in place. Sew a round of bias binding all the way round the outside edge, starting and finishing at the centre of one long edge.

5 Cut a 10cm length from the remaining binding and press under the ends. Fold in half widthways and slip stitch the folds together. Sew the ends securely to the point where the binding meets to make a hanging loop.

 top tip → IF YOU'RE WORKING WITH A FABRIC THAT HAS A DIRECTIONAL DESIGN, LIKE THE STRIPES ON THIS 'FLORAL GINGHAM', PLAN THE POSITION OF THE PATTERN PIECES SO THAT THE DESIGN RUNS CENTRALLY ALONG THE BACKING AND MATCHES UP WITH THE MITTS AT EACH END. YOU MAY NEED EXTRA FABRIC FOR THIS.

Peg Bag

what you will need...

- 40 x 75cm cotton duck
- child-size coat hanger
- 1.5m bias binding
- matching sewing thread
- sewing kit
- sewing machine

SKILL LEVEL

Hanging out the washing is so much easier when your pegs are close to hand, as our grandmothers knew well. Here's another practical exercise in using bias binding: this time you can learn how to neaten inside curves, by stitching around the opening on this pretty and practical peg bag.

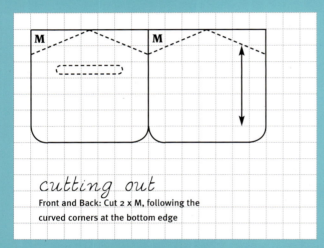

cutting out

Front and Back: Cut 2 x M, following the curved corners at the bottom edge

1 Lay the front face downwards and place the hanger centrally across the top, so that the base of the hook lines up with the edge. Draw along the top edge of the hanger, then cut along this line. Fold in half widthways to check the shape is symmetrical and trim as necessary.

2 Following the guideline on the cutting out diagram, draw in a narrow slit with rounded ends, 25cm up from the bottom edge. Work a line of reinforcing machine stitch 3mm outside the line. Using sharp embroidery scissors, cut out the centre to make the opening.

3 Neaten the opening with bias binding, sewn on by hand. So that the binding lies flat at the two ends you will need to pleat the centre and fan out the folded edges into a curve. Stitch the binding to the right side first, then the wrong side.

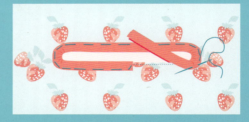

4 Pin the front to the back with wrong sides facing. Trim the top edge of the back so that it is the same shape as the front and tack the two pieces together.

5 Bind the outside edge of the peg bag, as shown on pages 20–21, starting at one side of the top point and remembering to leave a small gap for the hook. Insert the hanger through the opening and wriggle it about until the hook goes through the gap.

top tip →

IF YOU CAN'T FIND A 30CM COAT HANGER, YOU COULD TRY SHORTENING A STANDARD ONE. MEASURE UP AND MARK A CUTTING LINE 15CM FROM THE HOOK ON EACH ARM. CUT THE ENDS OFF CAREFULLY WITH A SMALL HACKSAW AND SMOOTH OFF ANY ROUGH EDGES WITH SANDPAPER.

Lavender Bags

SKILL LEVEL

Lavender has long been valued both for its fragrance and as a deterrent to moths. These hanging hearts and birds are filled with the dried buds, and will bring their gentle perfume to your wardrobe and linen cupboard. Sew them by hand or machine, for yourself or as presents for friends or family.

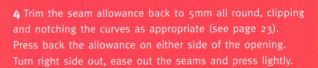

what you will need...

- 2 x 20cm squares of floral print cotton
- 35g dried lavender per bag
- 1 small button
- 15cm narrow tape
- paper and tracing paper
- matching sewing thread
- sewing kit
- sewing machine

templates
Large heart, page 157 and Large bird, page 159

1 For the bird bag, trace off the body and wing outlines and cut them out. Pin the body template to the wrong side of the main fabric and draw around the edge. Cut out roughly, leaving about 1cm all round.

2 Cover the wing with the other fabric, following the turned edge appliqué method on page 29. Pin the wing to the right side of the bird making sure it lies in the correct position by holding the fabric up to the light. Slip stitch down.

3 With right sides facing, pin the front to the other fabric and machine stitch around the outline. Leave a 4cm gap along the straight edge at the back.

4 Trim the seam allowance back to 5mm all round, clipping and notching the curves as appropriate (see page 23). Press back the allowance on either side of the opening. Turn right side out, ease out the seams and press lightly.

5 Using a teaspoon, fill the bird with lavender, then slip stitch the opening.

6 Fold the tape in half to make a hanging loop and sew the ends to the bird's back, close to the top of the wing. Stitch on the button to make the eye.

7 The heart is made in the same way, with the opening along one straight edge, just above the point. Sew the hanging loop to the centre top.

top tip → SEWING CURVES ON A SMALL SCALE CAN BE FIDDLY, SO I CHEATED! INSTEAD OF CUTTING OUT THE FRONT AND BACK, THEN JOINING THE EDGES, SIMPLY DRAW THE MOTIF ONTO A PIECE OF FABRIC, TACK ANOTHER PIECE TO THE BACK, SEW TOGETHER AROUND THE OUTLINE AND TRIM THE SEAM.

Coat Hangers

SKILL LEVEL

Give your best frocks the special treatment they deserve, and prevent the shoulders from creasing, with these quick-to-make hangers. They have been padded in thrifty style by binding the wooden arms with old tights: you could also use strips cut from an old t-shirt or jumper.

what you will need...

- 20 x 65cm floral fabric
- wooden coat hanger
- padding: old tights or top cut into 10cm strips
- 60cm bias binding
- matching sewing thread
- sewing kit

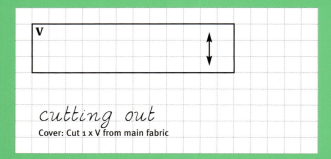

cutting out
Cover: Cut 1 x V from main fabric

1 Bind the padding around the coat hanger. Starting at one end, wrap it tightly towards, and then past, the hook. Sew on new lengths when needed and secure the ends with a few stitches.

2 Cut a length of binding 2cm longer than the hook. Press under a 5mm turning at one end. Fold in half lenthways and slip stitch the folded end and the long edges together to form a tube. Slide the open end over the hook and sew the raw ends to the padding.

3 Press a 1cm turning at the short edges and a 2cm turning along the long edges of the cover. Fold in half widthways and mark the centre point.

4 Slip stitch the folds at each short edge. Sew the top edges on the left side together, from the corner to the centre point. Use 5mm running stitches, worked 5mm down from the folds.

5 Slide the hanger into the cover. Pull up the thread so that the fabric gathers over the padding. Even out the folds and fasten off the thread. Gather the other side in the same way.

6 Make a bow from the remaining bias binding, trim the ends and stitch to the cover at the base of the hook.

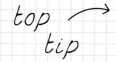

top tip → A LENGTH OF DOUBLE-SIDED TAPE FIXED ALL THE WAY ACROSS THE ARMS OF THE HANGER WILL STOP THE PADDING FROM SLIPPING ABOUT AS YOU WIND IT IN PLACE.

Lavender Pillow

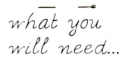

what you will need...

- 35 x 85cm floral fabric
- 300g dried lavender
- 1.8m 5cm-wide lace
- 8 x 1cm buttons
- matching sewing thread
- sewing kit
- sewing machine

SKILL LEVEL

Keep this scented pillow on your bed and the soothing qualities of lavender will always bring you the sweetest dreams. To keep the contents evenly distributed and to give it an upholstered look, the front and back have been stitched together at four central points and trimmed with mother of pearl buttons.

cutting out

Front and Back: Cut 2 x N

1 Mark the four button positions on both pieces, as shown on the diagram. With right sides facing, pin the two together. Machine stitch, with a 1cm seam allowance, leaving a 10cm gap in the centre of one edge.

2 Press the seam allowance back on either side of the gap. Clip the corners and turn right side out. Ease the corners into shape and press the seams.

3 Fill the bag with lavender by pouring it through a funnel made from a rolled-up sheet of paper. Slip stitch the gap to close.

4 Sew a button onto a cross at the front, then pass the needle right through to the back, so that it comes out at the corresponding mark. Add another button and stitch the two together through the pillow several times. Do the same at the other three crosses.

5 Pin the lace along one side edge of the pillow. Measure and mark off the next 10cm, then pin along the top so that the spare lace forms a loop at the corner. Pin the lace to the other two edges and join the ends.

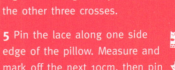

6 Slip stitch the lace to the seams. Sew a line of running stitches along the straight edge of each loop as you reach it and pull up the thread to gather the lace. Slip stitch the gathers securely to the corner.

top tip →

YOU CAN INTERPRET THIS PROJECT IN SEVERAL WAYS, BY VARYING THE SIZE AND SHAPE (A SQUARE OR LARGE HEART PERHAPS) OR BY CUTTING THE FRONT AND BACK FROM DIFFERENT FABRICS AND USING DIFFERENT TYPES OF BUTTONS ON EACH SIDE TO MAKE THE PILLOW REVERSIBLE.

Quilted Hottie

SKILL LEVEL

This hand-quilted hot water bottle cover, made from pink paisley fabric, was inspired by traditional feather eiderdowns. It is trimmed with a pale turquoise print and fastens with a rouleau loop and a pearl button. Snuggle up close and your hottie will keep you warm and snug on the coldest winter night.

what you will need...

- 50 x 60cm paisley fabric
- 50 x 60cm polyester or cotton batting
- 50 x 60cm backing fabric
- 15 x 40cm binding fabric
- matching sewing thread
- 50cm narrow velvet ribbon
- 1 x 12mm button
- sewing kit
- sewing machine

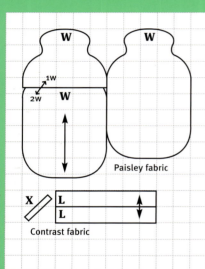

Paisley fabric

Contrast fabric

drawing up the pattern

Top Front: Use piece W, with line 1w as the bottom edge

Main Front: Use piece W, with line 2w as the top edge

Back: Use piece W, tracing around the entire outline

cutting out

Top Front: Cut 1 from paisley fabric

Main Front: Cut 1 from paisley fabric

Back: Cut 1 from paisley fabric

Binding: Cut 2 x L from contrast fabric

Button Loop: Cut 1 x X from contrast fabric, on the bias

top tip → THE PATTERN DIAGRAM IS FOR A STANDARD SHAPE, BUT CHECK THAT YOUR OWN HOTTIE LIES COMFORTABLY WITHIN THE MARKED SEAM LINE, WITH AT LEAST 2CM EXTRA ALL ROUND. INCREASE THE LENGTH OR WIDTH IF NECESSARY FOR A PERFECT FIT.

Quilted Hottie

1 You will find all you need to know about hand quilting in the techniques section, so refer back to page 29 for the next two steps. Start by marking a 3cm diamond grid on the right side of each of the three cover pieces.

2 Cut out a piece of batting and a piece of backing fabric, each of which is slightly larger all round than the main front panel. Tack the three layers together, quilt along the lines and around the outside edges, then trim. Make up the other top front and back in the same way.

3 Bind the straight edges of the two front panels with the contrast strips, as shown on page 20.

4 See page 25 for how to make a rouleau buttonhole from the bias strip. Trim it down to 6cm and fold in half to form a loop. Sew the ends securely to the wrong side of the top front panel, half way along the straight edge.

5 Place the back panel, right side up, on your work surface. Lay the top front panel, face down, across the top so the curved edges are lined up exactly. Position the front panel over them both so that the bottom and side edges match.

6 Pin the three pieces together around the outside edge.

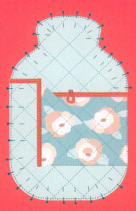

Tack and machine stitch, leaving a 1cm seam allowance. Clip and notch the curves (see page 23), then turn right side out and ease the curves into shape.

7 Cut the ribbon in half and tie each piece in a little bow. Cut off the ends at a sharp angle and sew one to each side of the neck. Sew the button to the centre of the front panel, just below the loop.

top tip →

THIS PROJECT IS AN EXCELLENT WAY TO LEARN HOW TO HAND QUILT, BUT IF YOU DON'T FANCY ALL THAT EXTRA STITCHING YOU COULD SIMPLY CUT THE BATTING AND BACKING TO THE SAME SIZE AS THE THREE COVER PIECES AND MAKE A PLAIN BUT PADDED COVER!

Bath Hat

SKILL LEVEL

what you will need...

- 60cm square of floral print
- 60cm square of waterproof fabric
- 2m bias binding
- 2m narrow lace
- 1m hat elastic
- 2 small safety pins
- matching sewing thread
- sewing kit
- sewing machine

This flowery bath hat is so pretty that you won't ever want to put it away in your bathroom cupboard. It is very easy to make, from a surprisingly large gathered circle of cotton duck or lighter weight cotton, which is lined with waterproof fabric and trimmed with a frill of broderie anglaise.

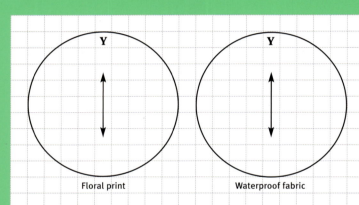

Floral print

Waterproof fabric

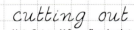

cutting out

Hat: Cut 1 x Y from floral print

Lining: Cut 1 x Y from waterproof fabric

1 Pin the lining to the wrong side of the hat and tack them both together all the way around the circumference.

2 Open out one fold of the bias binding and turn under 1cm at the end. With right sides together, tack the binding all around the circumference so that the unfolded raw edge lies along the outside edge of the hat. You'll find details of how to do this on page 21.

3 Trim the other end of the binding to 1cm when you've got all the way round and turn it under so that the two ends butt closely together. Trim the seam allowance back to 3mm.

4 Turn the folded edge of the binding to the wrong side and slip stitch the fold along the curved seam line.

5 Sew the straight edge of the lace to the right side of the hat along the bottom edge of the binding, with the scalloped edge facing outwards. Trim and seam the two ends.

6 Tie the elastic securely to a safety pin. Use another pin to fasten the loose end of the elastic close to the gap in the binding, so that it won't disappear as you gather up the hat.

7 Thread the elastic through the gap and around the binding, pulling it up as you go. Check that you have a comfortable fit, then knot and stitch the ends together. Trim to 2cm and slide the knot so that it is hidden within the binding.

top tip → I USED A WOVEN SHOWER CURTAIN MATERIAL TO MAKE THE WATERPROOF (BUT NOT WATER-TIGHT!) LINING FOR THE HAT. THIS IS SOFTER AND MORE COMFORTABLE TO WEAR THAN OTHER FABRICS WITH A PLASTICISED FINISH.

Needlecase & Pincushion

SKILL LEVEL

If you've got the sewing bug, you'll need plenty of different needles for plain stitching, embroidery and quilting. Store them safely in the pages of this handy book, then make the adorable pincushion to match. Don't put your needles in the cushion however – they may disappear into the filling!

what you will need...

- 40 x 35cm floral print cotton duck
- 30cm square felt
- bondaweb
- thin card
- pinking shears
- press stud
- 25cm narrow ribbon
- polyester toy filling
- matching sewing thread
- sewing kit
- sewing machine

template

Small heart, page 157

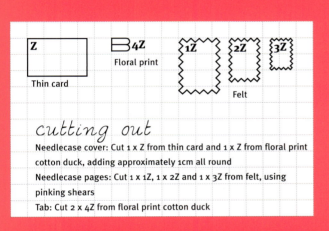

cutting out

Needlecase cover: Cut 1 x Z from thin card and 1 x Z from floral print cotton duck, adding approximately 1cm all round

Needlecase pages: Cut 1 x 1Z, 1 x 2Z and 1 x 3Z from felt, using pinking shears

Tab: Cut 2 x 4Z from floral print cotton duck

1 To make the pincushion, trace round the heart template onto the wrong side of the floral fabric. Cut out roughly, 1cm from the line. Cut another piece of fabric the same size and tack the two together with right sides facing.

2 Machine stitch around the outline, leaving a 4cm gap in one straight side. Trim the allowance to 6mm, then clip and notch it as shown on page 23. Press the allowance back on both sides of the gap and turn right side out.

3 Stuff the pincushion with your chosen filling, packing it down firmly through the gap. Close the gap with slip stitch.

4 Tie the velvet ribbon into a small bow and trim the ends into fishtails. Sew the bow to the centre top of the finished heart pincushion.

 **top tip**

ALTERNATIVE PINCUSHION FILLINGS OVER THE YEARS HAVE INCLUDED SAWDUST; CLEAN SHEEP'S FLEECE WHICH CONTAINS NATURAL LANOLIN; COFFEE GROUNDS TO PREVENT RUST, AND SAND OR EMERY POWDER WHICH GIVE YOU A HEAVIER CUSHION AND KEEP THE POINTS SHARP.

Needlecase
& Pincushion

1 To make the needlecase, cut a rectangle of Bondaweb 1cm larger on each side than the card cover. Iron this to the floral fabric and cut out around the edge. Peel off the backing paper.

2 Place the fabric on your ironing board with the Bondaweb facing upwards, then position the card centrally on top.

3 Fold the corners of the fabric over the card, gently pressing them down in turn with the tip of your iron. Now fold the sides over and iron each one so that the corners are neatly mitred.

4 Turn the cover the other way up and, protecting the surface with a piece of spare fabric, iron it gently so the fabric fuses onto the card. Stitch the recessed half of the press stud halfway down the right side, 2cm in from the edge.

5 Stitch the other half of the press stud to the round end of one tab, on the right side. Tack and machine stitch the two tabs together around the long and curved edges, leaving a 5mm seam allowance. Notch the allowance around the curve and turn right side out.

6 Trace the cover lining (1Z) onto the paper side of the Bondaweb. Cut out roughly, then iron it onto the felt. Cut along the pencil line with pinking shears.

7 Pin the other two pages centrally on top and machine stitch together down the centre. Peel off the backing paper from the first page, then press it onto the cover.

top tip

BUY SEVERAL PACKETS OF NEEDLES IN VARIOUS SHAPES AND SIZES AND TRANSFER THEM TO YOUR COMPLETED NEEDLECASE, KEEPING ONE TYPE ON EACH FELT PAGE. YOU'LL ALSO FIND IT USEFUL TO ADD A FEW ASSORTED SAFETY PINS AND PERHAPS A NEEDLE THREADER.

Knitting Bag

what you will need...

- selection of dress weight cotton fabrics
- old envelopes and paper
- 55 x 125cm floral print
- 2 round bag handles
- matching sewing thread
- sewing kit
- sewing machine

template
Hexagon, page 156

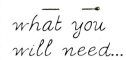

SKILL LEVEL

Hexagon patchwork, with its characteristic honeycomb pattern, was hugely popular in Victorian times and once again in the Seventies, when it was used to create countless bedcovers and cushions. It's time for another revival of this absorbing hand technique: start off with this useful knitting bag.

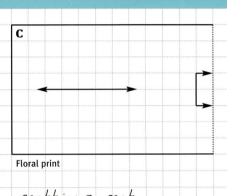

C

Floral print

cutting out
Lining: Cut 1 x C from floral print, on the fold

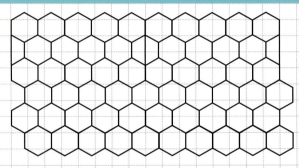

Layout for Hexagons and Half hexagons

1 Make 60 paper hexagons using the template as a guide, and cut two of them in half, from point to point.

2 Cut out a piece of fabric 1cm larger all round than the hexagon. Don't worry about being too accurate – just make sure it is big enough to cover the template comfortably.

3 Pin a hexagon centrally to the wrong side of the fabric. Turning down one edge at a time and making a neat fold at each angle, tack the surplus fabric to the paper.

top tip →

IF YOU WANT YOUR DESIGN TO HAVE AN OVERALL THEME, KEEP TO A LIMITED COLOUR PALETTE, AS I DID. FOR A MORE RANDOM, HAPHAZARD LOOK, JUST GO FOR ALL THE FABRICS YOU CAN FIND: TAKE A LOOK AT THE FABULOUS VINTAGE BEDSPREAD ON PAGES 86–87 TO SEE WHAT I MEAN!

Knitting Bag

4 Join the first two patches by lining them up with right sides facing, and slip stitching through two adjacent edges. Make small, closely spaced stitches and pass the needle through the fabric only, not the papers. Sew two sides of the third hexagon into the angle between the first two.

5 Continue building up all 62 patches into a mosaic, following the layout diagram. Stitch the first 40 together in four staggered rows of ten.

6 Sew half-hexagons at the ends of the fifth row and, working inwards, add four more hexagons to each side and two more half-hexagons in the centre, but don't join these two patches together.

7 For the sixth row, sew five hexagons at each end without joining the two in the centre.

8 Press the finished patchwork and fold it in half with right sides facing. Join the edges of the hexagons at the ends of the bottom three rows, to make the bag.

9 Unpick all the papers (you can reuse these for another project). Trim a shallow triangle from the edge of each hexagon on the top and bottom rows to make straight edges, taking care not to cut into the seams.

10 Fold the bag, wrong side out, so that the openings lie at the side edges. Pin the front and back together along the bottom edge and machine stitch, leaving a 1cm seam allowance. Turn the right side out.

11 Fold the lining in half lengthways, with right sides facing, and pin the side edges together. Make a 25cm seam, from the corner upwards on each side, 5cm from the edge. Trim 10cm from the top edge. Press down the remaining seam allowances at the sides, then press under 1cm along the top edges.

12 Slip the lining inside the bag. Pin and slip stitch the folded side edges to the patchwork. Machine stitch the top edge of the patchwork to the lining at the front and back, where they meet.

13 Fold the top edge of the front lining over to the bag, passing it through the first handle. Pin the folded edge to the patchwork as you go, just below the line of machine stitching. Slip stitch in place, then repeat at the back.

top tip →

PATCHWORK ORIGINATED AT A TIME WHEN NEW MATERIALS WERE EXPENSIVE AND OFTEN HARD TO COME BY. MAINTAIN THE TRADITION — AND YOUR GREEN CREDENTIALS — BY SAVING ALL YOUR OFFCUTS, ALONG WITH YOUR FAMILY'S OLD GARMENTS, TO MAKE YOUR HEXAGONS.

Knitting Needle Case

what you will need...

- 45 x 50cm floral print
- 45 x 55cm spotted fabric
- 45cm nylon zip
- 75cm bias binding
- matching sewing thread
- sewing kit
- sewing machine

SKILL LEVEL

Don't be put off by the idea of sewing in a zip – it's not nearly as complicated as you might think! I chose a bright red one for this long thin knitting needle case, which echoes the colour of the roses and stands out well against the spotty lining.

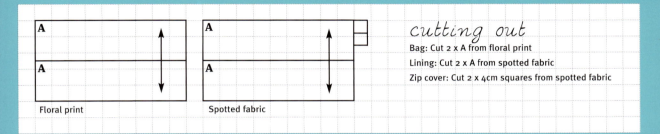

Floral print   Spotted fabric

cutting out

Bag: Cut 2 x A from floral print

Lining: Cut 2 x A from spotted fabric

Zip cover: Cut 2 x 4cm squares from spotted fabric

1 With right sides facing, pin and machine stitch one long edge of a lining piece to a bag piece, with a 5mm allowance. Press the seam away from the lining.

2 Fold along the seam line with wrong sides together, and press so that 5mm of the lining is visible above the top edge of the bag. Trim the bottom edge of the front so that it is the same depth as the lining. Join the other two pieces in the same way.

3 Fold the two small squares in half. Tack one across each end of the closed zip, with the folds facing inwards. Double check the length against the bag and adjust if necessary.

4 Open the zip. Tack one side of the bag to one side of the zip so that the teeth lie just below the top edge. Do the same on the other side and close the zip.

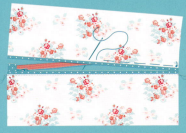

5 Fit a zip foot and, from the right side, machine stitch the zip to the bag, 3mm below the seam line. Sew across the zip at each end, 1cm from the edge.

6 Fold the bag with right sides facing, so that the zip lies in the middle. Tack the side and bottom edges together, then machine stitch leaving a 1cm seam. Trim the allowance to 4mm and bind to neaten (see page 20). Turn right side out.

top tip → THE FINISHED SIZE OF 43CM MEANS THAT THIS BAG IS LONG ENOUGH FOR MOST STANDARD KNITTING NEEDLES, BUT IF YOU HAVE GOT SOME EXTRA BIG PAIRS AMONGST YOUR COLLECTION, INCREASE THE LENGTH ACCORDINGLY SO THAT THEY WILL FIT IN.

Girl's Apron

SKILL LEVEL

It's not always easy to keep children clean when they're in the kitchen, but here are two aprons that may help! The girl's version has contrasting bound edges whilst the boy's one overleaf is quicker to make and a perfect beginner's project. Swap the fabrics as you wish, to suit your sewing skills – and your child.

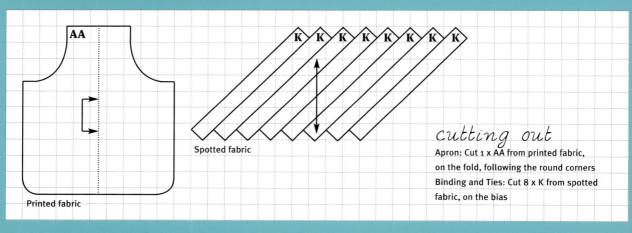

AA

Spotted fabric

Printed fabric

cutting out

Apron: Cut 1 x AA from printed fabric, on the fold, following the round corners

Binding and Ties: Cut 8 x K from spotted fabric, on the bias

1 You'll find all you need to know about bias binding on pages 20–21. Following the steps, join the spotted strips, then use them to bind around the neck and the lower half of the apron. Top stitch 3mm from the edge.

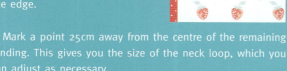

2 Mark a point 25cm away from the centre of the remaining binding. This gives you the size of the neck loop, which you can adjust as necessary.

3 Open out one fold of the binding and pin the first mark to the left edge of the neck, with raw edges together. Pin and sew the binding to the apron, following the instructions for inside curves. Do the same at the other side.

4 Tack the two folded edges of the binding together around the neck loop.

5 Trim the ties to the same length, and press under 1cm at each end. Tack the folded edges together. Starting at the end of one tie, and finishing at the other, top stitch all the way along the binding, 3mm from the edge.

6 Make the pocket from the remaining spotted fabric, as for steps 1 and 2 of the pincushion on page 77. Slip stitch the gap and press. Pin the pocket to the apron and sew down along the straight edges with neat top stitches.

top tip

GIVE YOUR APRON A CO-ORDINATED LOOK BY PICKING OUT A COLOUR FROM THE MAIN FABRIC TO USE FOR THE POCKET AND BINDING. I MATCHED THE BLUE POLKA DOT FABRIC TO THE STRAWBERRY FLOWERS, AND AS A BONUS, THE SPOTS ECHO THE SEED PATTERN ON THE RED FRUIT.

Boy's Apron

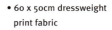

what you will need...

- 60 x 50cm dressweight print fabric
- 60 x 50cm white cotton
- 45 x 50cm red cotton
- bondaweb
- stranded embroidery thread in matching colours
- 2 D-rings
- matching sewing thread
- sewing kit
- sewing machine

SKILL LEVEL

Make this apron for the junior cowboy of the family, as even tough guys have to stay tidy sometimes. Curved seams, like those on either side of the bib, can be a bit tricky if you have to hem or bind them, but this apron's made in a special cheat's way which avoids any complicated techniques. Yee hah!

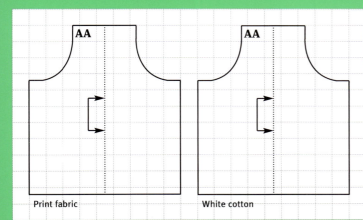

Print fabric

White cotton

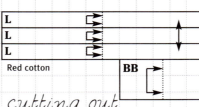

Red cotton

cutting out

Apron: Cut 1 x AA from print fabric, on the fold, following square corners

Backing: Cut 1 x AA from white cotton, on the fold, following square corners

Neck Loop and Ties: Cut 3 x L from red cotton, on the fold

Pocket: Cut 1 x BB from red cotton, on the fold

1 Pin the front to the lining around the side and bottom edges, with right sides facing. Seam together, 1cm from the edge, leaving the neck open. Clip the corners, notch the curves (see pages 22–23). Turn right side out. Press under the seam allowance at the neck and slip stitch the edges together.

2 Make a 1cm double seam along the top of the pocket and top stitch both edges. This will lie at the front. Press under a 1cm seam at the other sides, so that the fabric is turned to the back.

3 Press the pocket in half lengthways to mark the centre. Cut a few motifs from the offcuts and appliqué them with Bondaweb (see page 28). Edge each shape with straight stitches. Embroider the lassoes in chain stitch and the grass with straight stitches.

4 Sew the pocket in place and add a line of stitching down the centre.

5 Make two red strips into ties, as on page 27, neatening them at both ends. Sew one to each side of the apron with decorative reinforcing stitching.

6 Cut 10cm from the third strip, and make a tie from each piece. Slip the short length through the two D-rings. Fold in half and stitch the ends to the left corner of the neck edge as before. Sew the other tie to the right corner and loop the end through the rings.

top tip

THE COMIC STRIP COWBOYS ARE GREAT FUN TO DO AND TO WEAR. IF YOU ARE MAKING A MORE GIRLY APRON YOU COULD MAKE A SIMILAR POCKET WITH LEAVES AND BLOOMS CUT FROM FLOWERED FABRIC, OR USE ONE OF THE MOTIFS AT THE BACK OF THE BOOK FOR A SIMPLER DESIGN.

Stanley Picture

SKILL LEVEL

Stanley, my Lakeland Terrier, has become something of a design icon in his own right. He even has a special fabric to himself, called 'Mini Stanley'. This iron-on appliqué picture is based on one of the motifs in that print and shows him proudly sporting his best vintage floral coat and a spotty collar.

what you will need...

- bondaweb
- 35 x 45cm red star fabric
- 20 x 80cm blue spotted fabric
- scraps of floral and green fabric
- small button
- matching sewing thread
- 1m piping cord
- 18 x 26cm block of wood, padded with wadding on one side
- hammer and tacks or staplegun
- sewing kit

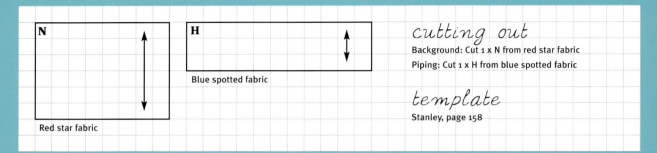

N
Red star fabric

H
Blue spotted fabric

cutting out

Background: Cut 1 x N from red star fabric
Piping: Cut 1 x H from blue spotted fabric

template

Stanley, page 158

1 Trace the main Stanley outline onto Bondaweb, reversing the image if you wish him to face to the right. Following the steps on page 28, cut him out from blue spotted fabric, and iron him centrally onto the red fabric.

2 Add a matching ear, then make his collar from green spotted fabric and his coat from the floral print. Sew on the button for his eye.

3 Place the finished appliqué face downwards and position the wooden block on top, making sure that it lies centrally over Stanley. Turn back the top edge and tack or staple it onto the wood. Now turn back the opposite edge, stretching it slightly and fix that down too. Secure the side edges in the same way.

4 To make the piping, press the strip of spotted fabric in half lengthways and cut along the fold. Sew the two pieces together and press the seam open, then cover the cord as shown on page 23.

5 Tack the piping around the edge of the fabric-covered block, joining the round, and then staple or tack the loose fabric to the back.

top tip

LOOK OUT FOR A CHARACTERFUL OLD CARVED FRAME AS AN ALTERNATIVE WAY TO DISPLAY YOUR PICTURE: IT DOESN'T MATTER IF THE GLASS IS MISSING OR IF THERE ARE A FEW KNOCKS AND CHIPS AS YOU CAN EASILY REVIVE THE WOODWORK WITH A COAT OR TWO OF PAINT.

Bird Mobile

SKILL LEVEL

Mix and match your leftover scraps of fabric to make these little bobbing birds, switching them around on wings and bodies. A jumble of mini prints always works well, so I chose three favourites, featuring roses, buds and stars, then added a paisley and a vintage rose print in the same colour palette.

what you will need...

- 45cm square mini print fabric
- scraps of other fabrics
- polyester toy filling
- black 3mm rocaille beads
- strong white beading thread
- 2 25cm garden sticks
- curtain ring or split ring
- matching sewing thread
- sewing kit
- sewing machine

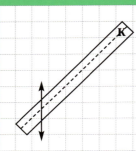

cutting out

Binding: Cut 1 x K from floral print, on the bias

Cut the strip in half lengthways

template

Small bird, page 159

1 Trace the bird's body and wing outlines onto paper and cut out. Draw round the body template onto the wrong side of a piece of fabric. Cut out roughly and, with right sides facing, pin to a second piece of the same fabric. Tack close to the outline.

2 Stitch around the outline, leaving a 3cm gap along the back. The lavender bird diagram on page 65 will show you how to do this.

3 Cut out, leaving a 6mm seam allowance. Press back the allowance along the opening, then clip and notch the curves. Turn right side out, stuff gently with toy filling and close the gap with slip stitch. Sew a bead to each side of the head for the eyes.

4 Make two wings in the same way. Turn right side out, press and slip stitch to the finished bird.

top tip

GIVE EACH OF YOUR FLOCK ITS OWN INDIVIDUAL CHARACTER BY VARYING THE POSITION OF THE HANGING THREADS, AND THE ANGLE AT WHICH YOU SEW THE WINGS.

Bird Mobile

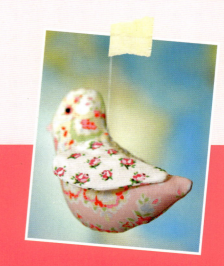

5 Bind each stick with a bias strip, wrapping it diagonally, and stitching down the ends. Hold them together in a cross, and bind the centre with thread or a very narrow strip of fabric. A few stitches, worked through the bindings, will keep the sticks securely fixed.

6 Stitch a 30cm length of beading thread to the end of each arm of the cross and knot the loose ends together. Tie the ends to the ring and trim.

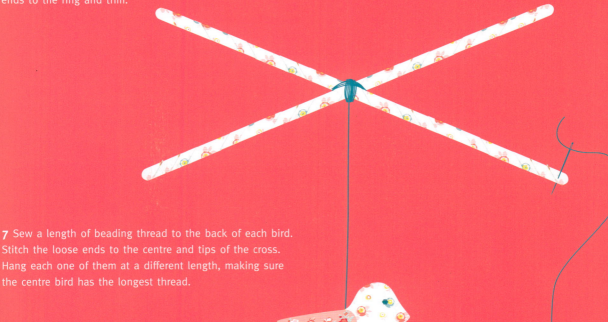

7 Sew a length of beading thread to the back of each bird. Stitch the loose ends to the centre and tips of the cross. Hang each one of them at a different length, making sure the centre bird has the longest thread.

top tip → THE BIRDS ARE GOING TO APPEAL TO EVERYBODY WHO SEES THEM, BUT FOR SAFETY'S SAKE, PLEASE KEEP THE MOBILE WELL OUT OF THE REACH OF THE SMALLEST MEMBERS OF YOUR FAMILY.

Stanley Toy

what you will need...

- 20cm square printed fabric
- 20cm blue spotted fabric
- 1m red ricrac
- tiny button
- scraps of red and green felt
- green embroidery thread
- filling
- sewing kit

template
Stanley, page 156

SKILL LEVEL

Lucky mascot Stanley is one of the smallest projects in the book, but – as you may expect – I have to admit that it is my favourite! He's stitched completely by hand, and can be made in an afternoon. This pet print was just the right fabric to use, but you could vary the look with spots on both sides or a mini floral design.

1 Cut out a paper Stanley template. Pin to the wrong side of the printed fabric so that his nose is pointing left. Trim the seam to 5mm, then notch and clip as on page 23. Fold the seam allowance over and tack it to the paper. Press and remove the paper.

2 Make the back in the same way, with Stanley facing to the right. Slip stitch the ricrac around the edge, so that the scallops project beyond the fold.

3 Pin the front to the back, sandwiching the ricrac between the two. Slip stitch together, leaving a gap along Stanley's tummy. Stuff the body with your chosen filling, a spoonful at a time, then close the gap.

4 Cut out the ear template and make two shapes from printed fabric as for the body. Slip stitch them together and sew in place along the top edge only. Add a narrow strip of felt for the collar.

5 To make his nametag, write 'Stan' on the red felt and work tiny back stitches over the letters. Cut out, using a coin to give you a neat circle, and sew the tag to the collar. Finish off with a tiny button for Stanley's eye.

top tip →

BEAN BAGS ARE USUALLY STUFFED WITH LENTILS OR RICE, TO GIVE THEIR CHARACTERISTIC WEIGHT AND TEXTURE. SUCH FILLINGS, HOWEVER, WON'T STAND UP TO THE DAMP SO YOU COULD USE THE NEWER ALTERNATIVE – SPECIALLY MADE NYLON BEADS FROM GOOD CRAFT SUPPLIERS.

Cot Quilt

SKILL LEVEL 🪡🪡🪡

Here are the birds again, this time sitting alongside their elephant friends on a charming cot quilt. The time and skill involved in stitching patchwork makes it a true labour of love, so this would be a wonderful present for a newborn. The pink and blue colour scheme makes it suitable for a girl or boy.

what you will need...

- 65 x 140cm floral print
- 45 x 140cm pink spotted fabric
- 55 x 140cm blue spotted fabric
- 80 x 120cm cotton batting
- 80 x 120cm backing fabric
- sewing kit
- sewing machine
- twin needle for machine (optional)

templates

Elephant, page 155 and Small bird, page 157

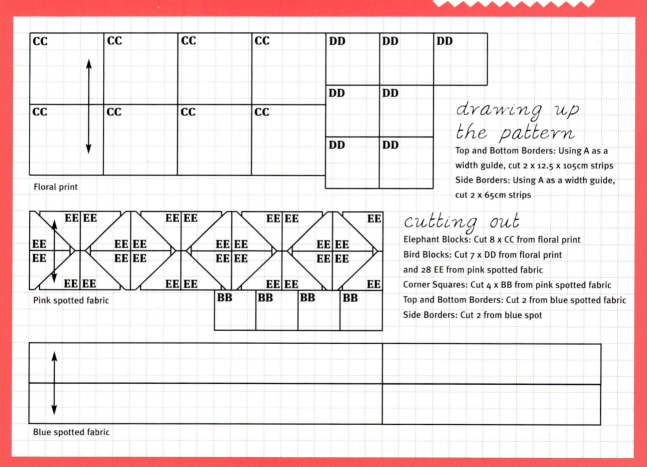

drawing up the pattern

Top and Bottom Borders: Using A as a width guide, cut 2 x 12.5 x 105cm strips
Side Borders: Using A as a width guide, cut 2 x 65cm strips

cutting out

Elephant Blocks: Cut 8 x CC from floral print
Bird Blocks: Cut 7 x DD from floral print and 28 EE from pink spotted fabric
Corner Squares: Cut 4 x BB from pink spotted fabric
Top and Bottom Borders: Cut 2 from blue spotted fabric
Side Borders: Cut 2 from blue spot

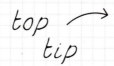

top tip → DEPENDING ON YOUR SKILL AND PATIENCE YOU CAN OMIT THE TWIN STITCHING AND CROSS STITCHES, AND INSTEAD HAND QUILT THE ENTIRE SURFACE OF THE PATCHWORK, OUTLINING EACH OF THE BLOCKS, AND IF YOU'VE TIME, THE ELEPHANTS AND THE BIRDS.

Cot Quilt

The seam allowance throughout is 1cm

1 Referring to page 28, cut out eight Bondaweb elephants from blue spotted fabric, four facing right and four left. Iron them centrally on to the large squares. Add blue tails and pink ears and eyes. Straight stitch around each shape, with matching thread. Embroider the eyes with black cross stitches.

2 Fix a blue bird to each of the small squares, three facing right and four of them facing to the left. Give each one a pink wing and an embroidered eye. Sew a pink triangle to each side of the square and press the seams inwards.

3 With right sides facing, pin the blocks together in five rows of three: three rows with the elephants on the outside, facing inwards, and two rows with the birds at the outside, also looking at each other. Machine stitch together.

4 Press all the seams towards the elephant blocks, then join the five rows together matching the seams exactly. Fit the twin needle to your sewing machine and work a line of double stitching over each long seam.

5 Sew the side borders to the quilt and press the seams open. Sew the remaining four spotted squares to each end of the top and bottom borders. Press the seams open, then pin and stitch in place, matching the seams at the corner squares.

6 Press the seams open and machine stitch along the top and bottom edges of the patchwork, as before. Press a 1cm turning along each outside edge.

7 Lay the quilt out flat with the right side facing downwards. Place the batting centrally across it, with the backing fabric on top. Pin the three layers together. Turn over and work a cross stitch across the corners of each block to secure the layers.

8 Finish off by turning the surplus fabric to the back, folding the corners over neatly. Pin down and slip stitch the fold to the backing.

top tip →

ANYTHING THAT COMES INTO CONTACT WITH BABIES AND SMALL CHILDREN WILL UNDOUBTEDLY NEED TO BE LAUNDERED AT REGULAR INTERVALS, SO DON'T FORGET TO WASH AND PRESS YOUR FABRIC BEFORE YOU START TO AVOID ANY SHRINKAGE OR COLOUR RUNS AT A LATER DATE.

Heart Quilt

SKILL LEVEL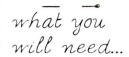

Making an appliqué quilt on the scale of this stunning hearts and flowers design, has always been a major undertaking, but contemporary techniques mean that it will take much less time than you may expect! You will find detailed step-by-step instructions for iron-on appliqué on page 28.

what you will need...

- 145 x 140cm white cotton
- 65 x 125cm floral print fabric for the border
- 75 x 140cm each of three different print fabrics
- 150 x 180cm print fabric for the backing (join as necessary)
- 150 x 180cm cotton batting
- 3m x 44cm-wide bondaweb
- quilter's safety pins (optional)
- quilting thread
- matching sewing thread
- sewing kit
- sewing machine

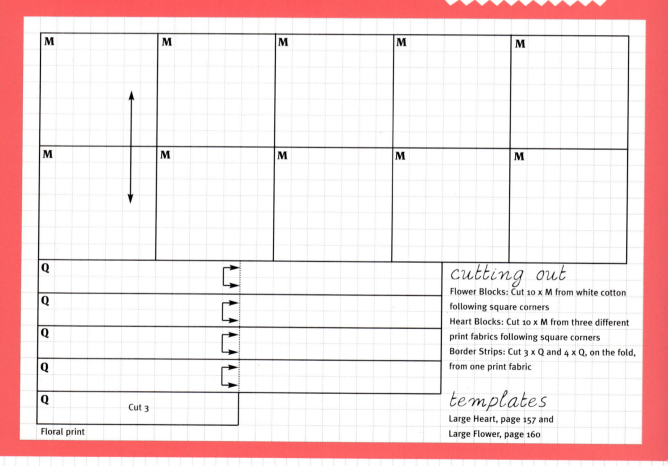

cutting out

Flower Blocks: Cut 10 x M from white cotton following square corners

Heart Blocks: Cut 10 x M from three different print fabrics following square corners

Border Strips: Cut 3 x Q and 4 x Q, on the fold, from one print fabric

templates

Large Heart, page 157 and Large Flower, page 160

THE FINISHED QUILT MEASURES 142 x 175CM — THE PERFECT SIZE TO GO OVER A STANDARD SINGLE BED. ADD ONE OR MORE ROWS OF SQUARES TO THE SIDE EDGE IF YOU NEED TO MAKE IT WIDE ENOUGH FOR A QUEEN, DOUBLE OR A EVEN KING-SIZED BED.

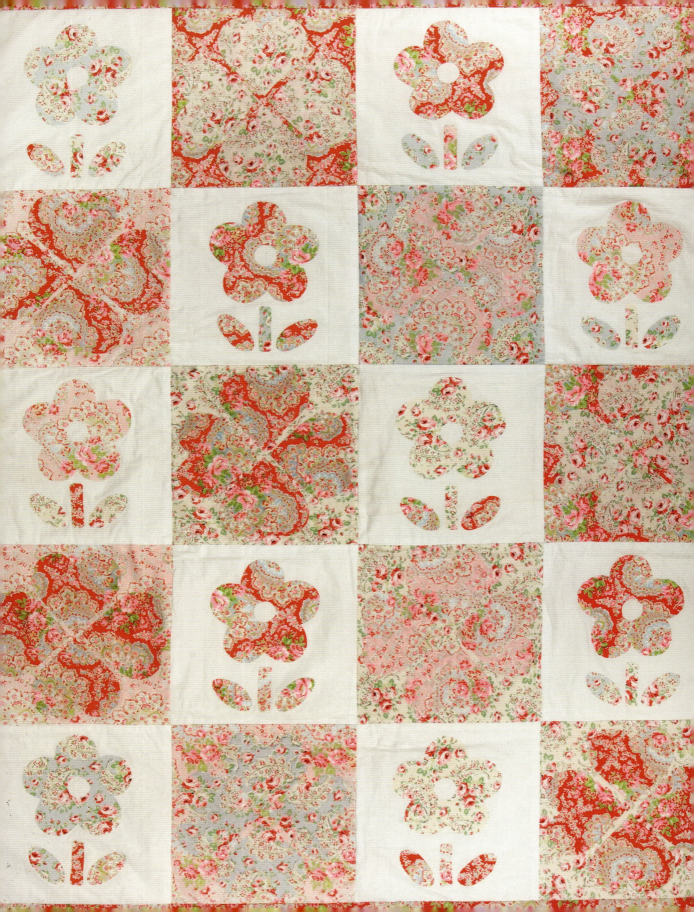

Heart Quilt

1 To make a flower block, cut a flower, two leaves and a stalk, each from a different print. Iron onto a white square. Select a new combination for each of the ten blocks. Edge the shapes with straight stitch, worked in matching thread.

2 Appliqué four matching hearts to each of the printed squares, positioning them centrally, with points facing inwards. Mix and match the prints so that all ten blocks look different.

3 Alternating hearts and flowers, arrange the completed blocks in five rows of four, in a chequerboard pattern.

4 Join the horizontal rows, leaving a 1cm seam allowance. Press all the seams open. Pin the top two rows together, matching the seams exactly, then stitch 1cm from the edge. Press seams open. Join the other three rows in the same way.

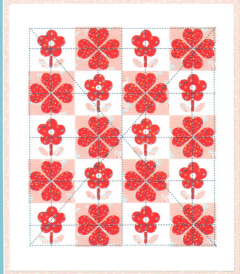

5 Spread out the backing, face downwards. Lay the wadding on top, then place the quilt top centrally over the two. Starting from the centre, pin or tack all three layers together. Firstly work out towards the four corners, then to the midpoint of each side.

6 Now work a row of tacking or pin a line along the centre of each row of blocks, so that you end up with a grid pattern across the surface, with a cross joining the corners. Finish by sewing or pinning all around the outside edge of the quilt top.

7 Using quilting thread and a short needle, stitch along each seam line: quilters call this 'stitching in the ditch'. If you prefer to sew by machine use a 'walking foot' to prevent puckering. Trim the backing and batting to 5cm all round.

8 Leaving a 1cm allowance, join all the border strips and press the seams open. Cut two 170cm lengths from this strip and press under a 1cm turning along one long edge of each.

9 With right sides facing and raw edges together, pin and stitch the 170cm side border strips to the side edges of the patchwork, leaving 2cm overlapping the border at each end. Press outwards. Add two 145cm top and bottom border strips in the same way.

10 Pin the overlapping border to the back of the quilt and slip stitch in place along the folded edges.

top tip

I CHOSE ALL THREE DIFFERENT VERSIONS OF MY VINTAGE-INSPIRED 'ROSE PAISLEY' PRINT TO MAKE THIS QUILT. THIS UNEXPECTED COMBINATION GIVES A UNIQUE AND SUBTLE APPEARANCE TO THE HEART BLOCKS, WHERE THE COLOURS BLEND HARMONIOUSLY.

Aeroplane Blanket

what you will need...

- 160cm square fleece fabric
- 2 skeins of red tapestry yarn
- large crewel needle
- 15 x 20cm each red, green, blue and yellow felt
- Bondaweb
- matching sewing thread
- sewing kit

templates

Aeroplane, page 158

SKILL LEVEL

Working with felt appeals to children and adults alike because it is so quick and easy to use. It comes in bright primary colours and has the advantage of not fraying, even when cut into intricate shapes. This cosy blanket is a great project to make together, as a way to learn about appliqué and stitching.

1 Turn up and tack down a 1cm double hem all around the outside edge of the fleece square.

2 Using a large crewel needle threaded with tapestry yarn, work a round of blanket stitch to keep the hem in place.

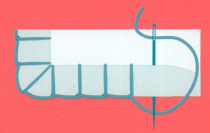

3 Following the detailed steps for iron-on appliqué on page 28, trace off the various parts of the aeroplanes onto Bondaweb, reversing one of the motifs. You can follow the colours I used or make up your own variation.

4 Lightly iron down the bodies of the aircraft first, using a pressing cloth to protect the surface of the felt and fleece. Add the windows, wings and tails.

5 Finish off by stitching around each individual shape with small straight stitches in thread to match each of the different colours of felt.

top tip

I APPLIQUED THIS TRIO OF JET LINERS ONTO A BACKGROUND OF SOFT FLEECE, BUT THEY WOULD ALSO CHEER UP AN OLD WOOLLEN BLANKET OR PLAIN BEDCOVER. IF YOU HAVE AN AVIATION ENTHUSIAST IN THE FAMILY, YOU COULD ADD A WHOLE FLEET TO A SET OF MATCHING CUSHIONS.

Beanie Cushion

what you will need...

- 1m x 130cm calico
- 7 litres of polystyrene beads
- 1m x 130cm printed cotton fabric
- 30cm zip
- 15 x 25cm spotted fabric
- matching sewing thread
- sewing kit
- sewing machine

SKILL LEVEL

Squashy bean bags are fun to have in bedrooms or playrooms. This one has a toddler-sized handle, so its young owner can drag it from place to place, then nestle down. The cover is bound to get grubby, so I inserted a zip for easy removal.

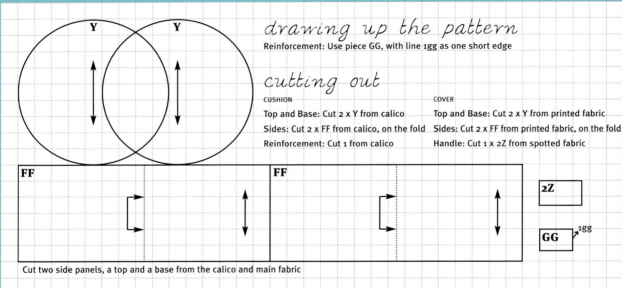

drawing up the pattern

Reinforcement: Use piece GG, with line 1gg as one short edge

cutting out

CUSHION

Top and Base: Cut 2 x Y from calico

Sides: Cut 2 x FF from calico, on the fold

Reinforcement: Cut 1 from calico

COVER

Top and Base: Cut 2 x Y from printed fabric

Sides: Cut 2 x FF from printed fabric, on the fold

Handle: Cut 1 x 2Z from spotted fabric

Cut two side panels, a top and a base from the calico and main fabric

The seam allowance throughout is 2cm

1 Join the short edges of the calico sides, leaving a 20cm gap in one seam. Press the seams open and press back the unstitched allowance. Add the top and base, as shown on page 23. Turn right side out, fill with beads and join the gap.

2 Make up the handle as on page 27, then join the ends and press the seam open. Pin to the centre of the cover top, on the right side. Pin the reinforcement to the wrong side, directly behind the handle. Machine stitch the handle in place.

3 Press under 3cm along one left and one right edge of the side panels. Sew the zip between these edges (see page 25) and slip stitch the folds together for 2.5cm at each end.

4 Open the zip and add top and base as before. Turn right sides out and press lightly. Insert the cushion and do up zip.

top tip

GETTING THE FILLED CUSHION INSIDE THE COVER MAY PROVE TO BE A BIT OF A STRUGGLE, BUT I PROMISE YOU THAT IT WILL GO IN EVENTUALLY! EASE THE BEADS THROUGH THE OPEN ZIP AND MAKE SURE THAT THE CUSHION IS THE RIGHT WAY UP.

Duffel Bag

SKILL LEVEL

Whether it's sports kit, swimming towels, school books or holiday clothes, busy families always seem to have endless amounts of 'stuff' to move around from place to place. Make everybody's life a little easier with this roomy drawstring duffel, which should appeal to even the coolest kids!

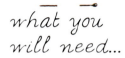

what you will need...

- 50 x 110cm print cotton duck
- 30cm square striped fabric
- 20cm square red felt
- scraps of green and blue felt
- bondaweb
- 1m thick cotton cord
- matching sewing thread
- sewing kit
- sewing machine

template
Elephant, page 155

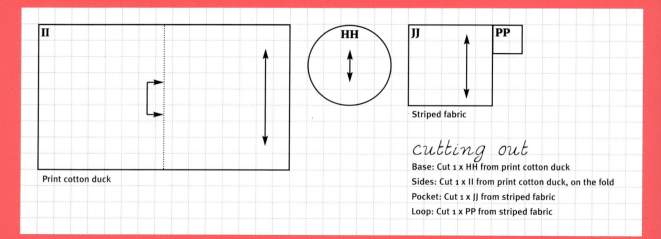

II — Print cotton duck

HH

JJ — Striped fabric

PP

cutting out

Base: Cut 1 x HH from print cotton duck

Sides: Cut 1 x II from print cotton duck, on the fold

Pocket: Cut 1 x JJ from striped fabric

Loop: Cut 1 x PP from striped fabric

The seam allowance throughout is 1.5cm.

1 As shown on page 28, appliqué the felt motif to the pocket and edge the main pieces with satin stitch. I added a green blanket to the basic design, to match those on the 'Circus Elephant' fabric.

2 Sew a 1cm double hem at the top of the pocket, then press under a 1cm turning along the other three edges.

3 Zigzag the sides of the side panel. Sew the completed pocket to the centre, 10cm up from the bottom edge. Reinforce the seams at the top corners with extra stitches.

4 Mark a point 10cm down from the top corner on each side edge. Press a 1cm then a 5cm turning along the top edge. Unfold the second turning and with right sides facing, pin the side edges together from the marked points to the bottom corner. Machine stitch this part of the seam, reinforcing both ends, and press open.

top tip →

IF YOU WOULD LIKE TO MAKE A SMALLER VERSION OF THIS BAG, FOR A YOUNGER CHILD PERHAPS, YOU COULD EASILY ADAPT THE BOLSTER CUSHION PATTERN. SHORTEN THE WIDTH OF THE RECTANGLE TO THE HEIGHT REQUIRED, REMEMBERING TO INCLUDE AN EXTRA 6CM FOR THE CASING.

Duffel Bag

5 Refold the second turning and pin it to the top edge of the bag to make the drawstring casing. Machine stitch close to the fold.

6 Fold the loop fabric in half, then press the side edges to the centre crease and top stitch. Fold in half lengthways and stitch both ends to the bottom of the seam, on the right side.

7 Clip the circular base and sides, following the instructions on page 23 and pin together with right sides facing.

8 Seam with two rounds of machine stitch. Trim the allowance back to approximately 8mm and zigzag to neaten. Turn the bag right side out.

9 Fasten one end of the cord to a safety pin and thread it through the drawstring casing. Take the pin through the loop, then stitch the ends of the cord securely together.

top tip → I DECORATED THE POCKET WITH A BRIGHTLY COLOURED ELEPHANT, TO GO WITH THE FABRIC I CHOSE FOR THE BAGS. IF YOU ARE GOING TO USE A DIFFERENT PRINT YOU COULD SELECT EITHER THE FLOWER, BIRD OR AEROPLANE MOTIFS AS AN ALTERNATIVE.

Shoulder Bag

what you will need...

- 60 x 70cm cotton duck
- matching sewing thread
- 3 2cm buttons
- matching stranded embroidery thread
- sewing kit
- sewing machine

SKILL LEVEL

This versatile little bag is just the right size to carry your essential items, either during the day or for an evening out, and the buttons mean that you can easily adjust the length of the strap. I gave it a slightly more vintage and worn-in look by washing and tumble-drying, to soften up the new fabric.

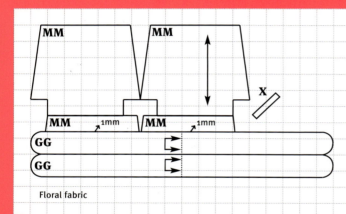

Floral fabric

drawing up the pattern

Facing: Use piece MM, with line 1mm as the bottom edge

cutting out

Front and Back: Cut 2 x MM
Facing: Cut 2
Strap: Cut 2 x GG, on the fold
Button loop: Cut 1 x X, on the bias

The seam allowance throughout is 1cm

1 Zigzag the side and bottom edges of the front and back. Pin, then seam the two pieces together along these edges, with right sides facing.

2 Press the seam allowances open. Join the corners in a 't-junction' as shown on page 22 and neaten the seam allowance. Turn right side out.

3 Make up the button loop, following the rouleau instructions on page 25. Trim it to 8cm and stitch the ends together to form a loop. With raw edges matching and the loop facing downwards, stitch the ends of the rouleau to the centre top of the back, on the right side.

top tip → IF YOU DON'T FANCY MAKING BUTTONHOLES, SIMPLY DECIDE YOUR STRAP LENGTH, THEN SEW THE TWO ENDS DIRECTLY ONTO THE SIDES OF THE BAG. YOU CAN THEN ADD THE BUTTONS AS A DECORATIVE FEATURE.

Shoulder Bag

4 Join the side edges of the facings, with right sides together. Press the seams open and press under a 1cm allowance along the bottom edge.

5 Slip the facing over the top of the bag with right sides together. Line up the side seams, then pin and machine stitch around the top edge. Turn the bag wrong side out.

6 Turn the facing over to the wrong side of the bag and press around the top edge. Tack the bottom edge of the facing to the bag and stitch it down, 3mm from the fold.

7 Top stitch around the opening.

8 Pin tack and stitch the two strap pieces together with right sides facing, leaving an 8cm gap along one edge. Press the seam allowance back on each side of the gap. Notch the seam allowance at the curved ends, as shown on page 23.

9 Turn the strap right side out and ease out the curves. Slip stitch the gap. Press, then top stitch 3mm from the edge. Work two buttonholes at each end, either by hand or machine.

10 Sew one button to the centre front and one to each side seam, positioning them centrally between the two lines of stitching, then button the strap in place.

top tip YOU COULD GIVE THE BAG A MORE STRUCTURED LOOK BY ADDING A LINING AND A SOLID BASE AS I DID FOR THE SHOPPER BAG VARIATION ON THE NEXT PAGES.

Shopper Bag

SKILL LEVEL

The shoulder bag on the previous pages, which also stars on the front cover of this book, turned out to be such a useful shape and size that I just had to come up with a variation! This rather more structured version has a solid base, a contrasting lining and a shorter, fixed handle made from cotton webbing.

what you will need...

- 45 x 75cm floral print cotton duck
- 35 x 75cm contrasting print for lining
- 10 x 20cm rectangle of thick card
- magnetic bag fastener or large press stud
- 40cm 4cm-wide webbing
- matching sewing thread
- sewing kit
- sewing machine

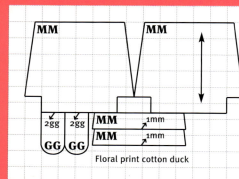

drawing up the pattern

Facing: Use piece MM with line 1mm as the bottom edge
Tab: Use piece GG with line 2gg as the straight edge

cutting out

Front and Back: Cut 2 x MM from floral print cotton duck
Facing: Cut 2 from floral print cotton duck
Tab: Cut 2 from floral print cotton duck
Lining: Cut 2 x MM from lining print

The seam allowance throughout is 1cm

1 Make up the bag and lining as for the first two steps of the shoulder bag, but don't turn the lining right side out. Place the cardboard at the bottom of the main bag, then slip the lining inside, matching up the side seams.

2 Attach the projecting part of the fastener to the curved end of one tab, on the right side, and 2.5cm up from the end. Tack the second tab on top with right sides facing.

3 Machine stitch around the long and curved edges of the tabs, leaving a 6mm seam allowance. Clip around the curve (see page 23) and turn right side out. Press lightly, avoiding the fastener, and top stitch the seam.

4 Pin the straight end of the tab to the centre top edge of bag, on the right side, with raw edges matching.

5 Pin the webbing centrally to the sides of the bag, so that 3cm at each end projects above the top edge.

6 Make up and sew on the facing as in steps 4 to 6 of the shoulder bag. Work a rectangle of reinforcing stitches across each side seam, as shown on page 26.

7 Fix the recessed part of the fastener to the centre front of the bag, 5cm down from the opening.

8 Finish off the handle by pinning the two edges of the webbing together for 20cm along the centre. Stitch 3mm from the edge.

top tip → YOU WILL NEED TO SEW THROUGH SEVERAL LAYERS OF THICKER FABRIC, PLUS THE COTTON WEBBING, FOR THIS PROJECT. TO MAKE SURE THAT THE STITCHES REMAIN EVEN YOU SHOULD FIT AN EXTRA STRONG NEEDLE TO YOUR SEWING MACHINE.

Large Tote

what you will need...

- 65 x 140cm floral print
- 55 x 85cm spotted fabric
- stranded embroidery thread
- button
- matching sewing thread
- sewing kit
- sewing machine

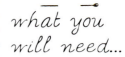

SKILL LEVEL

This practical tote features my absolute favourite fabric pairing of large-scale roses and spots. It has a useful outside pocket and is roomy enough to carry books and files, or even a laptop, but it would also make a stylish and eco-conscious alternative to plastic carriers when you're out shopping.

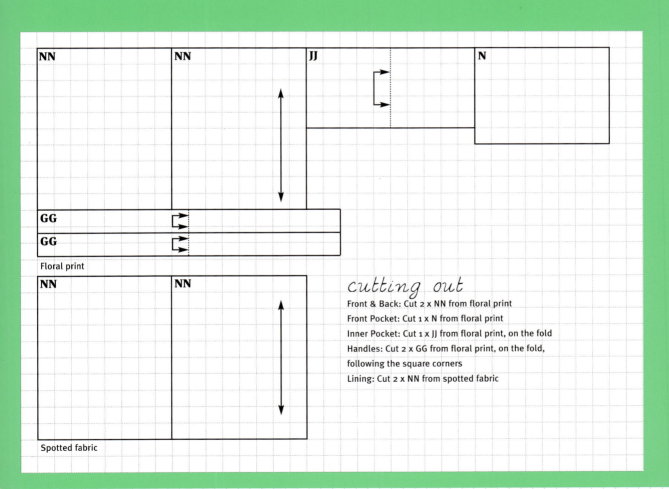

Floral print

Spotted fabric

cutting out

Front & Back: Cut 2 x NN from floral print

Front Pocket: Cut 1 x N from floral print

Inner Pocket: Cut 1 x JJ from floral print, on the fold

Handles: Cut 2 x GG from floral print, on the fold, following the square corners

Lining: Cut 2 x NN from spotted fabric

top tip → I MADE THE TOTE AND THE LINING FROM COTTON DUCK, WHICH MAKES IT VERY DURABLE, BUT YOU COULD LEAVE OUT THE LINING AND THE INNER POCKET TO MAKE A LIGHTER WEIGHT SHOPPING BAG THAT CAN BE FOLDED UP AND CARRIED IN YOUR HANDBAG.

Large Tote

The seam allowance throughout is 1cm

1 Press under 1cm, then a further 3cm along the top of the front pocket, then top stitch both folds. Make a buttonhole in the centre of the hem.

2 Pin and stitch the pocket to the front bag piece, with raw edges matching. Pin the back of the bag to the front, with right sides together. Machine stitch side and bottom edges. Press under a 1cm, then a 4cm turning around the opening.

3 With right sides facing, sew the side and bottom edges of the two lining pieces together. Press the seam allowances inwards. Trim 5cm off the top edge.

4 Stitch a narrow double hem along one short edge of the inner pocket. With right sides facing, fold in half widthways so that the hem lies 5cm from the other short edge. Pin and seam. Trim the corners, turn right side out and press.

5 Mark a vertical line 7cm in from the right edge and machine along it to divide the pocket. Turn under the unstitched seam allowance at the top corners and slip stitch it down.

6 Pin the top edge of the pocket to the top of the lining, centring it on the back edge. Slip the lining inside the bag and fold the turning over to conceal the raw edges.

7 Make up the handles, neatening the short ends, as shown on page 27. Pin and tack the ends of one handle to the inside back of the bag, so that the edges line up with the pocket. Tack the other handle in the corresponding position on the front.

8 Work a round of stitching 6mm down from the top edge, then a second round, 3cm from the top edge. Work reinforcing stitching over the ends of the handles, as shown on page 26.

9 Finish off by sewing the button to the front of the bag, directly behind the buttonhole.

top tip → YOU CAN ADJUST THE STITCH LINE ON THE INNER POCKET SO THAT YOU HAVE A PERFECT FIT FOR YOUR PHONE AND PURSE, OR MAYBE ADD A NARROW CHANNEL FOR A PEN OR PENCIL.

Inside-out Tote

what you will need...

- 75 x 140cm cotton duck
- 15 x 65cm spotted fabric
- 60cm 2.5cm wide webbing
- 2m bias binding (optional)
- matching sewing thread
- sewing kit
- sewing machine

SKILL LEVEL

This ingenious folding bag is designed with two sets of handles, one in the usual place at the top, and a second pair positioned half-way down the sides. Fold the upper half of the bag to the inside if you just need the standard shopper shown opposite, or open it out completely for bulk purchases – see overleaf!

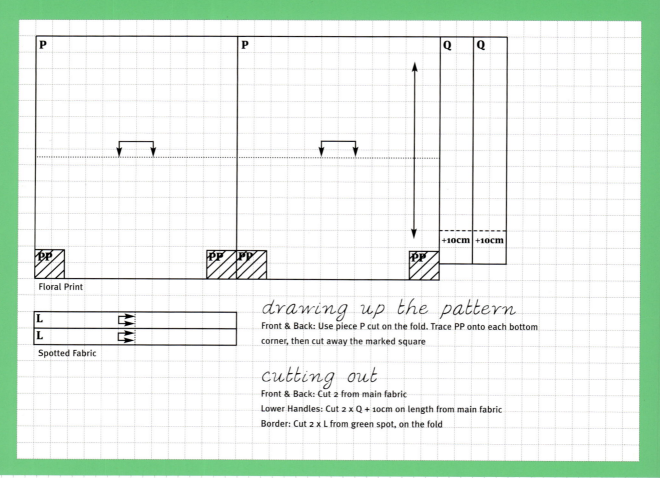

Floral Print

Spotted Fabric

drawing up the pattern

Front & Back: Use piece P cut on the fold. Trace PP onto each bottom corner, then cut away the marked square

cutting out

Front & Back: Cut 2 from main fabric

Lower Handles: Cut 2 x Q + 10cm on length from main fabric

Border: Cut 2 x L from green spot, on the fold

top tip → I BOUND THE INSIDE SEAMS WITH BIAS TAPE TO GIVE THEM EXTRA STRENGTH, BUT YOU COULD ALSO FINISH THEM WITH A ZIGZAG OR OVERLOCKED STITCH SO THAT THEY WILL NOT FRAY.

Inside-out Tote

The seam allowance throughout is 1cm

1 Fold and press a turning 30cm down from the top edge of the front and back pieces to mark the positions for the lower handles.

2 Make up the two lower handles as shown on page 27, then trim each one to 65cm.

3 Position one handle across the front of the bag so that the top edge lies along the crease. Pin the two ends to the side edges of the bag then pin down a 22cm length at the left and right, leaving a 21cm unattached length in the centre.

4 Mark a 3cm rectangle at each end of the unstitched part. Top stitch the top and bottom edges of the pinned parts of the handle and work reinforcing stitching (see page 26) within the rectangles. Do the same on the back of the bag.

5 With right sides facing, pin and stitch the front and back together along the side and bottom edges, leaving the cut out corners free. Bind or overlock the seam allowances.

6 Join the corners with a t-junction seam, as explained on page 22. Fold one seam allowance to the left and one to the right at the point where the two lines of stitching meet, so that you do not have a bulky join.

7 Pin and stitch the ends of the two border strips together, with right sides facing. Press the seams open and press a 1cm turning around one edge.

8 Matching the seams, pin the border around the top edge of the bag, so that the right side faces the wrong side of the bag and the raw edges are aligned.

9 Cut the webbing in half to make two 30cm handles. Measure a point 22cm in from each top corner. Slip the ends of the handles under the border at these points: the ends should project above the top edge for 2cm. Tack the handles securely in place.

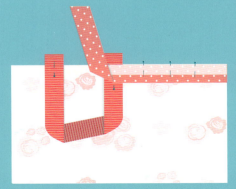

10 Turn the bag right side out and fold the border over. Tack down the folded edge, then top stitch both this and the top edge. Work rectangular reinforcing stitches over each end of the handle.

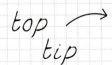

top tip → WHEN THE BAG WAS COMPLETE, I ONCE AGAIN DID MY SPECIAL TRICK OF WASHING IT ON A HOT CYCLE AND THEN TUMBLING UNTIL DRY, TO CREATE A SOFTER, MORE RELAXED APPEARANCE.

Quilted Purse

what you will need...

- 55 x 35cm floral print
- 55 x 35cm cotton batting
- 55 x 35cm plain fabric
- 35cm ricrac
- large button
- matching stranded embroidery thread
- pencil and clear ruler
- matching sewing thread
- contrasting sewing thread for quilting
- sewing kit
- sewing machine

SKILL LEVEL

The appeal of this project lies in the combination of carefully thought out details: the scalloped edge of the yellow ricrac insertion; the lines of pink quilting stitches; the hand-stitched buttonhole loop and the subtle gleam of a pearl button.

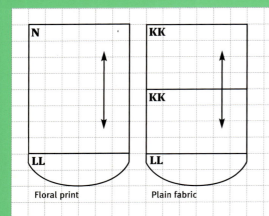

Floral print   Plain fabric

cutting out

Front & Back: Cut 1 x N from floral print

Flap: Cut 1 x LL from floral print

Bag lining: Cut 2 x KK from plain fabric, following square corners

Flap lining: Cut 1 x LL from plain fabric

The seam allowance throughout is 6mm

1 Mark the quilting lines on the main bag and the flap by ruling a diagonal grid of 2.5cm squares on the right side of each piece.

2 Trim 6mm from each side of the flap pattern, then cut a piece of batting to this size. Tack the batting centrally to the wrong side of the flap and quilt the marked lines.

3 Tack a length of ricrac around the flap, so that the edge of the braid lies along the curved edge. Pin the flap lining to the right side of the flap.

top tip →

IF YOUR FABRIC HAS AN OBVIOUSLY DIRECTIONAL DESIGN, CUT THE FRONT AND BACK PIECE WITH THE DESIGN RUNNING LENGTHWAYS. MAKE SURE THAT YOU SEW THE FLAP ONTO THE CORRECT END, OR THE PATTERN WILL APPEAR UPSIDE DOWN ON THE FRONT OF THE BA

Quilted Purse

4 Machine stitch along the curved edge. Clip the seam allowance (see page 23) and turn right side out. Ease out the curves and press lightly.

5 Quilt the front and back piece of the bag as for the flap. With right sides facing, pin and stitch the straight edge of the flap to the top back edge of the bag.

6 Fold the bag in half lengthways with right sides facing and tuck the flap inside. Pin and stitch the side seams.

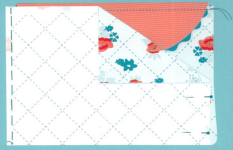

7 Stitch the two bag lining pieces together along the side edges. Press the seam allowances inwards, then press in a 1cm turning along the bottom edges. Turn right side out.

8 Slip the lining inside the bag so the right sides are facing and the seams aligned. Pin the top edges together so that the flap is sandwiched between the two. Machine stitch all around the opening.

9 Turn the bag right sides out through the opening and ease it into shape. Close the gap in the lining with small, neat slip stitches.

10 Work a buttonhole loop at the edge of the flap and sew the button to the front of the bag, in line with the loop.

top tip

I CHOSE A CLASSIC GRID PATTERN FOR THE HAND-QUILTING, THE SAME AS I USED ON THE HOTTIE. YOU COULD VARY THE STITCH PATTERN, DEPENDING ON YOUR FABRIC: IF YOU'RE WORKING WITH STRIPED FABRIC, FOR EXAMPLE, TRY QUILTING ALONG THE PARALLEL LINES.

T-Junction Washbag

SKILL LEVEL

I have always enjoyed finding new and unexpected uses for old fabrics, and this zip-up washbag started its life as a fifties sundress with a flouncy skirt! The wide turquoise and white stripes of the soft cotton are just perfect for the structured shape, which is finished off at the corners with t-junction seams.

what you will need...

- 30 x 80cm cotton fabric
- 30 x 65cm shower curtain fabric
- 40cm nylon zip
- 70cm bias binding
- 10 x 20cm medium weight iron-on interfacing
- matching sewing thread
- sewing kit
- sewing machine

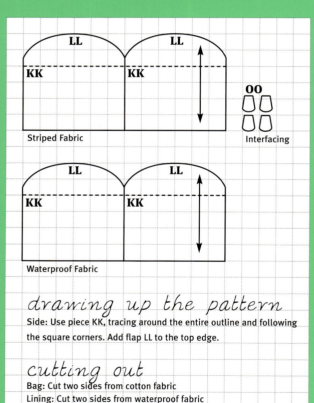

Striped Fabric

Interfacing

Waterproof Fabric

drawing up the pattern

Side: Use piece KK, tracing around the entire outline and following the square corners. Add flap LL to the top edge.

cutting out

Bag: Cut two sides from cotton fabric
Lining: Cut two sides from waterproof fabric
Tabs: Cut 4 x OO from interfacing

1 Tack the lining pieces to the wrong side of the bag pieces, around all four edges.

2 Open out the zip and pin one straight edge along one curved edge of the bag, with right sides together. The zip is longer than the bag, so leave an equal overlap at each end.

3 Fit a zip foot to the machine and stitch down, 5mm from the teeth. Do the same at the other side. Press the seams outwards and top stitch, close to the stitch lines.

4 With right sides facing, pin and stitch the side and bottom edges together through all four layers. Leave 1cm unstitched at each top corner.

5 Join the bottom corners with a 't-junction seam' as shown on page 22. Turn right side out and slip the ends of the zip through the gaps at the top of the side seams. Slip stitch to close. Trim and bind the inside seams.

6 Iron the tabs onto the remaining fabric and cut out, leaving a 6mm margin all round. Tack this to the back, then slip stitch the tabs together in pairs, around the side and bottom edges. Trim the ends of the zip to 2cm and ease them through the top of the tabs. Stitch in place.

top tip → IF, LIKE ME, YOU CHOOSE STRIPES, YOU WILL NEED TO ALLOW A LITTLE EXTRA FABRIC SO THAT EVERYTHING MATCHES. MAKE SURE THE DESIGN LINES UP ON FRONT AND BACK, AND CUT FOUR IDENTICAL TABS WITH THE STRIPES RUNNING HORIZONTALLY.

Drawstring Washbag

what you will need...

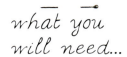

- 60 x 80cm patterned cotton fabric
- 35 x 45cm waterproof fabric
- 70cm fine piping cord
- 70cm contrast bias binding
- 70cm white bias binding
- matching sewing thread
- ruler
- sewing kit
- sewing machine

SKILL LEVEL

Here's another quirky recycled dress fabric – this time a painterly Sixties pattern of brightly coloured squares. I found a length of bias tape that proved to be the perfect match for the vivid green and used this to bind the main seam. The drawstring cords are made from two long rouleaux, cut from the main fabric.

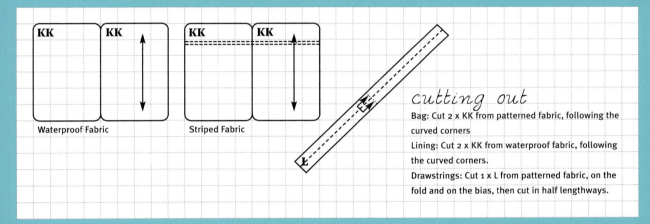

Waterproof Fabric   Striped Fabric

cutting out

Bag: Cut 2 x KK from patterned fabric, following the curved corners

Lining: Cut 2 x KK from waterproof fabric, following the curved corners.

Drawstrings: Cut 1 x L from patterned fabric, on the fold and on the bias, then cut in half lengthways.

1 Mark two points on each side, 6 and 7cm down from the top edge of one bag piece. Using a fading pen, rule between both sets of points, so that you have two parallel lines across the right side.

2 Pin the top part of the bag piece to a lining piece, with right sides facing. Leaving a 1cm allowance, machine stitch around the top edge between the upper two points, reinforcing both ends of the stitching.

3 Make a 1cm snip into both layers of fabric, at the ends of the lower line. Clip the corners, press the seam allowances inwards and turn right side out.

 top tip →

THIS PROJECT INTRODUCES YOU TO PIPED SEAMS AND ROULEAUX TIES – TWO SLIGHTLY MORE ADVANCED TECHNIQUES THAT ARE MUCH USED IN DRESSMAKING AND SOFT FURNISHINGS. DON'T BE PUT OFF HOWEVER, AS THE BAG IS NOT NEARLY AS TRICKY AS IT MAY LOOK AT FIRST!

Drawstring Washbag

4 Machine stitch along both lines to make the drawstring channel, then make up the second side in the same way.

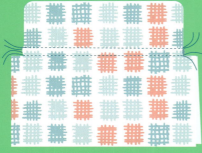

5 Cover the piping cord with the contrast bias binding, as shown on page 23. With raw edges matching and an overlap of about 3cm at each end, pin the piping to the right side of one bag piece. Fold the loose cord outwards at an angle.

6 Tack the second side to the first, with right sides facing.

7 Fit the zip foot to your machine and sew the two sides together, close to the edge of the cord. Stitch over the angled ends of the piping. Trim the piping and clip corners.

8 Neaten the seam allowance by covering it with the white bias binding, then turn right side out and press lightly.

9 Make up the two drawstrings as shown on page 25. Fasten a small safety pin to the first one and pass it through the gap between the two lines of stitching and along the drawstring channels on the front and back of the bag. Thread the second rouleau from the other side. Knot the ends of both cords and trim.

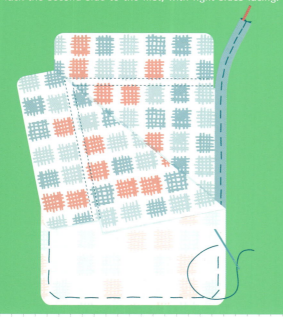

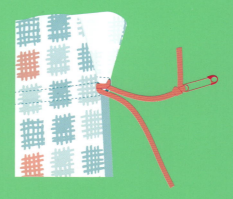

top tip

THE DRAWSTRINGS ARE MADE FROM VERY NARROW TUBES OF FABRIC: IF YOUR CHOSEN MATERIAL IS TOO THICK YOU WILL NOT BE ABLE TO DRAW IT THROUGH TO MAKE THE ROULEAUX, SO LOOK OUT FOR A FINE MATCHING COTTON INSTEAD. YOU COULD ALSO USE THIS FOR THE PIPING.

Jewellery Roll

what you will need...

- 25 x 80cm cotton duck
- 20cm nylon zip
- 1.5m bias binding
- 1 medium press stud
- 50cm fine piping cord
- matching sewing thread
- sewing kit
- sewing machine

SKILL LEVEL

Keep all your bracelets, necklaces and brooches safe when you're out and about, by tucking them into the various compartments of this practical jewellery holder, then slide your rings onto the fabric tube. This project would make a great gift for all ages. It is perfect to take travelling or keep your precious jewels tucked away in a drawer.

```
KK          KK          PP  PP
  1kk                   PP
Cotton duck
```

drawing up the pattern

Inside: Use piece KK, following the curved corners at the left edge. Cut along line 1kk so you have two pieces.

Outside: Use piece KK, following the square corners at the right edge. Trim 4cm from the left edge.

cutting out

Inside: Cut both parts from main fabric

Outside: Cut 1 from main fabric

Pockets: Cut 2 x PP from main fabric

Ring Holder: Cut 1 x PP from main fabric, on the fold

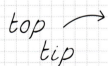

top tip → IF YOU WANT TO MAKE A MORE PADDED JEWELLERY ROLL YOU COULD SANDWICH A LAYER OF COTTON OR POLYESTER WADDING BETWEEN THE INSIDE AND OUTSIDE PIECES.

Jewellery Roll

1 Press under a 2cm turning along the right edge of the narrow inside piece and the left edge of the wide piece. Sew the zip between these folded edges (see page 25) and trim the projecting ends.

2 Stitch a narrow hem along one edge of each pocket and press a 6mm turning under the other three edges. With the hems on the left, pin them both to the right hand side of the inside piece, 2cm from the edges. Machine stitch down, close to the folds. Close the zip.

3 Press a 1cm turning along one long edge of the ring holder. Starting at the opposite edge, roll it up tightly with the right side outwards. Pin, then stitch down the fold. Neaten one end, with the seam at the back. Sew the projecting part of the press stud across the seam, 1cm up from the bottom edge.

4 Flatten out the open end of the ring holder. Pin, then stitch it securely to the top edge of the inside piece, 7cm to the right of the zip. Sew the second part of the press stud to the lower edge of the inside, in line with the first part.

5 Pin the outside piece to the completed inside with wrong sides facing and trim to the same width. Machine stitch 6mm from the outer edge. Trim the seam allowance back to 3mm.

6 Using a fading pen, rule a line across the inside, 1cm to the right of the ring holder. Machine stitch along this line.

7 Starting at the centre left, neaten the outside edge with bias binding, stitching it down by hand or machine. Ease the folded edges round the curved corners, stretching it gently. Turn the binding under at a 45 degree angle at the square corners.

8 For the tie, cover the piping cord with the rest of the bias binding. Press under 1cm at one end, then wrap the binding over the cord. Slip stitch the folded edges together, neatening the other end in the same way. Fold the tie in half to find the centre and stitch this point securely to the centre left edge.

top tip

Specs Case

what you will need...

- 35 x 25cm printed fabric
- 35 x 50cm velvet
- 25 x 35cm cotton batting
- 75cm fine piping cord
- small button
- matching sewing thread
- matching stranded embroidery cotton
- sewing kit
- sewing machine

SKILL LEVEL

A round of vibrant pink piping gives a new twist to this classic spectacle case, and shows how you can transform an everyday item into something really individual by changing just one small design element. The case has a soft velvet lining and an inner padded layer to protect your specs or sunglasses.

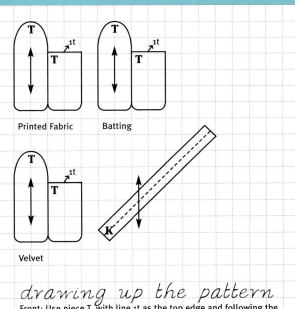

Printed Fabric   Batting

Velvet

drawing up the pattern
Front: Use piece T, with line 1t as the top edge and following the curved corners

cutting out
Back: Cut 1 x T from printed fabric, following the curved corners

Front: Cut 1 from printed fabric

Back Lining: Cut 1 x T from velvet

Front Lining: Cut 1 front from velvet

Piping: Cut 1 x K from velvet, on the bias, then cut in half lengthways

Batting: Cut one front and one back

1 Join the two bias strips, as shown on page 21 and use it to cover the piping cord (see page 23). Matching the raw edges, tack the piping around the outside edge of the back piece, starting at the centre bottom edge. Cross the two ends over where they meet, and trim the overlap.

top tip

THE VELVET PIPING HAS A GRAPHIC QUALITY, WHICH EMPHASISES THE OUTLINE OF THE CASE. THE BRIGHT PINK VELVET REALLY MAKES IT STAND OUT AGAINST THE GENTLE DOVE GREY BACKGROUND, SO PICK A STRONG COLOUR FROM YOUR MAIN FABRIC TO ACHIEVE THE SAME EFFECT.

Specs Case

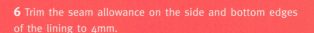

2 Press a 1cm turning along the top edge of the front piece. With right sides facing, pin and tack the front to the back around the side and bottom edges. Fit a zip foot and stitch together. Trim the seam allowance to 6mm, clip the corners and turn right side out.

3 Trim away a margin of 1cm all around the outside edges of the front and back pattern pieces and use these as a guide to cut the batting. Tack the back batting centrally to the wrong side of the back lining, so there is a 1cm allowance all round.

4 Press a 1cm turning along the top edge of the front lining. Pin the batting to the wrong side, leaving a 1cm allowance all round. Fold the turning over the batting and tack.

5 With right sides together, pin, tack and machine stitch the front and back lining pieces together, leaving a 1cm seam allowance.

6 Trim the seam allowance on the side and bottom edges of the lining to 4mm.

7 Fold the surplus lining around the flap to the back of the batting, pleating it a little as you go around the curve, and tack it down.

8 Slip the finished lining inside the case, so the wrong sides are together. Ease the corners of the lining into place.

9 Slip stitch the top straight edge of the front to the top of the lining. Tack the flap lining back on to the flap and slip stitch it down around the curved edge, next to the piping.

10 Work a buttonhole stitch loop at the centre edge of the flap as shown on page 25. Sew a button to the front of the completed case, in line with the loop.

top tip

THE HANDMADE BUTTONHOLE LOOP, IN THE SAME GREY AS THE MAIN FABRIC, IS A WONDERFUL FINISHING TOUCH. IT IS NOT DIFFICULT TO DO, BUT IF YOU HAVEN'T USED THIS STITCH BEFORE, IT'S WORTH TAKING TIME TO PRACTISE THE TECHNIQUE ON A PIECE OF SPARE FABRIC.

iPod® Case

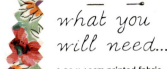

what you will need...

- 20 x 40cm printed fabric
- 25cm square brushed cotton
- 25cm square cotton batting
- 30cm 4cm-bias tape
- 30cm fine cord
- spring cord toggle
- matching sewing thread
- sewing kit

SKILL LEVEL

Traditional sewing techniques and the newest technology come together in this sweet little padded bag – the perfect safe home for your mobile phone or MP3 player. The drawstring fastening is made from nylon cord and secured with a spring toggle, which you can find at any good haberdashers.

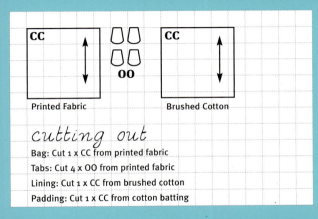

CC

OO

CC

Printed Fabric

Brushed Cotton

cutting out

Bag: Cut 1 x CC from printed fabric
Tabs: Cut 4 x OO from printed fabric
Lining: Cut 1 x CC from brushed cotton
Padding: Cut 1 x CC from cotton batting

1 Fold the bag in half with right sides facing. Pin, then seam the side and bottom edges together, leaving a 1cm allowance.

2 Press open the top 6cm of the side seam. Press a 2.5cm turning around the top edge, then turn the bag right side out.

3 Press a 2.5cm turning at each end of the bias tape, then press it in half lengthways with the turnings on the inside.

4 Tack the tape around the bag opening, with raw edges on the inside and 6mm of the folded edge projecting above the top edge. Line folded ends of the tape up with the side seam.

5 Pin the lining to the padding and make up as in step 1. Press the seam allowances inwards, then press a 2.5cm turning around the top edge. Slip the lining inside the bag, positioning it so that the side seam is opposite the opening.

6 Tack the top edge of the lining to the top edge of the bag, stitching through the tape. Slip stitch the edges together.

7 Fasten a safety pin to one end of the cord and thread it through the tape channel. Slip two ends through the toggle.

8 Press under a 1cm turning along each tab piece, straightening off the curve at the bottom edges. Pin together in pairs and slip stitch the side and bottom edges. Push the ends of the cord through the openings and close with slip stitch.

top tip →

I WAS LUCKY ENOUGH TO COME ACROSS A BINDING TAPE IN EXACTLY THE SAME SHADE OF ORANGE AS THE DETAILS ON THE DAISY PETALS, BUT IF YOU CAN'T FIND THE COLOUR YOU'RE LOOKING FOR, YOU CAN SIMPLY CUT A 4CM-WIDE BIAS STRIP FROM PLAIN FABRIC.

Addresses

Fabric and haberdashery shops

Bedecked
5 Castle Street, Hay-on-Wye,
Hereford HR3 5DF
01497 822 769
www.bedecked.co.uk

Cloth House
47 Berwick Street,
London W1F 8SJ
020 7437 5155 and
98 Berwick Street,
London W1F 0QJ
020 7287 1555
www.clothhouse.net

Creative Quilting
32 Bridge Road, East Molesey,
Surrey KT8 9HA
020 8941 7075
www.creativequilting.co.uk

Harts of Hertford
113 Fore Street, Hertford,
Hertfordshire SG14 1AS
01992 558 106
www.hartsofhertford.com

John Lewis
300 Oxford Street, London W1A 1EX
and branches nationwide
08456 049 049
www.johnlewis.com

MacCulloch & Wallis
25–26 Dering Street,
London W1S 1AT
020 7629 0311
www.macculloch-wallis.co.uk

The Makery Emporium
16 Northumberland Place,
Bath BA1 5AR
01225 487 708
www.themakeryonline.co.uk

Mandors
134 Renfrew Street,
Glasgow G3 6ST
0141 332 7716
www.mandors.co.uk

Merrick & Day
Redbourne Road,
Redbourne,
Gainsborough,
Lincolnshire DN21 4TG
01652 648 814
www.merrick-day.com

Millie Moon
24–25 Catherine Hill,
Frome,
Somerset BA11 1BY
01373 464 650
www.milliemoonshop.co.uk

Our Patterned Hand
49 Broadway Market,
London E8 4PH
020 7812 9912
www.ourpatternedhand.co.uk

Peabees Patchwork Bazaar
1 Hare Street,
Sheerness,
Kent ME12 1AH
01795 669963

Rags
19 Chapel Walk,
Crowngate Shopping Centre,
Worcester WR1 3LD
01905 612330

Sew and So's
14 Upper Olland Street,
Bungay,
Suffolk NR35 1BG
01986 896147
www.sewsos.co.uk

Tikki
293 Sandycombe Road,
Kew, Surrey TW9 3LU
020 8948 8462
www.tikkilondon.com

Sewing Classes

Alison Victoria School of Sewing
71 Market Street, Ashby de la Zouch,
Leicestershire LE65 1AH
www.schoolofsewing.co.uk

Heatherlea Design
01332 661 562
www.heatherleadesign.com

Just Between Friends
44 Station Way, Buckhurst Hill,
Essex IG9 6LN
020 8502 9191
www.justbetweenfriends.co.uk

Liberty Sewing School
Regent Street,
London W1B 5AH
www.liberty.co.uk

The Makery Workshop
146 Walcot Street, Bath BA1 5BL
01225 421 175
www.themakeryonline.co.uk

Modern Approach Sewing School
Unit A, Astra Business Centre,
Roman Way, Ribbleton,
Preston PR2 5AP
07910 740 120
www.sewjanetmoville.co.uk

Sew Over It
78 Landor Road, Clapham North,
London SW9 9PH
020 7326 0376
www.sewoverit.co.uk

Sue Hazell Sewing Tuition
Southcombe House,
Chipping Norton,
Oxfordshire OX7 5QH
01608 644 877
www.sewing-tuition.co.uk

Studio London
Studio 1 & 5,
Trinity Buoy Wharf,
64 Orchard Place,
London E14 0JW
020 7987 2421

Thrifty Stitcher
Unit 21, 4–6 Shelford Place,
Stoke Newington, London N16 9HS
07779 255 087
www.thethriftystitcher.co.uk

Fairs

Great Northern Contemporary Craft Fair
Spinningfields, Manchester
www.greatnorthernevents.co.uk

Knitting and Stitching Show
Alexandra Palace, London and
RDS, Dublin and
Harrogate International Centre
01473 320407
www.twistedthread.com

Sewing for Pleasure
NEC, Birmingham
www.ichf.co.uk/sewingforpleasure

A few handy websites:

DMC
www.dmccreative.co.uk
Sewing and embroidery threads.

Etsy
www.etsy.com
An online marketplace for everything
handmade and vintage, including
fabric and other sewing supplies.

Cath Kidston Stores

Aberdeen
Unit GS20, Union Square Shopping Centre,
Guild Square, Aberdeen AB11 5PN
01224 591 726

Bath
3 Broad Street, Milsom Place, Bath BA1 5LJ
01225 331 006

Belfast
24–26 Arthur Street, Belfast BT1 4GF
02890 231 581

Bicester Village Outlet Store
Unit 43a, Bicester Village,
Bicester OX26 6WD
01869 247 358

Birmingham – Selfridges
Upper Mall, East Bullring,
Birmingham B5 4BP
0121 600 6967

Bluewater
Unit L003, Rose Gallery,
Bluewater Shopping Centre DA9 9SH
01322 387 454

Bournemouth
5–6 The Arcade, Old Christchurch Road,
Bournemouth BH1 2AF
01202 553 848

Brighton
31a & 32 East Street, Brighton BN1 1HL
01273 227 420

Bristol
79 Park Street, Clifton, Bristol BS1 5PF
0117 930 4722

Cambridge
31–33 Market Hill, Cambridge CB2 3NU
01223 351 810

Canterbury
6 The Parade, Canterbury CT1 2JL
01227 455 639

Cardiff
45 The Hayes, St David's, Cardiff CF10 1GA
02920 225 627

Cheltenham
21 The Promenade, Cheltenham GL50 1LE
01242 245 912

Chichester
24 South Street, Chichester PO19 1EL
01243 850 100

Dublin
Unit CSD 1.3, Dundrum Shopping Centre,
Dublin 16
00 353 1 296 4430

Edinburgh
58 George Street, Edinburgh EH2 2LR
0131 220 1509

Exeter
6 Princesshay, Exeter EX1 1GE
01392 227 835

Glasgow
18 Gordon Street, Glasgow G1 3PB
0141 248 2773

Guildford
14–18 Chertsey Street, Guildford GU1 4HD
01483 564 798

Gunwharf Quays Outlet Store
Gunwharf Quays, Portsmouth PO1 3TU
02392 832 982

Harrogate
2–6 James Street, Harrogate HG1 1RF
01423 531 481

Heathrow Terminal 4
Departure Lounge,
Heathrow Airport TW6 3XA
020 8759 5578

Jersey
11 King Street, St Helier, Jersey JE2 4WF
01534 726 768

Kildare Village Outlet Store
Unit 21c, Kildare Village, Nurney Road
Kildare Town
00 353 45 535 084

Kingston
10 Thames Street,
Kingston upon Thames KT1 1PE
020 8546 6760

Leeds
26 Lands Lane, Leeds LS1 6LB
0113 391 2692

Liverpool
Compton House, 18 School Lane,
Liverpool L1 3BT
0151 709 2747

London – Battersea
142 Northcote Road, London SW11 6RD
020 7228 6571

London – Chiswick
125 Chiswick High Road, London W4 2ED
020 8995 8052

London – Covent Garden
28–32 Shelton Street, London WC2H 9JE
020 7836 4803

London – Fulham
668 Fulham Road, London SW6 5RX
020 7731 6531

London – Kings Road
322 Kings Road, London SW3 5UH
020 7351 7335

London – Marylebone
51 Marylebone High Street, London W1U 5HW
020 7935 6555

London – Notting Hill
158 Portobello Road, London W11 2BE
020 7727 0043

London – Selfridges
Oxford Street, London W1A 1AB
020 7318 3312

London – Sloane Square
27 Kings Road, London SW3 4RP
020 7259 9847

London – St Pancras
St Pancras International Station,
London NW1 2QP
020 7837 4125

London – Wimbledon Village
3 High Street, Wimbledon SW19 5DX
020 8944 1001

Manchester
62 King Street, Manchester M2 4ND
0161 834 7936

Manchester – Selfridges
1 Exchange Street, Manchester M3 1BD
0161 629 1184

Marlborough
142–142a High Street,
Marlborough SN8 1HN
01672 512 514

Marlow
6 Market Square, Marlow SL7 1DA
01628 484 443

Newcastle – Fenwicks
Northumberland Street,
Newcastle Upon Tyne NE99 1AR
0191 232 5100

Oxford
6 Broad Street, Oxford OX1 3AJ
01865 791 576

Reading
96 Broad Street, Reading RG1 2AP
01189 588 530

St Albans
Unit 4, Christopher Place,
St Albans AL3 5DQ
01727 810 432

St Ives
67 Fore Street, St Ives TR26 1HE
01736 798 001

Tunbridge Wells
59–61 High Street, Tunbridge Wells TN1 1XU
01892 521 197

Winchester
46 High Street, Winchester SO23 9BT
01962 870 620

Windsor
24 High Street, Windsor SL4 1LH
01753 830 591

York
32 Stonegate, York YO1 8AS
01904 733 653

For up-to-date information on all Cath Kidston
stores, please visit www.cathkidston.co.uk

Acknowledgments

Many thanks to Lucinda Ganderton and Jessica Pemberton – for making all of the projects – Pia Tryde, Elaine Ashton, Laura Mackay and Bridget Bodoano. Thanks also to Helen Lewis, Lisa Pendreigh and Katherine Case at Quadrille Publishing.

Cath Kidston

Series Creative Coordinator: Elaine Ashton
Design Assistant to Cath Kidston:
Laura Mackay
Project Maker and Sewing Consultant:
Lucinda Ganderton
Sewing Assistants: Jessica Pemberton
and Lis Gunner

Editorial Director: Anne Furniss
Art Director: Helen Lewis
Project Editor: Lisa Pendreigh
Designer: Katherine Case
Photographer: Pia Tryde
Illustrator: Bridget Bodoano
Production Director: Vincent Smith
Production Controller: Aysun Hughes

If you have any comments or queries regarding the instructions in this book, please contact us at enquiries@quadrille.co.uk.

This edition first published in 2012 by
Quadrille Publishing Limited
Alhambra House
27–31 Charing Cross Road
London WC2H 0LS
www.quadrille.co.uk

Projects, templates and text copyright © Cath Kidston 2009
Photography © Pia Tryde 2009
Design and layout copyright © Quadrille Publishing Limited 2009

Cataloguing-in-Publication Data: a catalogue record for this book is available from the British Library.

ISBN 978 184949 205 8

Printed in China

Templates

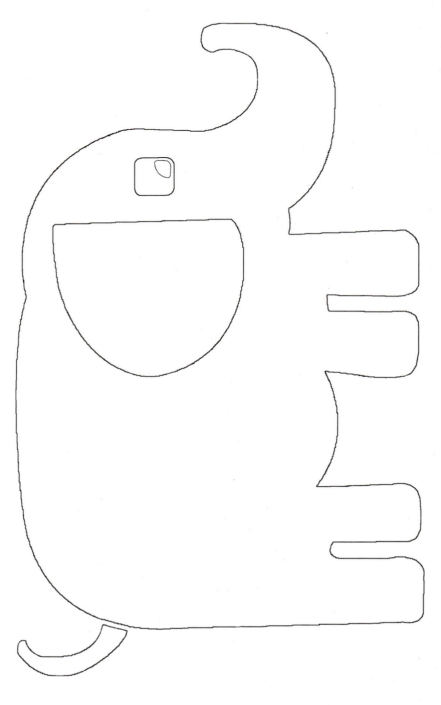

Elephant Template
needed for:
Cot Quilt pages 100–103
Duffel Bag pages 112–115

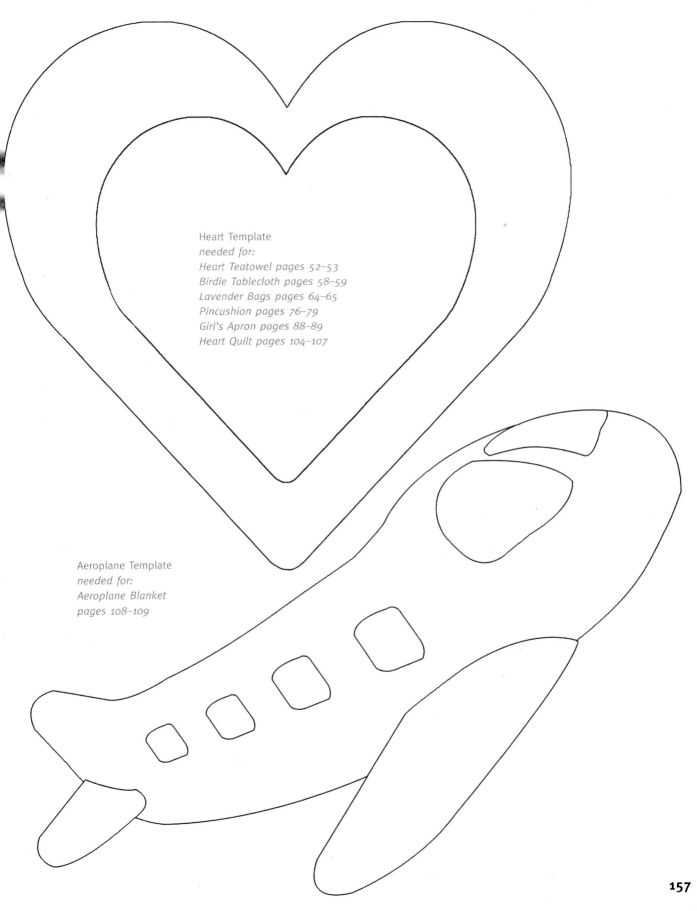

Heart Template
needed for:
Heart Teatowel pages 52–53
Birdie Tablecloth pages 58–59
Lavender Bags pages 64–65
Pincushion pages 76–79
Girl's Apron pages 88–89
Heart Quilt pages 104–107

Aeroplane Template
needed for:
Aeroplane Blanket
pages 108–109

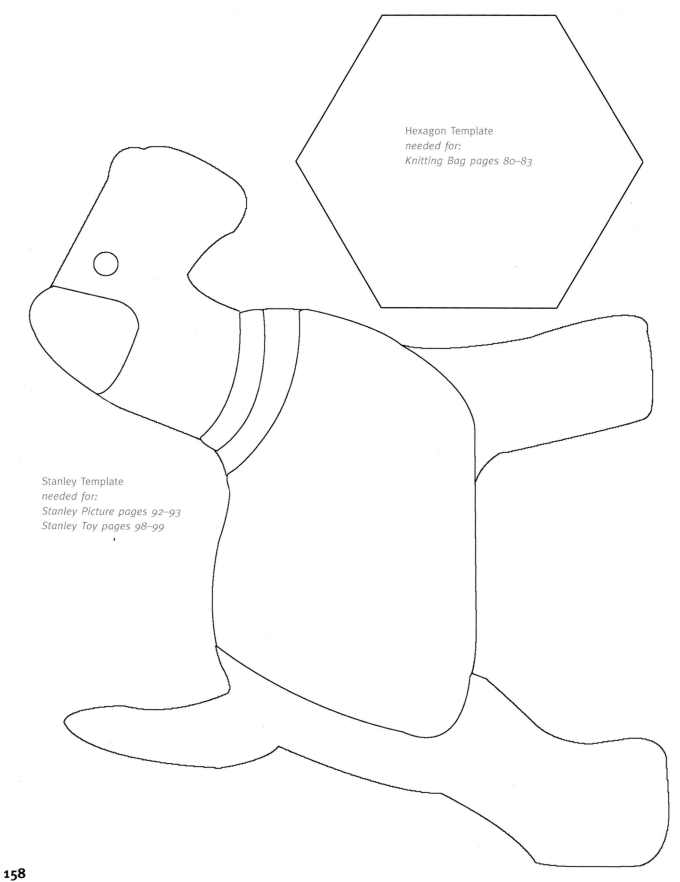

Hexagon Template
needed for:
Knitting Bag pages 80–83

Stanley Template
needed for:
Stanley Picture pages 92–93
Stanley Toy pages 98–99

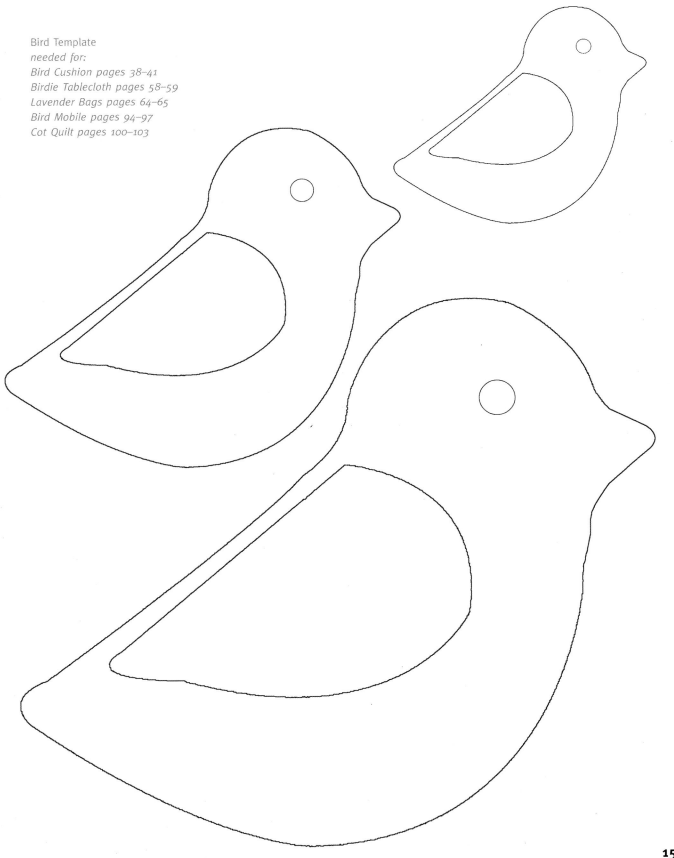

Bird Template
needed for:
Bird Cushion pages 38–41
Birdie Tablecloth pages 58–59
Lavender Bags pages 64–65
Bird Mobile pages 94–97
Cot Quilt pages 100–103

Flower Template
needed for:
Flower Cushion
pages 46–47
Heart Quilt pages
104–107

stitch!

Cath Kidston

stitch!

Cath Kidston

PHOTOGRAPHY BY PIA TRYDE

Quadrille
PUBLISHING

Introduction

The recent resurgence of interest in craft – and sewing in particular – has grown from a low-key trend into a much larger movement, and it now seems as if it's here to stay! It has been incredible to see just how many people, of all ages, are really enjoying making things by hand. A few years ago quite a few of my friends hadn't a clue how to sew on a button, let alone tackle any more advanced stitchery, so I find it very exciting that needlework has finally become mainstream.

My previous books, *Make!* and *Sew!* featured a wide variety of embroidery, appliqué and sewing projects inspired by my printed fabrics. When it came to planning *Stitch!* I wanted to take this exploration forward to the next level, and find a way of working these designs into step-by-step projects that focused on another traditional technique. Needlepoint tapestry was the natural choice. Thinking back to my childhood, tapestry was enormously popular, not least because it is so easily transported. My mother went everywhere with her sewing bag, and always had a project on the go, whether it was a cushion cover or a specs case. We also had an amazing rug, which my grandmother had made. She drew a picture of her house directly on to a large canvas and painstakingly filled in the outlines with carefully chosen coloured wools, using a variety of stitches.

What appeals to me about needlepoint is that the basics are very easy to learn and to put into practice, but the results are incredibly effective. Within a short time you can achieve a wonderful effect. Once I started translating my designs into charts, it immediately became apparent that they would also work perfectly as counted cross stitch patterns. I had less experience in this medium,

but soon discovered how much is possible... it is just as simple as needlepoint. All you need to do is to follow the chart and count your stitches as you go!

I had to narrow my selection down to a final total of fifteen prints and motifs, but you'll find plenty of familiar old favourites, like the cowboy and little house, alongside some exciting new designs. Each motif is interpreted in two ways, in different colour schemes, and I was delighted to find just how versatile they are, and how well their delicacy and detail translates into both cross stitch and needlepoint. The cherry border for example, is a wonderful repeated cross stitch design, but a single motif in tent stitch makes an equally effective badge.

All the technical background and stitches are detailed in the opening chapter so beginners will be able to tackle their first project with confidence and more experienced stitchers can brush up on their skills. Some pieces are quite quick to do, and easy for someone who is just starting out, whilst designs such as the floral chair seat and the striped rug may prove more a labour of love.

I hope I've made it easy for you to get started. I am now completely hooked on my latest tapestry (very often in front of the TV) and find it both a productive and a rewarding pastime. I hope you will find needlepoint and cross stitch just as enjoyable and addictive as I do!

Cath Kidston

Stitch! Basics

The next few pages cover all you need to know about needlepoint and cross stitch, from advice on materials and equipment to detailed, illustrated instructions for creating the stitches. I've added in plenty of hints and tips for successful finishing off, and some technical background information on how to make your completed needlework up into a finished project.

Needlepoint Basics

Some of the projects in this book are worked in cross stitch, while the others are embroidered on to canvas. But what is this second technique actually known as? Is it needlepoint, canvas work, tapestry or woolwork? There are as many opinions as there are names, and although the four terms are more or less interchangeable, I'm sticking with the first one!

Needlepoint is worked with wool (and sometimes embroidery thread) on an open weave canvas. This is covered completely by the stitches, so unlike cross stitch, the design always has a solidly stitched background. It's a wonderfully versatile technique; I've used it to create a variety of accessories and homewares, from a clutch bag to a floor rug.

All you need to get started are three items of equipment – a piece of canvas, a needle and some wool – and after a few practise stitches, you'll be able to reinterpret any of the designs in this book.

CANVAS

Needlepoint canvas is woven from tightly spun and stiffened cotton. It has a square weave of vertical and horizontal – warp and weft – threads which produce a mesh-like appearance. You stitch through the spaces between these threads. It is labelled according to how many holes there are every 2.5cm. This is known as the count: the lower the number, the larger the stitches will be. Therefore, 12-count canvas is on a smaller scale than 5-count rug canvas. The 'materials' list for each project specifies the size and count of the canvas required.

You can buy canvas in pre-cut lengths or off the roll in a white or antique (unbleached) finish. Always go for the best quality, which is less likely to distort as you sew: check that it isn't over-stiffened and that the threads show no sign of fraying.

There are three different types of canvas:

• Mono interlock canvas is used for half cross and tent stitch. The twisted mesh holds the stitches in place so they do not slide between the woven threads.

• Mono canvas is fine for straight stitch designs, like the bargello cushion and hippie bag and for working continental tent stitch. If you can find it, choose the 'de luxe' version.

• Duo or Penelope canvas is woven from pairs of thread, and is good for half cross stich. In traditional needlepoint it is used for the advanced techniques of tramming and petit point.

NEEDLES

Tapestry needles have a blunt tip so that they won't split the canvas threads or damage the previous stitches as you sew. They also have a long, wide eye to accommodate thick yarn. They come in various sizes to go with the different count canvases: the lower the number, the thicker the needle.

Buy a mixed pack and pick out a needle that goes through the canvas holes without forcing the threads apart, but that doesn't slip through too easily. A size 18 is the standard for 10-count canvas, a 20 is used for a 12- or 14-count and a finer size 22 for delicate 16-count. You might need a supersized 14 for the rug, which holds up to three lengths of wool at a time.

YARN

The wool needlepoint projects are worked with DMC tapestry yarn, a soft, single stranded 4-ply wool that is sold in 8m skeins. It is available in an inspiringly wide spectrum of colours, and the exact shades and quantities needed for each project are listed under 'materials'. (The equivalent colours from the Anchor range can be found on pages 154–5).

Stranded embroidery thread is an interesting alternative to wool. Sew with all six strands at the same time and thread the needle as shown for yarn. Mount the canvas on a frame to keep the stitches regular.

CUTTING THE YARN

You'll see that the skeins of wool are held together with two paper bands, the lower one wider than the other – don't be tempted to take these off as you'll soon get in a tangle. To use, hold the skein firmly by the narrow top band and gently pull the loose length at the bottom end.

The yarn has to pass back and forward through the canvas many times as you stitch. To prevent it becoming frayed, work with a length of around 50cm. Once you start stitching, you may find that the yarn starts to turn back on itself. If this happens, simply hold your work upside down and the needle will spin round as the yarn untwists.

THREADING THE NEEDLE

There is a special knack for getting the unwieldy end of your wool through the narrow eye of a tapestry needle. Hold it by the top end and with the other hand, fold the final 3cm of yarn over the point. Pull the yarn down to tighten and hold the resulting loop securely between your finger and thumb. Slide the needle out and push the eye down over the loop.

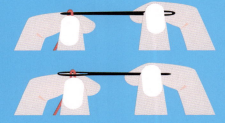

STARTING AND FINISHING

Now you're ready to go! As with so many aspects of needlepoint, there are several ways of starting and ending your stitches, but this is the method used by professional embroiderers and it gives the neatest finish.

• WASTE KNOT

Make a knot at the end of the yarn and take the needle through the canvas from front to back, about 2cm to the left of your starting point. As you work, the strand of yarn at the back will be anchored the canvas by the stitches. When it is covered, simply snip the knot close to the canvas.

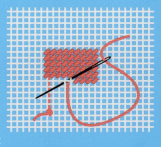

• WASTE END

If you are using a frame, you can finish off in a similar way. Bring the last 6cm of yarn up within an area that has yet to be stitched, 3cm from the end of the row. Make a short stich, leaving the tail on the right side. Unpick the stitch and trim the tail when the yarn at the back as been covered.

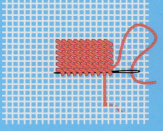

• WOVEN FINISH

The other way to finish off is to slide the needle under the back of the last 2cm of stitches. Trim the end close to the surface. This is sometimes easier if the canvas isn't mounted but it can create a slight ridge on the right side. You'll have to use this method with the last few lengths used in a design.

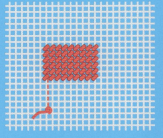

Basic Stitches

This is the simplest and most versatile needlepoint stitch, which is always used for charted designs. A small, slanting stitch, worked diagonally over the intersection of two canvas threads, it creates a smooth surface which resembles a woven fabric.

Just to confuse things, there are three ways of working tent stitch. They all look the same from the right side of the canvas, and all have different names! Which variation you use is really up to you, but I'll explain the different methods of construction and benefits of each one. In the instructions for the projects I usually suggest that you use half cross stitch, but you may prefer to work in tent or even basketweave – you choose!

HALF CROSS STITCH

This method is the most economical as it uses the least yarn, but this makes it marginally less hardwearing than the other two methods and produces a slightly flatter stitch. It can be sewn from side to side or up and down: on the reverse side you will see rows of short vertical or horizontal stitches. It should always be worked on interlock or duo canvas.

Bring up the needle at the top of the stitch and take it down diagonally, over one intersection to the left. Come up again one thread above, to start the next stitch and continue to the end of the row.

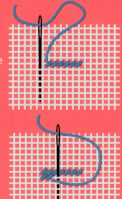

The next row is worked below or above this row, from left to right. You may find it helps to turn the canvas upside down, so you are always making stitches in the same direction.

TENT OR CONTINENTAL TENT STITCH

My favourite method. It's very quick to work without a frame, as you can push the needle in and out in a single scooping action for each stitch. It can also be worked in horizontal or vertical rows of plump stitches. On the back of the canvas it appears as a line of longer sloping stitches, and because it uses more wool, it gives a thicker finish. You can use mono, interlock or duo canvas.

Work the first row from right to left. Start at the bottom of the first stitch and take the needle up diagonally to the right, over one intersection. Bring the point out to the left, behind two intersections, and through the next hole. Carry on to the end of the row.

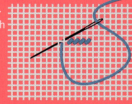

The next row is worked above or below the first in the opposite direction, from left to right. Again, try turning the canvas the other way up, so that the direction of the stitches remains constant.

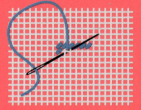

BASKETWEAVE TENT STITCH

This is worked diagonally, on either mono or duo, as it doesn't distort the canvas very much. It is often recommended for backgrounds and, because it has a padded reverse side, was traditionally used for seat covers. The back lives up to its name, having a dense interwoven appearance. It takes about twice as much thread as half cross stitch.

Starting at the top right corner, work the first two stitches vertically as for continental tent stitch. Make the third stitch next to the first, and the fourth next to the third.

Advanced Stitches

Most of the needlepoint in this book, especially the more detailed designs based on my fabric prints, is worked entirely in tent stitch, which creates an almost pixillated image. There are, however, many other needlepoint stitches which will add texture and detail: here are the ones that I have used.

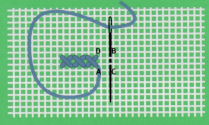

CROSS STITCH

To give them a raised appearance, needlepoint cross stitches are sewn singly, rather than in two stages. Work over two intersections for 12- or 10-count canvas, but over a single intersection with double yarn for 5-count rug canvas.

Make a slanting upwards stitch from A to B then a second one from C to D. Repeat to the end of the row.

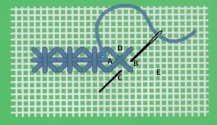

DOUBLE CROSS STITCH

This stitch is also known, rather poetically, as Leviathan stitch or Smyrna cross. It's made by stitching an upright cross over a single cross stitch. It's worked over four thread intersections.

Make a single cross stitch, then work a horizontal stitch from A to B and a vertical stitch from C to D. Start the next double cross at E, then continue in the same way.

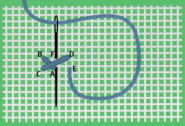

LONG ARMED CROSS STITCH

This border stitch consists of a row of overlapping asymmetrical crosses which produce a solid, plait-like outline. It's worked over two horizontal and four vertical intersections.

Start the row with a diagonal stitch from A to B. The first cross is worked from C to D and then E to F. Come out again at A ready for the next cross.

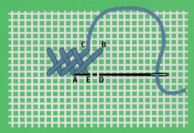

PLAIT STITCH

A wider version of long armed cross, work this stitch over two, three or four horizontal intersections, depending on the required width.

The first cross is made from A up to B and the second from C down to D. Start the next cross at E, and repeat along the row.

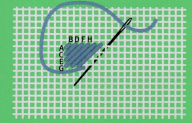

SLOPING GOBELIN STITCH

This is a versatile stitch that can be worked over two, three or four intersections. I used blocks of it for the brick walls of the House Cushion and vertical lines for the roofs, reversing the direction of the slant on alternate rows.

Depending on the depth of the row, start with one, two or three upwards slanting stitches in the top left corner, worked from A to B, C to D and E to F. G to H is the first full stitch – repeat this to the end of the row and fill in the triangular space with more shorter stitches.

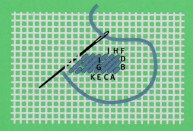

CUSHION STITCH

These little squares are made up of five graduated diagonal stitches. You can work them all in the same direction or alternate the slant on every other row to vary the effect. Both methods were used for the two Spot Cushions on page 38.

The first square is worked from A to B, C to D, E to F, G to H and I to J. Continue working from right to left, starting the next square at K. The rows of stitches can also be worked from vertically, but the squares must always line up.

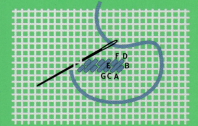

MOSAIC STITCH

A smaller variation of cushion stitch, this is a versatile filling, which I used for the Electric Flower Cushion on page 59 and the Spot Doorstop on page 120. Mosaic stitch can also be worked vertically and you can vary the direction of the slant if you wish.

Work the first square from A to B, C to D and E to F. Start the next square at G and carry on stitching from right to left.

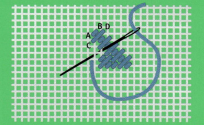

FLORENCE STITCH

Made up of diagonal rows of alternate long and short stitches, this useful filling adds an interesting texture.

Start the first row at top left with two diagonal stitches from A to B and C to D. Repeat these as many times as necessary, working downwards. The next row is worked upwards, so that the long and short stitches interlock. Vary the length of the stitches to fill the space.

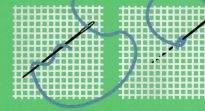

FRENCH KNOTS

I couldn't resist using these little round knots in the window boxes of the House Cushions, although they are not usually found in needlepoint. Practise a few to get the hang of the technique first.

Wrap the yarn twice around your needle to make two loops. Keeping the yarn taut, push the point down through the canvas, one thread away from the hole where it emerged.

Cross Stitch
Basics

Cross stitch has long been a popular embroidery technique. It is simple and versatile, easy to learn and because you work on to a fabric with a square, grid-like weave, all your stitches will be perfectly regular, right from the start.

I wanted this book to bring a fresh approach to an old favourite, and I had an interesting time going through all my designs, in search of those that would translate well into cross stitch. I particularly like the bright and breezy yacht motif and interpreted it on two different scales. The tiny sprigged lavender bag and spotty tea cosy are perfect for beginners (and both very quick to work) but for a longer term commitment you could choose the endearing little house picture. The great thing is that the basic technique is just the same for all four.

FABRIC
Most of the projects are worked on slightly stiffened cross stitch fabric, also known as Aida cloth, that is specially designed for cross stitch. It has a block weave, which gives the surface a pattern of woven squares with holes at the corners. Each stitch is worked over a single block. The closer together the holes, the finer the stitches will be and therefore, the more detailed the design. Like canvas, cross stitch fabric is graded by the number of holes per 2.5cm or inch. I used a larger scale 8-count per inch for yacht, a medium 11-count for the rose bouquet knitting bag and a finer 14-count Aida for the lavender bags. It comes in a white, ecru and range of pastel and brighter colours

SOLUBLE CANVAS
This is a wonderful innovation which gives you the freedom to stitch cross stitch designs on to garments, fine lawn, or denim – in fact, any fabric that doesn't have an even weave. It looks like a fine transparent plastic and is punched with a series of small holes that lie in a grid pattern, equivalent to 14-count Aida. Simply cut out a piece slightly larger than your finished design and tack it securely to the background fabric. Embroider your design as usual, then wash the finished project in warm water to dissolve the canvas. Do make sure fabric is pre-shrunk before you start to stitch, just in case.

NEEDLES
As with needlepoint, work with a blunt tipped needle that will not damage the cloth or split the stitches. Fine tapestry needles are sometimes labelled as cross stitch needles: pick a size 26 for 14-count Aida or a size 24 for 11-count. You can even add a touch of luxury to your work by using gold-plated needles, which glide easily through the fabric! If you are using soluble canvas you'll need an ordinary embroidery needle with a long eye and a sharp point to pierce the background fabric.

STANDARD EMBROIDERY THREAD
All of the cross stitch projects are worked in stranded thread, or floss. This lustrous cotton is produced in a wonderful range of colours, and I've picked out shades that match my own distinctive palette. It comes in 8 metre-long skeins and consists of six finely spun strands of smooth cotton, which are loosely twisted together. These can be separated and recombined, depending on the size of stitch required. Fine 14-count designs on Aida and soluble canvas use just two, 11-count designs use four strands and for larger-scale 8-count you need all six strands. In the 'materials' list for each project you will find details of the amount of thread needed and a reference for each colour. The numbers refer to the DMC range, but equivalent shades from two other manufacturers – Anchor and Madiera – are listed on pages 154–5.

Getting Started

PREPARING THE THREAD

The skeins of thread are designed to unravel easily, but make sure you pull in the right direction, or you'll get in a tangle. Hold the skein by the short band at the top and pull down on the loose end of thread from the bottom end. You will need a length of around 50cm to work with – any more and it will fray before you finish and your stitches will look untidy.

Hold the middle of the cut length gently but firmly between finger and thumb and carefully pick out the end of a single strand with the other hand. Pull the strand out of the bundle, maintaining the tension so that the other five threads don't snag up. Remove the number of individual threads you need in this way and lay them out together, side by side. Thread all of them through the needle at the same time, using the same technique as for tapestry yarn on page 15.

STARTING AND FINISHING

It may sound a bit obvious, but you should always start and end a length of thread in the correct way. Knots leave lumps and bumps on the back of the fabric, and badly finished 'tails' have a habit of working loose. Follow these methods and your work will always be smooth and even.

INVISIBLE START

When working with an odd number of strands, there's an ingenious way to start off without a knot. Cut a metre length of thread and separate out one, two or three strands. Fold the strand or strands in half and thread the cut ends through your needle. Take the needle down at A, the starting position of the next half cross stitch and bring it back up in the finish position B, leaving the loop on the surface of the fabric. Slip the needle through the loop and

pull the thread gently to form the first half cross stitch. Take the needle back down through B, then carry on stitching as usual. Be careful not to pull the loop too tightly or the fabric will distort. One word of warning – make sure you are in the right place if starting this way, as it's not easy to undo!

WASTE KNOT

When you are working with an odd number of strands, use a waste knot as for needlepoint. Thread the needle and knot the other end. Take the needle down from the front, about 3cm from the point where the next stitch begins, in a position where the loose thread will be trapped on the wrong side by the cross stitches. Carry on stitching towards the knot and clip it close to the surface when the thread is anchored.

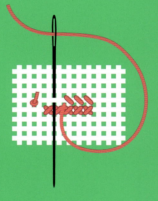

FINISHING OFF

Turn the work over once you finish the last stitch. Slide the needle horizontally under the upright stitches at the back for about 2cm, then pull it through so the thread lies under the stitches. Clip the end, leaving a tuft of about 3mm. Do not pull the thread tightly or the final stitch will go out of shape.

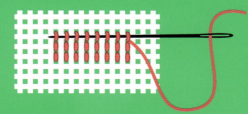

HOW TO CROSS STITCH

Each cross stitch is made up of two diagonal half cross stitches, one worked over the other. To give a professional look to your embroidery, work them so that the second halves of the cross all lie in the same direction – it doesn't really matter which way this is, as long as they all match.

CROSS STITCH ROWS

This is the quickest way to cover large areas and is economical with thread. The reverse side appears as rows of short upright stitches. Work in horizontal rows, from right to left to right or left to right – it doesn't matter which way, as long as the second stitches of each cross all lie in the same direction to produce a smooth, regular surface. You may find it easier to work in vertical rows to fill in some parts of a design.

Start at the bottom right corner, at A and take the diagonally up to B to make the first half cross stitch. Repeat this to the end of the row.

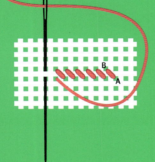

Start the second row of stitches at C and take the needle down at D. Carry on stitching from left to right, until all the half stitches are covered.

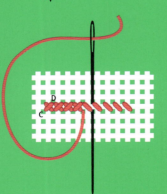

SINGLE CROSS STITCHES

Come up at A and take the needle diagonally across and up to B to make the first half cross stitch. The second stitch is worked from C to D. You can work a short row in this way, starting the next cross at C and working from right to left.

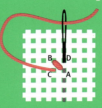

DIAGONAL LINES

Each cross stitch in a diagonal line is worked individually. You may need to use this technique for letters or for angled outlines. Make the first stitch from A to B and C to D, then come out at E to start the next one. This is worked from E to F and G to C. Repeat this, making sure all the top stitches lie in the same direction.

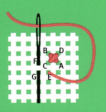

Getting Ready
To Stitch

PREPARING THE BACKGROUND

Whether you're about to embark on a needlepoint or a cross stitch project, you'll need to prepare your background fabric before you start sewing. Aida cloth might be creased and canvas still curved from the roll, so the first thing to do is to press it well. If you are going to use soluble canvas, launder the garment or fabric it if has not yet been washed.

Although it may seem time consuming, it's worth taking time to neaten the edge of Aida cloth with a narrow hand-stitched hem or a machine zigzag, to prevent it fraying. If you are not using a frame, bind all four sides of your canvas with masking tape, otherwise the yarn will snag on the rough edges (and if you are using a frame, and are feeling virtuous, you can bind just the side edges). Do make sure that you don't use a low-tack tape however, or it will simply peel off!

MARKING THE CENTRE

Most projects begin with the instruction to mark the centre of the fabric. This gives you a guideline for positioning the stitches, which corresponds with the vertical and horizontal centre lines marked on each chart. It also helps to ensure the grain lies straight within the frame. Fold the canvas or cloth into quarters and sew a line of running stitch over each crease. Use a bright coloured sewing thread and stitch along a single line of holes: this is easily unpicked when your work is complete.

FRAMING UP

Keeping the fabric under tension within a frame helps to keep your stitches regular. This is especially true with needlepoint; some distortion is inevitable when a diagonal stitch is worked over a canvas with a square weave, and for stitches like bargello and cushion which are made over several threads of canvas. Even so, the decision whether to use a frame or not is a matter of personal preference. Sewing without one means your work is more easily portable. Like many others, I find it more relaxing to sit back in an armchair with my canvas in my lap (and something interesting on the television of course!).

SEWING WITH A FRAME

Working with a frame requires a two-handed sewing method, with one hand above the canvas to push the needle down and the other hand poised below, ready to push it back up to start the next stitch. Which hand goes where depends on whether you are left or right handed, so if you haven't sewn this way before, try some practise stitches until you find a rhythmic action that is comfortable for you.

If you have an old-fashioned floor-standing frame or a hoop on a stand that can be clamped to a table, make sure that it is set at the right level, so that you don't have to lift your arms too high, or hunch over it. Scroll and stretcher frames can be propped up against a table, across the arms of a chair or over your knees if you prefer to sit on the floor.

You should always stitch in good light. Natural daylight is ideal, but good task lighting, directed over your shoulder, is fine during the dark evenings. Just be sure not to let any shadows fall across your work and always double check the codes of each colour thread as they can look quite different by artificial light.

TYPES OF FRAMES

If you do mount your canvas, it should be in a rectangular frame to maintain the square weave of the canvas or fabric. There are two types to choose from:

STRETCHER FRAMES

These consist of two pairs of narrow wooden struts, which slot together at the corners. You can interchange the pairs to create different shaped frames. Painters use these stretcher frames to mount their canvas, and a wide range of sizes can be found at your local art supplier. The smallest frames are very useful for small-scale projects like the pencil cases.

Pick a frame that is the same size as your canvas – you can always allow a wider margin so that the canvas fits the frame exactly. Fix the centre point of each side of the canvas to the frame with drawing pins or a staple gun, pulling it slightly to create a little tension, then pin out towards the corners. If the centre markings are going out of true, simply adjust the pins to straighten up the grain of the fabric.

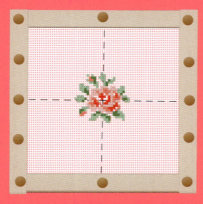

ROLLER FRAMES

Also called scroll frames, these are made up of two lengths of dowel, along each of which is stapled a length of cotton webbing. They are held together with two short side struts, which have a v-shaped slot at each end, and are secured by screws and wing nuts. The canvas can then be rolled up as you work: if you are working a large-scale design, only part of it will be visible.

The frame should be no more than 20cm wider than your canvas. Stitch the webbing centrally to the top and bottom edges, then slot on the struts. Adjust the rollers so that the centre point of the canvas lies in the middle of the frame and then tighten the wing nuts at the top. Roll the bottom bar until the canvas is taut and secure the other two wing nuts. Lace the side edges of the canvas over the struts with strong thread so that it feels like a drum. As your stitches progress, you will need to turn the rollers and re-do the lacing so that the unworked canvas sits within the centre of the frame.

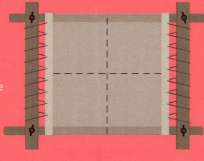

EMBROIDERY HOOPS

Cross stitch fabric can also be mounted in a rectangular frame, but most embroiderers like to use a lighter weight wooden hoop, in which the fabric is sandwiched between two wooden rings. The inner ring is solid and the outer one open, and held in place with an adjustable screw. Hoops are available in diameters from 10cm to 40cm: find a size that will leave plenty of fabric around your stitches.

Loose the screw to remove the outer ring. Spread the fabric centrally over the inner ring and slide the outer ring over the top. Gently pull each edge of the fabric to increase the tension. Check that the crossed stitch lines are still straight, then tighten the screw.

The only problem with a hoop is that it can leave indentations in your work. Binding the inner ring with cotton tape can help prevent this and it also stops the fabric from slipping. It's a good idea to take the fabric out of the frame each time you finish stitching. If you are working on a larger project, like the knitting bag, you may have to move the hoop so that part of it lies over completed stitches. Placing a sheet of tissue paper between the fabric and outer ring will reduce the pressure on the stitches: simply tear away the paper within the ring to reveal the area to be stitched next.

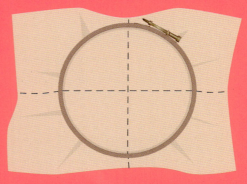

Starting to Stitch

I have given you detailed step-by-step instructions with each of the projects, showing how to stitch the individual charts, and then how to make up the finished embroidery. Whether this is simply mounting it in a frame, or turning it into a lined bag with handles, all the technical aspects are illustrated with clear diagrams.

The book has been designed for stitchers with varying levels of knowledge, from the novice to the expert. If you're just starting out I'd recommend one of the smaller projects – a pincushion or a badge – which are quick to make and which don't involve a lot of extra sewing. To help you choose, each project has been given a skill rating, from a basic 1, up to a more complicated 3. Experienced workers can always skim over some of the more basic advice.

Have fun with the designs and interpret them as you like. You may prefer to make the union jack cushion design up as a straightforward picture (and it would look fabulous in a scuffed vintage frame) or embroider the Stanley badge design directly on to a kid's denim jacket with soluble canvas. I have always thought that the electric flowers design would make a stunning rug, worked in repeated squares, in cross stitch on 5-count canvas with double yarn!

HOW TO READ A CHART
The charts for counted cross stitch and tent stitch are the same: a pattern of tiny coloured squares in a grid formation. Each of these squares represents a single cross stitch worked over one block of the cross stitch fabric, or a single tent stitch worked over one thread intersection. Like graph paper, the grid is divided by heavier lines every ten squares, which make it easier to count the stitches. The vertical and horizontal centre lines are marked with two arrows. These correspond with the two lines of tacking on the background fabric.

For other needlepoint stitches and for bargello designs, the coloured squares represent part of a longer stitch. The colours and exact stitches used are fully explained in the first steps of each project.

To save wear and tear on the book, you could photocopy the particular chart that you are working from, enlarging it a little to make it easier on the eyes. As with charted knitting patterns, crossing out or blocking off the areas that you have worked can help you keep track of your progress – and it gives you a great sense of achievement.

SHADE CARD
At the bottom of the chart is a key, which gives the reference number of the embroidery thread or yarn for each of the colours. It's a good idea to make a shade card before you start out on a project, to give you have a sample of every thread to match back with the numbers. Punch a line of holes along a strip of cardboard and fix a length of yarn through each one. You can then write the manufacturer's reference number alongside, so if the paper bands slip off, you'll always know which colour goes where.

It's a good idea to buy all the skeins needed at the same time, especially for larger areas like the background of the cowboy cushion, as colours can vary between dye lots. No two stitchers will use the same amount of yarn or thread, so the amounts given are generous and allow for a little unpicking.

UNPICKING
However carefully we count, we all make mistakes, and luckily misplaced or uneven needlepoint stitches are easily remedied.

With the tips of your embroidery scissors or an unpicker, cut through the centre of each stitch, taking care not to go into the canvas threads. Pull the resulting tufts out from the reverse side (tweezers might help if they get stuck) and use adhesive tape or a lint roller to get rid of any stray strands.

ORDER OF WORK

Thread your needle with the shade at the centre of the chart and start with the group of stitches that lies closest to the crossed lines. Count carefully and make one stitch for each square.

If the next area of the same colour lies less than 2.5cm away, take the thread behind the fabric and bring the needle up to start stitching. If it is further away, finish off and start again. Try not to carry long 'floats' or loose stitches across the back between blocks of stitches, as they can get tangled, and remember that darker threads will show through the holes of cross stitch fabric.

As a general rule, you should then continue working up towards the top edge and then down towards the bottom edge of the design. Some charts, however, will need to be worked in another order, and it's always easiest to stitch outlines first and then fill them in. The little house design is a good example of this, where you start off with the doors and windows, then add the details, whilst the bargello needlepoint designs both start at the top left corner. I've suggested a logical way of working for all of the projects, which may be helpful.

BLOCKING AND FINISHING

When the day eventually comes that you have completed your final stitch, remove your work carefully from the frame. All you need to do with cross stitch is to press it lightly from the wrong side to remove any creases, first placing it face down on a clean tea towel.

Needlepoint, however, may need a little more attention. You might find that your neat rectangular canvas has turned into a rhomboid. Don't worry... you can easily 'block' it to get rid of the distortion. The size, or stiffening agent, in the canvas threads is water soluble, so when it is damp the canvas can be pulled back into their original shape.

Make a paper template the same size as the finished piece and mark the centre point of each edge. Tape it centrally to a drawing board and cover with a piece of cling film or clear plastic that is about 5cm larger all round. Use a laundry spray to dampen the stitches and place the canvas face down on the cling film. Match the tacked centre lines with the midpoints of the template to square it up and place a drawing pin at each of these points, 2cm from the edge of the stitches. You may need to stretch it to make them line up exactly. Pull the four corners into position and pin them down, then add more pins at 2cm intervals. Leave the board in a warm place to dry naturally, then unpin the canvas.

AFTERCARE

You will have invested many hours in creating your cross stitch or tapestry projects, so take great care of them. Fine needlework produced by previous generations is now valued as heirloom pieces. Direct sunlight can cause fading, and remember that anything made from 100% wool is vulnerable to moth attack. If the stitches get grubby, use a vacuum cleaner with a soft brush attachment, or with the foot of an old pair of tights taped around the nozzle, to get rid of any loose dust or grit.

Small spots can be removed with gentle soap and a clean moist cloth, but washing isn't really advisable as it removes the stiffening and can felt or matt the stitches. However, if you need to take drastic action and a piece is really dirty, it can be gently rinsed in tepid water with soapflakes, then stretched out to dry naturally. Canvas should be pinned out on a board, as for blocking. Specialist dry cleaning is the best alternative, but can be expensive.

Sewing
Essentials

Many of the smaller projects can be stitched by hand (you may prefer to make up cushion covers this way too), but a sewing machine is required for some larger items, like the boat bag. This doesn't have to be the latest high tech invention, as all you need to do is a straight stitch and the occasional zigzag.

WORKBOX EQUIPMENT

In addition to the wool and needles used for embroidery, you will need some basic needlework tools and haberdashery. Keep these all together in a sewing basket, and store your work in progress and frame in an old cotton pillow case.

• a mixed packet of needles with a few long-eyed embroidery needles and some thicker sewing needles to start with.

• embroidery scissors, with short blades and a pointed tip are essential for cutting threads and trimming knots. Manicure scissors are good for unpicking and snipping stray stitches.

• household scissors are useful for cutting canvas and should also be used for cutting out paper patterns.

• dressmaker's shears, which have long angled blades, are necessary for accurate cutting of backing and lining fabrics.

• an unpicker, specially designed to cut safely through stitches, may prove helpful from time to time.

• long dressmaker's pins with round glass heads are strong enough to go through thick fabrics and will show up well against the stitches. Keep them to hand in a pincushion – if you haven't got one, this could be your first make!

• a tape measure is essential for calculating lengths of fabric.

• sewing threads should match the colour of the backing fabric or the predominant colour in the needlepoint. Number 50 mercerized cotton is a good all-purpose thread for natural fibres that will stitch through canvas and thicker fabrics. Pick a contrasting colour for tacking so that the stitches stand out.

FABRICS

Selecting the right trims and fabrics is a vital part of making up your projects: it's exciting when you come across the perfect velvet, linen or silk to back a cushion or line a bag. Sometimes I'll choose a material that perfectly co-ordinates with the threads, like the pink linen on the door stop, but I also like unexpected colour combinations that clash.

Search for backing fabrics that are similar in weight to the canvas or Aida cloth, such as antique linen, vintage upholstery fabric, velvet and my own cotton duck prints. Lining fabrics can be lighter, so hunt down suitable dressmaking or haberdashery cottons and silks. Although the inside of a bag isn't always visible, I love hidden details like the golden satin I used for the clutch bag lining.

CUTTING OUT

The materials list for each project includes the size of fabric required for backing and lining panels. One-off shapes like the lavender heart are given as templates, but for squares and rectangles you can make your own paper patterns. Do this by drawing the given measurements out on a sheet of squared dressmaker's paper and cutting along the grid lines. Pin the pieces to the right side of the fabric, so one edge lies parallel to the grain, then cut around the edge with shears.

CUSHION PADS

Ready-made pads, with feather or polyester fillings, come in a range of sizes. Not all of my cushion designs are standard shapes, so you may have to make your own pad... don't be daunted by this as it's very straightfoward. Cut two pieces of calico or ticking, each 2cm larger all round than the given pad size. Pin together around the outside edge, then machine stitch with a 2cm seam. Leave a 10cm gap in one size. Trim the corners and press back the seam allowance, including that along the opening. Turn right side out through the gap. Stuff the case with polyester cushion filler, a loose fibre from good furnishing suppliers. Pin the two sides of the opening and sew by hand or machine to close.

Finishing Touches

It's the details that give individuality to any piece of needlework, so I always like to spend time carefully planning my projects... and sometimes changing my mind along the way! I knew that the knitting bag handles were just right when I first saw them, but the bargello cushion on page 34 was originally edged with a vintage red braid. Later on I came across the jolly bobble fringing and knew that it was a much better alternative... so the woollen braid had to go. Don't ever be afraid to swap things round in the search for the perfect finishing touch!

PASSEMENTERIE

This evocative French word is defined as 'ornamental decoration or adornment' and encompasses the range of furnishing or dressmaking trims, from fringing to piping and braids.

• Piping, a loosely twisted cotton cord covered with a narrow bias strip of fabric, creates a coloured outline around the edge of a cushion or padded case. It is stitched in place between the front and back panels, either by hand or machine. This is an advanced technique but you can achieve a similar result by hand-stitching narrow cord along a finished seam. To finish, make a tiny slit in the seam, close to the corner, and push the ends of the cord through the gap and secure them with a few stab stitches.

• Bobble fringing has an irresistible, light–hearted appeal. As with piping, it can be stitched into a cushion cover as it's put together, but it's much easier to add afterwards, by hand. Position it so that the woven edging lies on the back panel then stitch along the top and bottom edges.

• Ric-rac is a narrow braid that is woven in a continuous wavy line. I trimmed the boat lampshade with this, stitching it behind the lower hem so only a little line of scallops is visible.

• Lace is too delicate to go on needlepoint, but if you can find any heavier edgings, they work well with cross stitch. I used a simple broderie anglaise for the lavender bag and a vintage guipure for the boudoir cushion. Sew by hand with small, unobtrusive stitches.

• Fringing works well with needlepoint. You'll find many extravagant versions sometimes a simple cotton fringe, like the one I used on page 38 is all you need. I customised this to suit the Spot Cushions: as it was too long, I trimmed it back to 1cm for a fresher look.

• Pompons always look bright and perky, so I couldn't resist adding one to the top of the tea cosy on page 28 (where there are also making-up instructions.) You can alter the size by varying the diameter of the cardboard foundation discs.

FINISHING OFF

The edging for your cushion or case should always be finished neatly. There is a special technique for overlapping the ends of piping, shown in detail within the relevant projects, and sometimes loose ends can simply be concealed at a corner. If you've used lace or a frilled edging you will have to join two cut ends, so allow an extra 2cm for the turnings. At the start, fold the first 5mm to the wrong side then stitch the bottom edge around the cushion. When you've gone all the way round, trim the surplus to 1.5cm. Turn back the final 5cm so that it lies towards the front before you stitch it down. Overlap the neatened ends by 1cm and sew the two layers together along the folds and the top edge.

Stitch! Projects

Editing and selecting the projects for this book was a nigh-on impossible task as there were so many possibilities! In the end I tried to choose as wide a range of techniques and ideas as possible, including a pincushion to make in an afternoon and a rug that could take a year. Whatever your skill set I hope you find inspiration and enjoyment in the thirty designs I finally chose.

Bargello Cushion

MATERIALS

40cm square 12-count mono canvas
tapestry frame
DMC tapestry wools in the following
   colours:
   white (blanc); yellow (7049);
   red (7106); pink (7202);
   green (7386); fawn (7411);
   blue (7802) – 2 skeins each
tapestry needle
34cm square floral print backing fabric
dressmaker's pins
sewing machine
sewing needle
matching sewing thread
140cm length braid or fringing
30cm square cushion pad

SKILL LEVEL: 1

The flowing waves of this traditional Bargello design are built up from blocks of vertical stitches of various lengths, worked in horizontal rows. The technique dates back to Renaissance Italy, but I've given my cushion a contemporary twist with a bright new colour palette and an unexpected flowery backing.

1 The vertical stitches mean the canvas will not distort, as tends to happen with diagonal stitches. If you prefer to work without a frame, simply bind the edges of the canvas with masking tape. Mark the starting point for the first row of stitches 7cm diagonally in from the top left corner.

2 Thread your needle with green yarn and bring it up at the starting point. Following the chart on page 37, on which each vertical block of coloured squares represents one straight stitch worked over six horizontal canvas threads, work the first row of green stitches.

3 The next row is worked in yellow and interlocks with the first. Start three threads down from the first green stitch: bring your needle up here and insert it at the base of the first stitch. Continue the row, working all the stiches in the same direction.

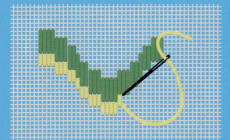

4 Continue the design for the cushion front, changing colours and altering stitch lengths as indicated on the chart. Fill in the gaps at the upper and lower edges to give a perfect square.

5 Once the design is complete, press lightly from the wrong side. Trim the excess canvas down to a 2cm margin all round.

6 With right sides facing, place the cushion front on top of the backing panel. Pin and tack the two together all round the outside edges. With the cushion front uppermost, sew along the line where the unstitched canvas and the stitching meet. Leave a 20cm opening along the lower edge.

top tip A WELL-CHOSEN EDGING FINISHES OFF A CUSHION IN THE SAME WAY THAT A GOOD FRAME ENHANCES A PAINTING.

I CHOSE THIS PERKY BLUE POMPON TRIM BECAUSE IT COMPLEMENTS THE COLOURS OF BOTH FRONT AND BACK.

Bargello Cushion

7 Clip a triangle from each corner – cut diagonally 5mm from the corner – then trim another narrow triangle from each side. Press back the seam allowances either side of the opening.

8 Turn the cushion cover right side out. Using the blunt end of a pencil, carefully ease the corners out into neat right angles.

9 Insert the cushion pad and pin together the two sides of the opening. Using a double length of thread, slip stitch the edges together by hand to close the gap.

10 Using small slip stitches and matching sewing thread, sew the braid to the cushion. Line up the bottom edge of the braid along the seam line as you sew. Gather the braid slightly at each of the corners and finish off theends as shown on page 30.

top tip TO MAINTAIN AN EVEN TENSION BARGELLO STITCHES MUST BE WORKED IN THE SAME DIRECTION – FROM BOTTOM TO TOP.

white (blanc)   red (7106)   green (7386)   blue (7802)

yellow (7049)   pink (7202)   fawn (7411)

Spot Cushion

MATERIALS

For the blue cushion
40cm square 10-count canvas
tapestry frame
DMC tapestry wool in the following
  colours:
   off-white (7510) – 2 skeins
   blue (7555) – 16 skeins
36cm square natural linen backing fabric
130cm length cotton fringing
30cm square cushion pad

For the red cushion
30cm square 10-count canvas
DMC tapestry wools in the following
  colours:
   red (7106) – 7 skeins
   off-white (7510) – 1 skein
26cm square natural linen backing fabric
90cm length cotton fringing
20cm square cushion pad

For both
tapestry needle
scissors
dressmaker's pins
sewing needle
matching sewing thread

SKILL LEVEL: 1

So far my versatile spot design has popped up on everything from a baby buggy and a bathmat to wallpaper and clogs. I couldn't resist finding just one more use for it – this time on two blue and red square needlepoint cushions. They work together well as a pair or piled on a sofa, alongside a row of floral print cushions.

1 Start both cushions in exactly the same way, following the chart on page 40. The outer square gives the size of the larger blue cushion; use the inner outline for the smaller red cushion. Working outwards from the centre of the canvas, stitch the spots in half cross stitch (see page 20) using the off-white yarn.

2 The blue background is worked in cushion stitch (see page 22). Start the first row at the top left corner, with a square block of five diagonal stitches. Continue along to the right corner, then stitch the following rows directly below, all in the same direction. You will need to make shorter diagonal stitches to fit around the spots.

3 The red background is worked in cushion variation stitch (see also page 22). You may find it easier to reverse the canvas, by holding it the opposite way up, when you are working the left-sloping stitches.

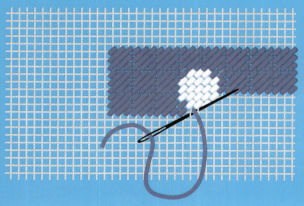

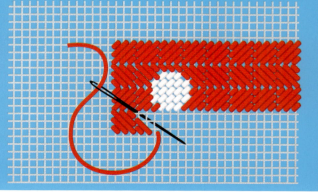

top tip CUSHION STITCH IS WORKED DIAGONALLY, WHICH DISTORTS THE CANVAS, SO THE BLUE CUSHION MAY NEED TO BE BLOCKED.

THE RED ONE USES CUSHION VARIATION STITCH, SO AS THE ROWS SLANT IN ALTERNATE DIRECTIONS IT WILL NOT NEED STRAIGHTENING OUT.

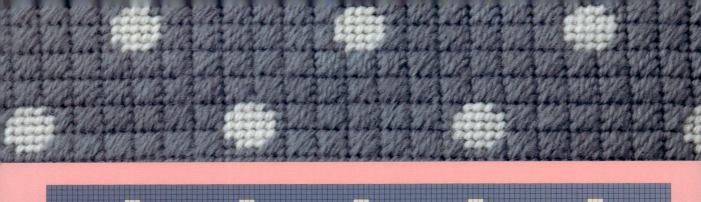

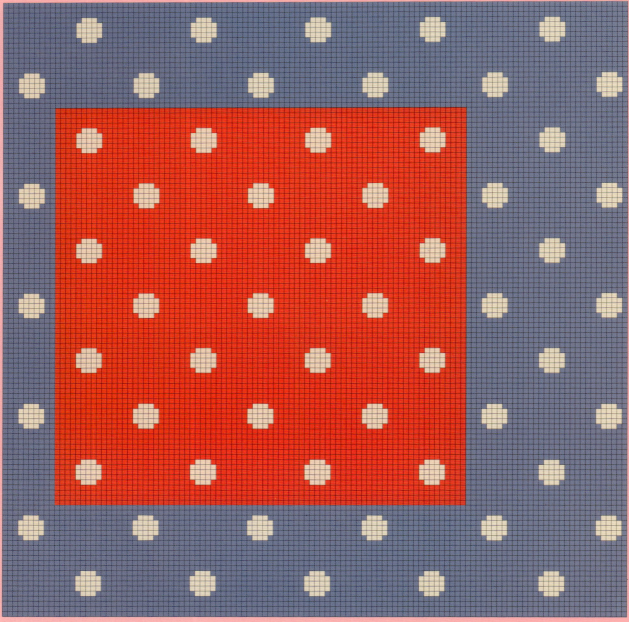

red (7106)   off-white (7510)   blue (7555)

Spot Cushion

4 Make up both cushions in exactly the same way. Once the design is complete, press lightly from the wrong side. Trim the excess canvas down to a 2cm margin all round. Place the cushion front right side down on a folded tea towel and press back 5mm of stitching at each corner at a 45 degree angle. Press back the edges to give a squared-off mitre at each corner.

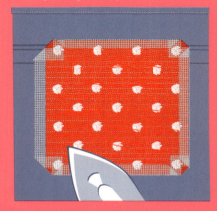

5 Press back and then unfold a 3cm turning along each edge of the backing panel. Press across the corners, squaring them off as before, then re-press the creases along all four edges. The backing panel should now be the same size as the front.

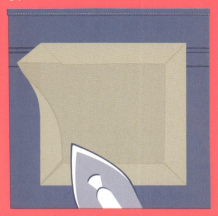

6 Starting at one corner, pin and tack the fringing to the wrong side of the backing panel, so the fringe lies beyond the neatened edge. Fold the woven part of the fringing at a 45 degree angle at the next three corners, and overlap the ends when you have completed the round. Cut off the loose end.

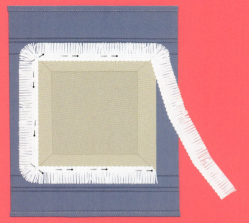

7 With wrong sides facing, pin the cushion front to the backing panel around three sides, so that the fringing is sandwiched between the two. Slip stitch these three sides together, passing the needle through the fringe. Insert the cushion pad, then pin, tack and stitch the fourth sides together.

top tip IF YOU CAN'T FIND THE PERFECT EDGING, DON'T FORGET THAT YOU CAN ALWAYS CUSTOMISE. THIS FURNISHING FRINGE COMPLEMENTED THE CUSHIONS PERFECTLY, BUT IT WAS A BIT TOO LONG... SO I SIMPLY TRIMMED IT DOWN WITH MY SHARPEST SCISSORS!

Provence Rose Pillow

SKILL LEVEL: 1

The little needlepoint pincushion on page 102 worked so well that I wanted to see how the rose motif looked as a repeat design… and I'm very pleased with the result. Re-coloured in shades of coral and jade green it makes an elegant cross stitch centre panel for this narrow boudoir cushion.

1 Mark the centre of the cross-stitch fabric. Bind the edges of the fabric with masking tape or mount it in a tapestry frame if you wish. The design is worked in cross stitch throughout using four strands of the embroidery thread. Following the chart on page 45, and starting in the centre of the fabric, work the first motif. Stitch the rose, then the leaves and the buds.

2 To make sure you get the correct distance between each rose, start the next two motifs by working the leaves nearest to the centre rose, leaving one unstitched square between them. Work a further three motifs on each side of the first rose.

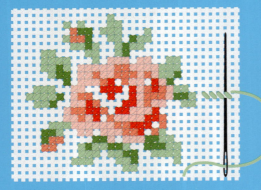

3 Next, work the pale blue decorative border along both the upper and lower edges, repeating it as many times as necessary to match the number of rose motifs.

MATERIALS
20 x 50cm 11-count cross-stitch fabric in white
DMC stranded cotton embroidery thread in the following colours: mid-green (562); light pink (963); coral (3705); light coral (3706); light cream (3865) – 1 skein each; light green (564) – 2 skeins; light blue (747) – 3 skeins
small tapestry needle
50 x 90cm blue fabric
24 x 40cm cushion pad (see how to make this on page 28)
90cm length lace edging
dressmaker's pins
sewing machine
sewing needle
matching sewing thread

Cutting out
from the blue fabric cut:
one 26 x 44cm front panel
two 26 x 28cm back panels

4 Once the design is complete, press lightly from the wrong side. Trim the excess cross-stitch fabric back to a 3cm margin along the long edges and a 2cm margin along the short edges. Place the cross-stitch panel right side down on a folded tea towel and press back the top and bottom turnings.

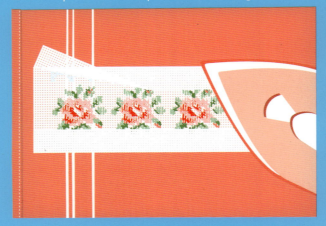

top tip YOU COULD ALSO USE THIS DESIGN AS AN EDGING FOR A FLUFFY WHITE TOWEL, ON A FABRIC BAG OR EVEN AROUND A LARGE DRUM-SHAPED LAMPSHADE.

Provence Rose Pillow

5 Cut the length of lace edging in half. Slip stitch the two pieces along the upper and lower edges of the cross-stitch panel. Start the repeat pattern at the same place on both edges so it is symmetrical.

6 Place the lace-edged fabric panel centrally across the cushion front. Pin along the upper and lower edges.

7 Using matching sewing thread, machine stitch the lace-edged fabric panel down. Sew carefully and slowly between the first two rows of cross stitches.

8 Press back a 1cm turning along one short edge of a backing panel, then fold it back once more and press again to make a double hem. Machine stitch the hem down, 5mm from the edge. Hem the second backing panel in exactly the same way.

9 With right sides facing and raw edges matching, pin one backing panel to the cushion front so the hemmed edge lies across the centre. Pin the second backing panel to the other side of the front, overlapping the hemmed edges.

10 Machine stitch all round the edge of the cushion, leaving a 2cm seam allowance. Trim the seam allowance back to 1cm and clip a small triangle from each corner to reduce the bulk. Turn the cushion cover right side out and insert the pad.

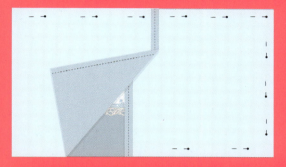

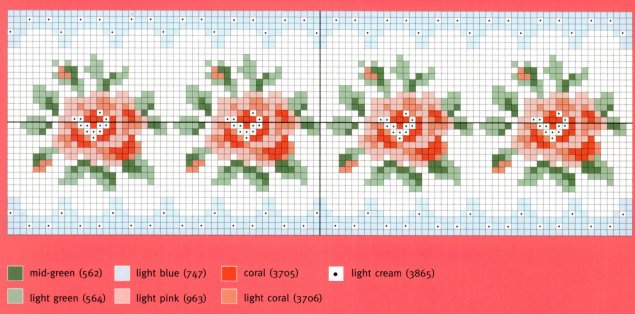

- ■ mid-green (562)
- ■ light green (564)
- ■ light blue (747)
- ■ light pink (963)
- ■ coral (3705)
- ■ light coral (3706)
- • light cream (3865)

top tip I FILLED IN THE LIGHT CREAM DOTS WITHIN THE BLUE BORDERS, BUT YOU COULD TRY LEAVING THESE UNSTITCHED TO CREATE A MORE LACE-LIKE FEEL.

Union Jack Cushion

SKILL LEVEL: 3

The design for the Union Jack pencil case on page 82 worked so well that I decided to develop it further, by continuing the floral sprig pattern to form a border around the central flag. A selection of more subdued shades gives the resulting cushion a softer vintage appearance, which is completed by the faded look of the denim piping.

MATERIALS

30 x 40cm 10-count canvas
tapestry frame
DMC tapestry wool in the following
   colours:
   dark red (7108); yellow (7455)
   – 1 skein each
   mid-pink (7223); beige (7230);
   green (7391) – 2 skeins each
   grey-blue (7705) – 3 skeins;
   dark pink (7758) – 8 skeins
tapestry needle
50cm square lightweight denim fabric
110cm length 6mm piping cord
two 24 x 22cm rectangles striped
   ticking backing fabric
20 x 30cm cushion pad
dressmaker's pins
sewing machine
matching sewing thread

1 Mark the centre of the canvas. Bind the edges of the canvas with masking tape or mount it in a tapestry frame. The design is worked in tent stitch throughout. Following the chart on page 48, work in the order given on page 82.

2 Once the central flag is complete, stitch the additional sprigs within the outer border and fill in the dark pink background. Once the whole design is complete, remove the canvas from the frame and block if necessary. Trim the excess canvas down to a 2cm margin all round.

3 Make a bias strip from the denim fabric to cover the piping cord. Draw a line at a 45 degree angle from the bottom left corner up to the right edge. Mark two more parallel lines above this, each 4cm apart. Cut along these lines.

4 With light blue sides facing, overlap the ends of the two denim strips at right angles and pin together. Machine stitch, leaving a 6mm seam allowance, then trim the spare triangles of denim at each end. Press the seam open and cut the strip down to 105cm. Press back a 1cm turning at one end.

top tip IF, LIKE ME, YOU ARE USING A TICKING TO MAKE THE BACKING, MAKE SURE THAT THE STRIPES
RUN ALONG THE LENGTH OF BOTH PIECES. THEY WILL THEN APPEAR UPRIGHT ON THE FINISHED CUSHION.

dark pink (7758)

green (7391)
yellow (7455)
grey-blue (7705)

dark red (7108)
mid-pink (7223)
beige (7230)

Union Jack Cushion

5 Fold the denim strip lengthways over the piping cord leaving a 'tail' of 2cm. Starting 3cm from the end, tack the two sides of the fabric together, leaving the final 3cm unstitched.

6 Starting at the centre of the lower edge of the needlepoint, tack the piping all round the cushion front. Position it so that the cord lies inwards and the tacking stitches run along the edge of the woollen stitches. Make a small cut into the denim at each corner so that the piping bends round at right angles.

7 Fold the neatened end of the denim strip over the raw end when they meet. Trim the piping cord so that the ends butt and stitch them loosely together. Fold the uppermost end of the piping back over and tack down.

8 Hem the backing panels following the instructions given in step 8 on page 44. With right sides facing and raw edges matching, pin and tack one backing panel to the cushion front so the hemmed edge lies across the centre. Pin and tack the second panel to the other side, overlapping the hemmed edges.

9 Fit a zipper foot to your sewing machine so the stitches lie alongside the piping cord. With the cushion front uppermost, sew all round along the line where the unstitched canvas and stitching meet. Clip a triangle from each corner to reduce the bulk. Press the seam allowances at front and back inwards.

10 Turn the cushion cover right side out, carefully ease the corners out into neat right angles, and insert the pad.

top tip THE 20 x 30CM PAD USED TO FILL THE CUSHION IS NOT A STANDARD SIZE THAT YOU CAN BUY READYMADE, BUT YOU CAN FIND OUT HOW EASY IT IS TO MAKE YOUR OWN ON PAGE 28.

Spray Flower Cushion

MATERIALS

30 x 45cm 11-count cross-stitch fabric in ecru

DMC stranded cotton embroidery thread in the following colours:
light green (772); ecru (842); mid-pink (899); green (992); dark pink (3350); turquoise (3766) – 2 skeins each;
light pink (604); light gold (676); brown (3857) – 1 skein each

fine tapestry needle

22 x 34cm linen backing fabric

dressmaker's pins

sewing machine

sewing needle

matching sewing thread

100cm length frilled edging

18 x 30cm cushion pad

SKILL LEVEL: 2

Here is one of my very favourite floral spray designs, this time making an appearance as a cross-stitch motif. I've re-interpreted it in bright summery shades of embroidery thread to make a luxurious boudoir cushion – the perfect gift for a best friend, sister, mother or aunt (providing you can bear to part with it).

1 Mark the centre of the cross-stitch fabric. Bind the edges of the fabric with masking tape or mount it in a tapestry frame if you wish. The design is worked in cross stitch throughout using all six strands of the embroidery thread. Following the chart on page 52, and starting in the centre of the fabric, work the large pink roses, then the smaller blue flowers, the leaves and finally the dots.

2 Once the design is complete, press lightly from the wrong side. Trim the excess fabric down to a rectangle measuring 22cm high x 34cm wide. To ensure the design remains central, measure a point 4cm from the first stitch on each side. Cut along the rows of holes in the fabric that line up with these points.

3 With right sides facing, place the backing panel on top of the cushion front. Pin and tack the two together all round the outside edges.

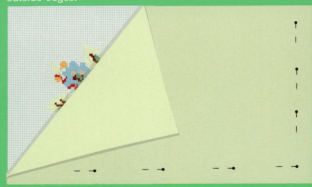

4 With the cushion front uppermost, machine stitch all round the edge of the cushion, leaving a 2cm seam allowance. Leave a 15cm opening along the lower edge. Sew a few extra diagonal stitches across each corner so that they will be slightly rounded.

top tip THE STITCHES ARE WORKED WITH SIX STRANDS OF THREAD TO CREATE A DENSE TEXTURE. IF YOU WISH TO MOUNT THE FABRIC, USE A RECTANGULAR FRAME OR A LARGE HOOP WITH A CIRCUMFERENCE OF 35CM OR MORE, SO THAT THE STITCHES WILL NOT GET DAMAGED.

light green (772)   dark pink (3350)   light pink (604)   brown (3857)

ecru (842)   mid-pink (899)   turquoise (3766)   light gold (676)

green (992)

Spray Flower Cushion

5 Clip a small triangle from each corner – cut diagonally 6mm from the corner stitches – then trim another narrow triangle from each side. Press back the seam allowances all round the cushion cover, including on either side of the opening along the lower edge.

6 Turn the cushion cover right side out. Using the blunt end of a pencil, carefully ease the corners out into neat rounded curves.

7 Insert the cushion pad. Pin and tack together the two sides of the opening. Slip stitch the edges together by hand to close the gap.

8 Fold over 1cm at one end of the frilled edging, then fold it once more to conceal the raw end. Stitch down the folded end. When adding the edging to the cushion cover, ensure that this folded end lies on the wrong side of the cushion.

9 Sew the frilled edging to the cushion by hand with matching sewing thread. Starting at the centre of the lower edge, use small slip stitches along the seam line. Gather the edging slightly at each corner.

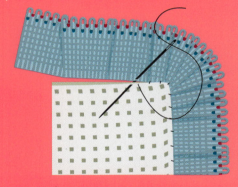

10 When the edging has been added to all four sides and you are back at the starting point, trim the loose unstitched end to 2cm and neaten as in step 8. Stitch the two neatened ends of the edging securely together.

top tip THE FILLING PAD IS STITCHED INSIDE THE CUSHION COVER TO GIVE A NEAT FINISH TO THE BACK. IF YOU NEED TO DRY CLEAN THE COVER AT ANY TIME, ALL YOU HAVE TO DO IS UNPICK THE STITCHES ALONG THE OPENING AND TAKE OUT THE PAD.

House Cushions

MATERIALS

three 40cm squares 10-count canvas
tapestry frame
DMC tapestry wool in the following
   colours:
   ecru; yellow (7472) – 4 skeins each
   pink (7004); dark blue (7306);
   mid-green (7386); red (7666) –
   3 skeins each
   pinky-red (7106) – 7 skeins
   dark cream (7141) – 10 skeins
   dark green (7541) – 6 skeins
   dark red (7544) – 1 skein
   brown (7622) – 8 skeins
   light green (7771); mid-blue (7802)
   – 2 skeins each
tapestry needle
30 x 80cm red check backing fabric
60 x 80cm calico
sewing machine
polyester cushion filling
210cm length bobble fringing
matching sewing thread

SKILL LEVEL: 3

This bolster – a highly desirable terrace of three cottages –
is a long-term project that will keep you occupied for weeks.
Like the striped rug, it is also a sampler, which introduces
some of the textured needlepoint stitches featured on pages
16–19. Have fun with this design. Either copy my choice of
stitches or improvise with your own.

1 All three sections of the cushion are worked in exactly the
same way. However, when stitching the second and third
canvases, remember to work the roofs in either red or mid-
green and the doors in either pink or light green. Mark the
centre of one piece canvas. Bind the edges of the canvas with
masking tape or mount it in a tapestry frame if you wish. The
design is worked in a combination of needlepoint stitches (see
pages 16–19). Following the chart opposite, and starting in
the centre of the canvas, work the door's outline and portico,
handle, studs and letterbox in half cross stitch. Add the brown
steps in mosaic or slanting gobelin stitch. Fill in the blue door
with mosaic stitch, the other steps and path in slanting gobelin
stitch and the porticos in mosaic or Florence stitch.

2 Next, work the window outlines in half cross stitch and
the sills in a single row of cushion stitch. Fill in the panes,
curtains and flowers in half cross stitch with a few French
knots, if you wish, to add texture to the petals.

3 Work the berries in half cross stitch and the bushes around
them in half cross or Florence stitch. Stitch the brown gutter
in mosaic or tent stitch. Fill in the blue roof in slanting gobelin
stitch and the sky in Florence stitch. (The blue house has sky
only on the right; the green house has it only on the left.)

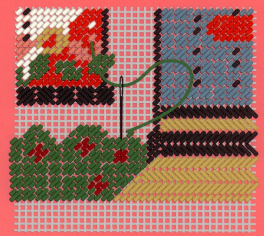

⬜	ecru (ecru)
🟨	yellow (7472)
🟧	pinky-red (7106)
⬜	dark cream (7141)
🟩	dark green (7541)
🟥	dark red (7544)
⬛	brown (7622)
🟧	pink (7004)

ROOF		**DOOR**	
🟦	dark blue (7306)	🟦	mid-blue (7802)
🟥	red (7666)	🟧	pink (7004)
🟩	mid-green (7386)	🟩	light green (7771)

4 Finally, fill in the wall with 'bricks' of eight slanting gobelin stitches worked over four canvas threads. Adjust the length of the diagonal stitches to fit around the other features and change the direction of each row.

5 Once the design is complete, remove the canvas from the frame and block if necessary. Trim each canvas down to a 2cm margin all round. With right sides facing pin the houses together in the right order, matching the edges of the needlepoint. Machine stitch along the edges of the stitching. Press the seams open.

6 Using the completed canvas as a template, cut out the backing panel and two pieces of calico for the cushion pad. Make up the cushion pad as shown on page 28.

7 With right sides facing, pin the 'terrace' to the backing panel. Machine stitch all round the edge of the cushion front, leaving one short end unstitched. Press the seam allowances inwards. Turn the cushion cover right side out. Insert the pad and pin together the two sides of the opening. Using a double length of thread, slip stitch the edges together by hand to close the opening. Hand sew the fringing all round the edge, neatening the edges as shown on page 30.

top tip IF YOUR TIME (AND MAYBE YOUR PATIENCE) ARE LIMITED YOU COULD MAKE UP THE CANVASES ONE AT A TIME AND TURN THEM INTO THREE DETACHED HOUSES.

Electric Flower Cushion

MATERIALS

45cm square 10-count canvas

tapestry frame

DMC tapestry wool in the following
  colours:
  mid-pink (7135) – X skeins
  dark pink (7136) – 6 skeins
  dark blue (7287) – 2 skeins
  green (7406) – 2 skeins
  yellow (7470) – 2 skeins
  off-white (7510) – 5 skeins
  light blue (7594) – 1 skein

tapestry needle

34cm square dark pink backing fabric

130cm fine piping

sewing machine

sewing needle

matching sewing thread

30cm square cushion pad

SKILL LEVEL: 2

My boldly graphic electric flowers design is the perfect showcase for introducing some new needlepoint stitches. The background and outlines are all worked in half cross stitch but the petals and flower centres are filled in with diagonal mosaic and Florence stitches, which gives them extra depth and texture.

1 Bind the edges of the canvas with masking tape or mount it in a tapestry frame if you wish. Mark the starting point for the first row of stitches 10cm diagonally in from the top left corner.

2 The design is worked in a combination of half cross, mosaic and Florence stitch and involves a lot of detailed counting. Following the chart on page 60, work the outline of the top left flower in half cross stitch. Fill in the centre and the petals with mosaic stitch.

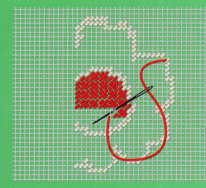

3 Contine to work the rest of the design, stitching the flower outlines first and then filling the centres and petals in with either mosaic or Florence stitch. The chart on page 60 is annotated to show exactly where each stitch is used. The smaller flowers are all worked in half cross stitch.

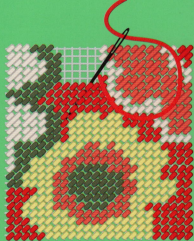

4 Once the flowers are complete, fill in the dark red background using half cross stitch.

5 Once the whole design is complete, remove the canvas from the frame and block if necessary. Trim the excess canvas down to a 2cm margin all round.

top tip STITCHING INSET PIPING CAN PROVE A LITTLE FIDDLY, SO YOU MAY PREFER TO HAND STITCH A CORD OR OTHER NARROW TRIMMING AROUND THE FINISHED CUSHION.

mid-pink (7135)	dark blue (7287)	yellow (7470)	light blue (7594)	F Florence stitch
dark pink (7136)	green (7406)	off-white (7510)		M mosaic stitch

Electric Flower Cushion

6 Starting at the centre of the lower edge, tack the piping all round the cushion front. Position it so that the join between the cord and braid runs along the edge of the woollen stitches. Overlap the ends of the piping and make a small cut into the braid at each corner so that the piping bends round at right angles.

7 With right sides facing, place the backing panel on top of the cushion front. Pin and tack the two together all round the outside edges.

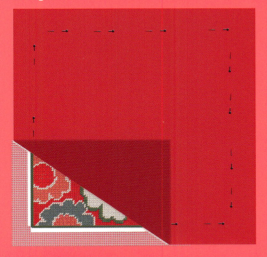

8 Fit a zipper foot to your sewing machine so the stitches lie alongside the piping cord. With the cushion front uppermost, sew all round along the line where the unstitched canvas and stitching meet. Leave a 20cm opening along the lower edge. Clip a triangle from each corner to reduce the bulk, then press back the seam allowances either side of the opening.

9 Turn the cushion cover right side out. Using the blunt end of a pencil, carefully ease the corners out into neat right angles.

10 Insert the pad and pin together the two sides of the opening. Using a double length of thread, slip stitch the edges together by hand to close the opening, passing the needle through the piping from front to back, just below the cord.

top tip ADD TO THE VIBRANT APPEARANCE OF THIS CUSHION BY USING A LUXURIOUS

BACKING FABRIC: I SOURCED A RICH VELVET TO MATCH THE DARK PINK YARN.

Bargello Hippie Bag

MATERIALS

42 x 46cm 12-count mono canvas
tapestry frame
DMC tapestry wool in the following
  colours:
  light blue (7294); off-white (7331);
  brown (7515) – 2 skeins each
  orange (7303) – 5 skeins
  dark blue (7336) – 3 skeins
  yellow (7485); green (7541) –
  4 skeins each
10 assorted skeins DMC tapestry wool
  or 80m knitting wool for strap
tapestry needle
36 x 40cm floral print backing fabric
36 x 80cm lining fabric

SKILL LEVEL: 1

From the Woodstock generation to Glastonbury, this fab needlepoint bag will appeal to flower children of all ages. Its unstructured shape gives plenty of room for knitting, shopping or even files and books. But why not just leave your work behind, sling it over your shoulder, and head off for a summer festival!

1 Bind the edges of the canvas with masking tape or mount it in a tapestry frame. Mark the starting point for the first row of stitches 8cm diagonally in from the top left corner.

2 Thread your needle with orange yarn and bring it up at the starting point. Following the chart on page 64, on which each vertical block of coloured squares represents one straight stitch worked over six horizontal canvas threads, work the first row of orange stitches. The next interlocking row is worked in yellow, with each stitch worked over five threads.

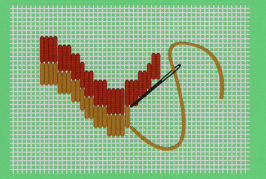

3 Continue the design for the bag front, changing colours and altering stitch lengths as indicated on the chart. To finish, fill in the gaps at the upper and lower edges to give a perfect rectangle.

4 Once the design is complete, press lightly from the wrong side. Trim the excess canvas down to a 2cm margin all round.

5 With right sides facing, place the bag front on top of the backing panel. Pin and tack the two together along both side and bottom edges. With the bag front uppermost, carefully machine stitch along the line where the unstitches canvas and the stitching meet.

6 Clip a triangle from both bottom corners – cut diagonally 5mm from the corner – to reduce bulk. Press back the seam allowances at front and back. Press under a 2cm turning around the bag's opening. Turn the bag right side out. Using the blunt end of a pencil, carefully ease the corners out. Press lightly.

7 Fold the lining in half and pin the side edges together. Machine stitch with a 2cm seam allowance, then press the seam allowances inwards. Press under a 4cm turning around the lining's opening.

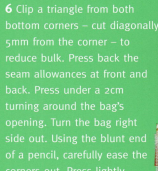

top tip TO ADD A HANDY INSIDE POCKET, PRESS A 1CM TURNING AROUND THREE SIDES OF A 20CM SQUARE OF LINING FABRIC.

MAKE A DOUBLE HEM ALONG THE FOURTH SIDE. SEW TO THE LINING BEFORE YOU MAKE IT UP, SO THE HEM LIES 10CM IN FROM ONE SHORT END.

orange (7303)   light blue (7294)

yellow (7485)   off-white (7331)

green (7541)   brown (7515)

dark blue (7336)

Bargello Hippie Bag

8 Slip the lining inside the outer bag, matching up the side seams. Pin the top edges together, ensuring that both the lining and the outer bag are on exactly the same level.

9 Overstitch the outer bag to the lining with a double length of matching sewing thread: pass the sewing needle between two woollen stitches and under the top thread of the canvas, and then through the top edge of the lining.

10 Cut 350cm lengths of yarn for the strap. Knot them 20cm from one end and secure the knot over a hook. Divide the threads into three groups of eight and plait them together – untwist the loose ends as you go, to avoid getting into a tangle. When the plait is 150cm long, knot the other ends together and trim both ends into a 6cm tassel.

11 Stitch one knot securely to a bottom corner of the bag and sew the plait along the seam line at the side, using a double length of sewing thread. Stitch all the way up one side of the plait, then back down the other for security. Sew the other end of the plait to the opposite side in the same way.

top tip FOR THE PLAITED STRAP, I RECYCLED LEFT-OVER YARNS FROM THIS AND OTHER PROJECTS, BUT USE ANY SPARE WOOL.

Spray Clutch Bag

MATERIALS

30 x 45cm 10-count canvas
tapestry frame
DMC tapestry wool in the following
    colours:
    mid-pink (7195) – 2 skeins;
    light pink (7221); dark blue (7296);
    light green (7376); dark green (7396);
    dark cream (7411); dark brown (7432);
    gold (7494); dark pink (7758) –
    1 skein each
    teal green (7927) – 4 skeins
tapestry needle
gold lining fabric: 22 x 34cm for the
    flap and 34 x 40cm for the bag
iron-on wadding: 19 x 29cm for the
    flap and 29 x 34cm for the bag
dark blue velvet: two 22 x 34cm
    rectangles for the bag
dressmaker's pins
sewing machine
matching sewing thread
sewing needle

SKILL LEVEL: 3

The muted colours of this floral clutch will add a touch of traditional elegance to any evening outfit. The sumptuous roses are stitched in warm coral tones on a teal background, and the softly padded bag is made from blue velvet, lined in an old gold silk to tone with the yarns used for the smaller flowers and leaves.

1 Mark the centre of the canvas. Bind the edges of the canvas with masking tape, or mount it in a frame if you wish. The design is worked in half cross stitch throughout. If you prefer use tent stitch, but remember to allow 30% extra yarn.

2 Following the chart on page 68, and starting in the centre of the canvas, work the large pink roses. Continue to work the design outwards with the smaller blue and gold flowers, green and gold leaves and spots. Finally, fill in the background with teal green.

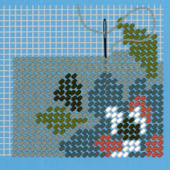

3 When the design is complete, remove the canvas from the frame and block if necessary. Trim the excess canvas down to a 2cm margin all round. Press the canvas back along the side and bottom edges, then unfold the creases. Press the bottom corners inwards at 45 degrees. Clip a triangle at each corner, refold to mitre and re-press.

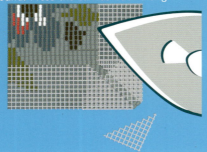

4 Position the iron-on wadding for the flap, adhesive side down, across the back of the needlepoint. Tuck the edges under the pressed-back canvas at the side and lower edges. Iron it in place, following the manufacturer's instructions.

5 Press a 2cm turning along the side and lower edges of the flap lining and mitre the corners. With wrong sides facing, pin the lining to the side and lower edges of the flap. Overstitch these edges together with matching sewing thread. Tack the unstitched lining to the canvas, 1.5cm from the top edge.

top tip TAKE A TIP FROM PROFESSIONAL DRESSMAKERS: NEVER PRESS VELVET FROM RIGHT SIDE, OR YOU WILL FLATTEN THE PILE. LAY A TOWEL OVER YOUR IRONING BOARD AND PLACE THE VELVET RIGHT (PLUSH) SIDE DOWN BEFORE STEAM PRESSING LIGHTLY FROM THE BACK.

mid-pink (7195)　dark green (7396)　dark pink (7758)

light pink (7221)　dark cream (7411)　teal green (7927)

dark blue (7296)　dark brown (7432)

light green (7376)　gold (7494)

68

Spray Clutch Bag

6 Pin the bag pieces together along the side and lower edges, with the plush sides facing. Machine stitch with a 2cm seam allowance, then press the seam allowances inwards. Clip a triangle from each bottom corner. Turn the bag right side out and lightly press. Pin and tack a 1.5cm turning around the opening.

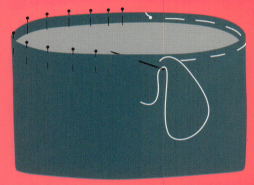

7 Fold the bag lining in half lengthways. Pin the sides and stitch with a 2cm seam allowance. Press the seam allowances inwards, then press back a 2cm turning around the opening.

8 Fold the lining wadding around the lining. Tuck the top edges under the turning at front and back, and pin in place. Press gently to fuse the two together.

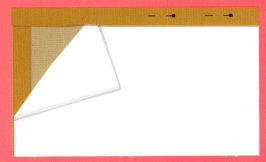

9 Slip the lining inside the bag, so that the top edge lies 5mm below the edge of the bag. Pin and tack the two together along the front edge.

10 Slot the top edge of the flap into the back of the bag, between the velvet and lining. Pin it in place, so that the row of tacking stitches lies 5mm below the folded top edges of the bag and lining.

11 Slip stitch the top edge of the lining to the flap, passing the needle through the canvas to hold it in place, but not through the velvet. Working from the other side, slip stitch the folded edge of the bag to the canvas, following a row of stitches to maintain a straight line.

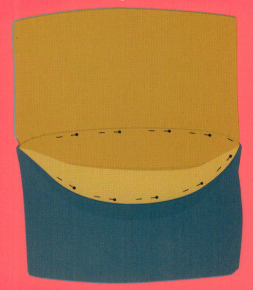

top tip USE PLENTY OF PINS AND SHORT TACKING STITCHES TO HOLD THE FRONT AND BACK OF THE BAG TOGETHER WHEN YOU ARE STITCHING THE SIDES, TO PREVENT THE TWO PIECES OF VELVET 'CREEPING' OUT OF ALIGNMENT WHEN YOU STITCH.

Sail Boat Beach Bag

SKILL LEVEL: 3

Here's a roomy bag with a seafaring air, that's big enough to carry everything that you need for a day on the beach. The pocket is made from 8-count cross-stitch fabric, which is satisfyingly quick to stitch. It gives the embroidery a solid look, which complements the striped ticking and spotty lining.

1 Mark the centre of the cross-stitch fabric. The design is worked in cross stitch throughout using all six strands of the embroidery thread. Following the chart on page 73, and starting in the centre of the fabric, work the main red sail. Continue to work the design outwards with the second sail, the masts and waves, then the clouds and gulls.

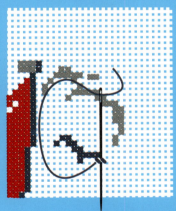

2 Once the design is complete, trim the pocket back to a 25 x 29cm rectangle, ensuring that the motif remains central. Position the iron-on interfacing, adhesive side down, on the wrong side of the stitched pocket, so that there is a 2cm margin all round. Iron the interfacing in place, following the manufacturer's instructions.

MATERIALS

30 x 35cm 8-count cross-stitch fabric in ecru
DMC stranded cotton embroidery thread in the following colours: dark red (498); red (817); blue-green (926); dark blue-green (930) – 1 skein each
small tapestry needle
21 x 25cm medium weight iron-on interfacing
100cm length 1cm-wide braid
100cm x 140cm striped ticking fabric
50 x 130cm spot lining fabric
100cm length 3cm-wide striped braid
dressmaker's pins
matching sewing thread
sewing machine

Cutting out

cut each piece so the stripes are centred and run from top to bottom.
front and back: two 40 x 50cm rectangles
sides: two 12 x 40cm strips
base: one 12 x 50cm strip
lining: one 40 x 117cm rectangle for the sides, plus one 12 x 50cm strip for the base

3 Press the corners of the pocket inwards at a 45 degree angle to mitre them, then press back each of the margins.

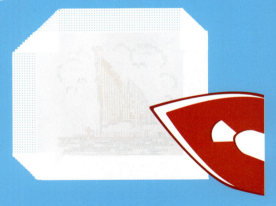

top tip I USED A RED AND WHITE TICKING FOR THE BAG BUT YOU MAY BE LUCKY ENOUGH TO COME ACROSS SOME OLD-FASHIONED STRIPED DECK CHAIR CANVAS, WHICH COMES IN TRADITIONAL SEA SIDE COLOURS.

Sail Boat Beach Bag

4 Starting at the centre lower edge, using small slip stitches and matching sewing thread, sew the braid to the pocket. Fold the braid at an angle around each corner and finish off the ends   as shown on page 30.

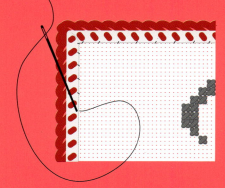

5 Pin the pocket centrally to the front bag panel, lining the side edges up with the stripes. Machine stitch along the side and lower edges, reinforcing both ends of the seam by working a few extra stitches in the opposite direction.

6 Now make the gusset. With right sides facing, pin one short end of each side strip to the short ends of the base. Machine stitch 1.5cm from the edge, leaving 1.5cm of fabric unstitched at each end of the seam.

7 Again with right sides together, pin one long edge of the gusset to the front panel, taking care to precisely match up the corners. Machine stitch the base, leaving 1.5cm of fabric unstitched at each end of the seam. Machine the side seams, starting from the top corners, and finishing 1.5cm from the bottom. Join the other long edge of the gusset to the back panel of the bag in the same way.

8 Turn the bag right side out. Using the blunt end of a pencil, carefully ease out the corners. Press the seams lightly, then press under a 2cm turning around the bag's opening.

9 With right sides facing, pin together the short edges of the main lining panel. Slip it inside the bag and, if necessary, adjust the width of the seam so that it fits perfectly. Machine stitch this side seam, then press the seam open. This seam lies along the centre back of the outer bag.

10 Fold the base lining panel in half lengthways to find the centre. With right sides together, pin this point to the back seam line of the main lining panel. Pin out to the corners, then pin the remaining three sides of the base panel to the lower edge of the main lining.

top tip IF YOU DON'T WANT TO MAKE YOUR OWN BAG, YOU COULD STITCH THE YACHT PANEL DIRECTLY ONTO A PLAIN CANVAS TOTE OR A SUMMER STRAW HOLDALL.

11 Make a 1.5cm cut into the main lining panel where it meets each corner so that the seam allowance lies flat against the base lining panel. Machine stitch the two together, all around the base, leaving a 1.5cm seam allowance.

12 Press the seams lightly, then press under a 2cm turning around the lining's opening.

13 Slip the lining inside the bag. Pin the two together all round the opening so that the top edge of the lining sits 5mm below the top edge of the outer bag.

14 Cut the braid in half to make the bag handles. Take the first length of braid and, 15cm in from the sides, tuck 4cm at each end between the outer bag and the lining. Pin and tack the ends in place. Repeat with the second length of braid on the other side.

15 Machine stitch all round the bag's opening, 1cm down from the top edge. To reinforce the handles, sew a rectangle with a cross inside over each of the four ends of the braid.

■ dark red (498)

■ red (817)

□ blue-green (926)

■ dark blue-green (930)

Bouquet Knitting Bag

SKILL LEVEL: 3

This is a really useful bag, which will easily accommodate your sewing and knitting projects, including the longest needles. It's made from red fabric and stitched with flamboyant cabbage roses. The design is reminiscent of Victorian Berlin work, but with a vivid new scheme – inspired by the rug in my hallway!

1 To find the starting point for the design, fold the cross-stitch fabric in half widthways. Now measure a point 20cm up from the bottom edge: this corresponds to the centre of the chart.

2 The design is worked in cross stitch throughout using four strands of the embroidery thread. Following the chart on page 76, and starting at the marked point on the fabric, work the large roses. Continue to work the design outwards with the smaller blooms, then the leaves and buds.

3 Once the design is complete, lightly from the wrong side to protect the stitches. Trim the fabric down to a rectangle measuring 45cm high x 40cm wide. With right sides facing, place the backing panel on top of the bag front. Pin and tack the two together along the side and lower edges. Measure 15cm down from the top on each side edge and mark with a pin.

MATERIALS

45 x 50cm 11-count cross stitch fabric in red
DMC stranded cotton embroidery thread in the following colours:
   lime green (166); olive green (830);
   pink (956); beige (3782) –
   2 skeins each
   red (891) – 3 skeins
   light orange (977); brown (3031);
   light green (3348) – 1 skein each
small tapestry needle
45 x 150cm brown cotton fabric for the backing and lining
pair of 20cm wide knitting bag handles with slots at the lower edge
dressmaker's pins
matching sewing thread
sewing machine

Cutting out

cut the brown fabric into three
   40 x 45cm rectangles

4 Machine stitch with a 2cm seam allowance from the marked point, leaving 15cm unstitched. Clip a triangle from the corners and press the corners inwards to mitre. Press back the seam allowances along the side and lower edges, including the unstitched parts. Press back a 2cm turning along the opening.

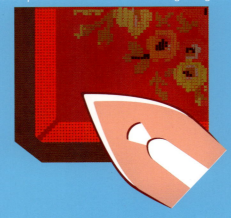

5 Turn the bag right side out and lightly press the seams.

top tip IF YOU ARE NOT A KNITTER, YOU MAY PREFER TO MAKE THIS DESIGN UP AS A FABULOUS SQUARE CUSHION OR AS A FRAMED PICTURE.

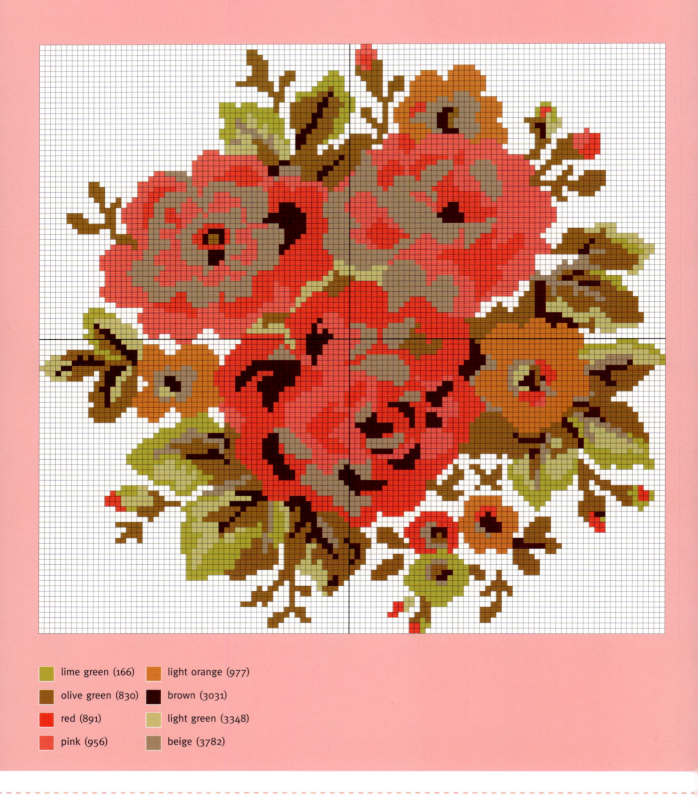

🟩	lime green (166)	🟧	light orange (977)
🟫	olive green (830)	⬛	brown (3031)
🟥	red (891)	🟨	light green (3348)
🟧	pink (956)	🟫	beige (3782)

Bouquet Knitting Bag

6 Join the two remaining brown fabric rectangles in exactly the same way to make the lining, leaving 15cm at the top of the side seams unstitched. Press back the seam allowances as for the bag.

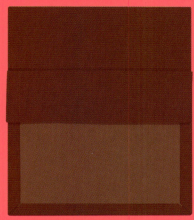

7 Slip the lining inside the bag. Pin the unstitched side edges of the bag to the lining. Starting 3cm down from the corners, oversew them together.

8 Now comes the tricky bit – fitting the bag onto the handles! Push one corner of the lining up, from back to front, through the slot at the bottom edge of one handle. Pin it to the corresponding front corner. Continue pushing the lining through the gap, pinning it to the bag front as you go. Oversew the two edges together along the folds. Sew the other handle to the back of the bag in the same way.

9 To keep the handle in position, work a row of small running stitches to join the bag and lining together, 3cm down from the top edge. Do this at the front and back of the bag.

top tip THESE HANDLES ARE MADE FROM TORTOISESHELL-LOOK PLASTIC, BUT IF YOU CAN'T FIND ANY SIMILAR, A PAIR OF NATURAL BAMBOO HANDLES WOULD LOOK JUST AS GOOD.

Union Jack Purse

MATERIALS

20 x 30cm 10-count canvas
tapestry frame
DMC tapestry wool in the following
  colours:
   yellow (7504) – 1 skein
   off-white (7510) – 2 skeins
   dark pink (7603) – 1 skein
   light pink (7605) – 1 skein
   red (7666) – 3 skeins
   blue (7802) – 2 skeins
   green (7911) – 1 skein
tapestry needle
sewing machine
16 x 23cm floral print backing fabric
20cm red zip
23 x 30cm spot print lining fabric
matching sewing cotton
sewing needle

SKILL LEVEL: 3

Here's my new take on an iconic and perennially fashionable design – a Union Jack purse, embellished with tiny floral sprigs and a dusting of polka dots. A flowered backing and a lining of blue spots continue the red, white and blue theme. Don't be put off by the zip – it's really very easy to sew it in by hand.

1 Mark the centre of the canvas. Bind the edges of the canvas with masking tape or mount it in a frame. The design is worked in tent stitch throughout and involves a lot of detailed counting. Following the chart on page 80, work the white borders to the central red cross.

2 It's always easiest to work the detailed areas first, then fill in the background around them. Work the six floral sprigs inside the central cross, then fill in the red background.

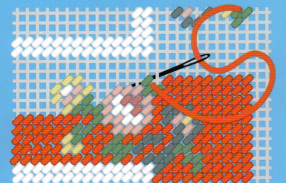

3 Next, work the red diagonals and flowers, then the white borders. Finish off by working the blue spotty triangles.

4 Once the design is complete, block the canvas if necessary. Trim the excess canvas back to a 2cm margin all round. With right sides facing, place the purse front on top of the backing panel and pin along the side and lower edges. With the purse front uppermost, sew all round these three edges along the line where the unstitched canvas and stitching meet.

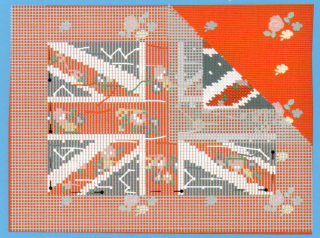

5 Clip a small triangle from each corner to reduce the bulk. Turn the purse right side out. Press under a 2cm turning around the top edge, then press the purse very lightly using a cloth to protect the surface of the stitches.

top tip I USED MY RED ROSE HABERDASHERY WEIGHT PRINT FOR THE BACKING. TO STAND UP TO EVERYDAY WEAR AND TEAR IT NEEDED TO BE A LITTLE HEAVIER, SO I FUSED THE FABRIC TO A PIECE OF CALICO WITH BONDAWEB BEFORE CUTTING IT TO THE EXACT SIZE.

Union Jack
Purse

	yellow (7504)		red (7666)
	off-white (7510)		blue (7802)
	dark pink (7603)		green (7911)
	light pink (7605)		

6 Fold the lining panel in half lengthways. Pin and machine stitch the side seams, leaving a 2cm seam allowance. Trim the seam allowance back to 6mm and press back. Press under a 2cm turning all round the top edge.

7 Open the zip fully so the pull lies at the closed end. Pin the right edge of the zip to the front of the purse, lining it up so that 6mm projects above the top edge and the teeth begin 1cm in from the corner. Tuck the other end of the zip into the purse, then pin the left edge of the zip to the back of the purse in the same way. Tack, then slip stitch in place using matching sewing thread.

8 Slip the prepared lining inside the purse. Line up the side seams, then pin the opening of the lining in place so it lies 6mm below the top edge of the zip. Slip stitch the folded edge of the lining to the zip with matching sewing thread.

top tip IF YOU DON'T WISH TO MACHINE STITCH THE PURSE, SIMPLY PRESS BACK THE CANVAS MARGIN AND THE SEAM ALLOWANCE

ON THE BACKING. HAND SEW THE TWO TOGETHER ALONG THE SIDE AND BOTTOM EDGES WITH A DOUBLE LENGTH OF MATCHING SEWING THREAD.

Stanley Pencil Case

MATERIALS

35 x 25cm 10-count canvas
tapestry frame
DMC tapestry wool in the following
   colours:
   beige (7520); tan (7525);
   black (7624) – 1 skein each
   grey (7626); red (7666) –
   3 skeins each
tapestry needle
50cm length 3mm piping cord
40 x 60cm grey flannel fabric for
   lining and piping
16 x 25cm red cotton backing fabric
25cm zip
matching sewing thread
sewing needle

SKILL LEVEL: 3

Stanley, my adorable but occasionally mischievous Lakeland terrier, has become a star in his own right. His distinctive portrait now appears on a sparkling crystal brooch and as a kidswear logo, and he even has his own fabric. For fellow fans, here's a trio of Stanleys striding across a zip-up pencil case.

1 Mark the centre of the canvas. Bind the edges of the canvas with masking tape or mount it in a frame if you wish.

2 The main part of the design is worked in tent stitch. Following the chart on page 84 on which each coloured square represents one tent stitch, work the central Stanley. Next, add his tan and black companion to the left and then his beige and tan friend to the right. Fill in the grey background with tent stitch.

3 The red border is worked in mosaic stitch (see page 18). Following the same chart on page 84 on which four red squares represents one mosaic stitch, work the first red mosaic stitch at the top left corner, in line with the grey tent stitch, and then continue the row towards the right. The red border is four mosaic stitches deep.

4 Once the design is complete, block the canvas if necessary. Trim the excess canvas down to a 2cm margin all round.

5 Press under, then unfold, a 2cm turning all round the backing panel. Mitre the corners to reduce the bulk by pressing the corners inwards, lining up the creases. Trim the tips from each of the corner triangles, and then re-press the creases. Press and mitre the corners of the stitched case front in exactly the same way.

6 Prepare a 48cm length of grey piping. Follow the instructions given for covering piping cord in steps 3 to 5 of the Union Jack Cushion on pages 47 and 49.

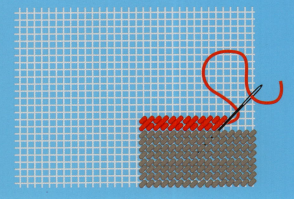

top tip WORKING WITH CANVAS, BACKING FABRIC AND A LINING, PLUS THE PIPING AND A ZIP CAN PROVE A BIT FIDDLY, SO I RECOMMEND STITCHING THE PENCIL CASE BY HAND TO ENSURE A NEAT FINISH.

Stanley
Pencil Case

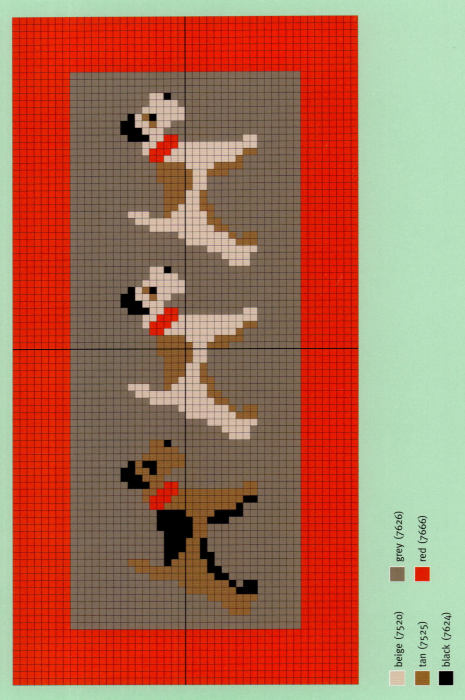

beige (7520)　tan (7525)　black (7624)　grey (7626)　red (7666)

7 Starting at one top corner of the case front, tack the piping along the side and lower edges. Position it so that the cord projects just beyond the pressed edges. Tuck the two loose ends behind the canvas, 6mm down from the top corners and trim. Make a small cut into the grey fabric at each corner so that the piping bends round at right angles.

8 With wrong sides facing, place the backing panel on top of the piped case front. Pin and tack along the side and lower edges. Slip stitch the folded edges to the piping by hand. Do the same on the front for a secure finish.

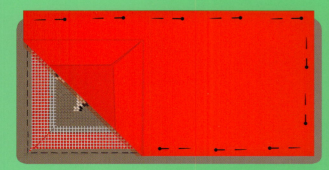

9 Open the zip fully so the pull lies at the closed end. Pin the left edge of the zip to the front of the case, lining up the tape so it sits just below the canvas. Tuck the ends into the case, then pin the right edge of the zip to the back in the same way. Tack, then slip stitch in place using matching sewing thread.

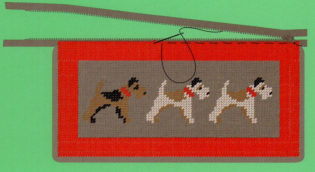

10 To make the lining cut two rectangles measuring 16cm high x 23cm wide from the remaining grey fabric. Pin and tack the two together along the side and lower edges. Machine stitch with a 6mm seam allowance. Press the seam allowance inwards. Press under a 3cm turning all round the top edge.

11 Slip the prepared lining inside the pencil case. Pin in place, matching the side seams and with the folded edge 6mm below the zip teeth. Slip stitch in place using matching sewing thread.

top tip THE 'INVISIBLE' ZIP IS DESIGNED SO THE TEETH LIE BEHIND THE TAPE AND CANNOT BE SEEN WHEN USED IN DRESSMAKING. IT LOOKS ESPECIALLY EFFECTIVE HERE AS THE DISCREET FINISH MATCHES THE PIPED EDGES, BUT AN ORDINARY ZIP WORKS JUST AS WELL.

Stripe Gadget Case

SKILL LEVEL: 1

Functional accessories don't always have to be utilitarian, as this sophisticated case proves. It's embroidered in tent stitch using six strands of thread, which gives a smooth, lustrous finish, and is backed with floral cotton. If you prefer a less pastel look, try using the colour scheme I picked for the Stripe Rug on pages 110–13.

MATERIALS

20 x 25cm 14-count canvas
masking tape
DMC stranded cotton embroidery
   thread in the following colours:
   beige (822); light green (927) –
   2 skeins each
   light blue (164); dark blue (3768);
   coral (893); lemon (677); pink
   (3326) – 1 skein each
fine tapestry needle
15 x 18cm lightweight iron-on wadding
15 x 18cm floral print backing fabric
18 x 24cm light blue lining fabric
dressmaker's pins
sewing needle
matching sewing thread

1 Bind the edges of the canvas with masking tape or mount in a small tapestry frame if you wish. Mark the starting point for the first row of stitches 7cm diagonally in from the top right corner.

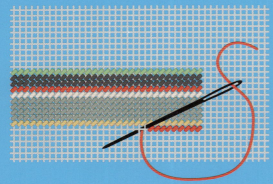

2 The design is worked in tent stitch throughout using all six strands of the embroidery thread. Following the chart on page 88, work each row of coloured stripes in turn.

3 Once the design is complete, remove the canvas from the frame and block if necessary. Trim the excess canvas down to a 1cm margin all round.

4 Position the iron-on wadding on the wrong side of the floral backing panel, adhesive side down. Iron it in place, following the manufacturer's instructions. Trim it down to the same size as the case front, adding a slight curve at each bottom corner.

5 Place the case front right side down on a clean folded tea towel and press back the margin around the side and lower edges. Press back a 2cm turning along the top edge. Fold back the bottom corners and press into gentle curves.

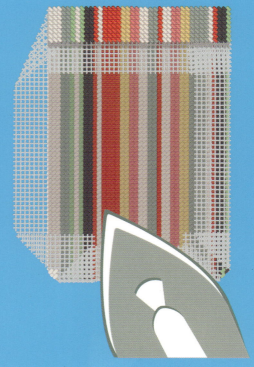

top tip THE BAG WAS DESIGNED TO FIT MY OWN SMARTPHONE. TO ADAPT THE SIZE FOR A LONGER OR NARROWER PHONE, OR YOUR MP3 PLAYER, SIMPLY INCREASE THE NUMBER OF STITCHES IN EACH ROW, OR REDUCE THE NUMBER OF ROWS YOU WORK.

beige (822)

light green (927)

light blue (164)

dark blue (3768)

coral (893)

lemon (677)

pink (3326)

Stripe
Gadget Case

6 Press back a 1cm turning around the side and lower edges of the backing panel and then a 2cm turning along the top edge. Use only the tip of your iron to press back the edges of the fabric; try to avoid ironing the wadding – or it will go flat! Tack the turnings down all round the backing panel, easing the fabric around the gently curved corners.

7 With wrong sides facing, place the backing panel on top of the case front and pin along the side and lower edges. Using a double length of matching sewing thread, neatly oversew these three sides together.

8 Press the lining panel in half lengthways. Trim it down to the correct size; the folded fabric should be exactly 2cm wider and 3cm deeper than the sewn case.

9 Machine stitch the side edges together, leaving a 2cm seam allowance. Press the resulting tube flat, so that the seam lies centrally on the uppermost side, then press the seam open.

10 Cut a small curve from each bottom corner, then machine stitch 1cm from the lower edge. Trim the seam allowance back to 4mm so the lining will fit neatly inside the case.

11 Press back a 1.5cm turning around the opening of the lining and tack it down.

12 Slip the prepared lining inside the case. With the seam at the centre back, pin and tack the lining in place. Oversew the edges of the lining and the case using a double length of matching sewing thread.

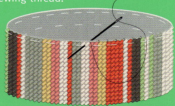

top tip YOUR PHONE SHOULD FIT SNUGLY INSIDE THE PADDED BAG, BUT FOR EXTRA SECURITY YOU CAN STITCH A BUTTON TO THE CENTRE FRONT, CLOSE TO THE OPENING AND INSERT A FASTENING LOOP OF FINE CORD OR ELASTIC INTO THE SEAM AT THE CENTRE BACK.

Electric Flower Specs Case

MATERIALS

20 x 30cm 14-count mono canvas
DMC stranded cotton embroidery
 thread in the following colours:
  red (349); green (469); yellow (733);
  pink (3805) – 1 skein each
  purple (915); lilac (3835) – 2 skeins each
  off-white (648) – 3 skeins
small tapestry needle
11.5 x 20.5cm green backing fabric
50cm square pink cotton lining fabric
90cm length fine piping cord
17 x 16cm iron-on lightweight wadding
sewing machine
matching sewing thread
sewing needle
dressmaker's pins

SKILL LEVEL: 3

There will be no more excuses for mislaid reading glasses if you keep them safe in this slip-in case. It's a return appearance for the Electric Flower print, this time re-worked in bright jewel colours. Like the Stripe Gadget Case, it's stitched on fine canvas with stranded embroidery thread to produce a silky, brocade-like surface.

1 Mark the centre of the canvas. Bind the edges of the canvas with masking tape or mount it in a tapestry frame if you wish. The design is worked in tent stitch throughout using all six strands of the embroidery thread. Following the chart on page 92, work the outlines of each flower, then add the coloured petals and centres and finally fill in the lilac background.

2 Once the design is complete, block the finished canvas if necessary. Trim the excess canvas back to a 2cm margin all round. Clip a small triangle from each corner – cut diagonally 5mm from the stitches. Press each corner in at a 45 degree angle, then press back the margin along each edge.

3 Prepare a 65cm length of pink piping. Follow the instructions given for covering piping cord in steps 3 to 5 of the Union Jack Cushion on pages 47 and 49.

4 Starting at the left bottom corner, slip stitch the piping around the edge of the case front. Work from the right side and position it so that the cord lies snugly against the edge of the stitching. Make a small cut into the pink fabric at each corner so that the piping bends round at right angles. Tuck both ends under the corner where they meet.

5 Press under, then unfold, a 2cm turning all round the green backing panel. Mitre the corners in exactly the same way as the case front. Check that the case front and the backing panel are the same size; adjust the turnings if necessary.

top tip TO MAKE A CASE TO FIT YOUR COOLEST SUNGLASSES, INCREASE THE
WIDTH BY ADAPTING THE COLOURS USED FOR THE CUSHION CHART ON PAGE 60.

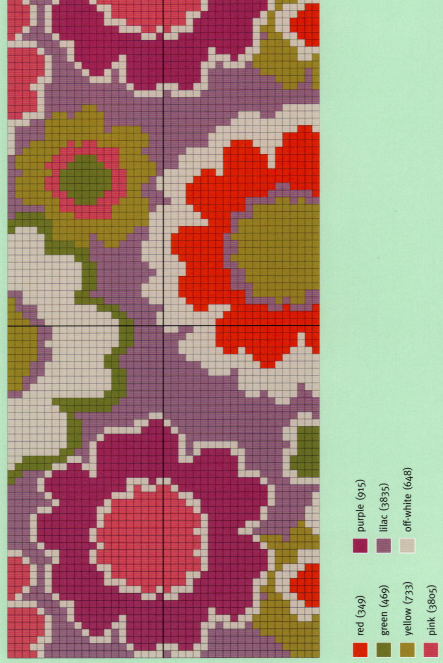

red (349)
green (469)
yellow (733)
pink (3805)

purple (915)
lilac (3835)
off-white (648)

Electric Flower Specs Case

6 Prepare a 10cm length of pink piping. Tack the piping along one short edge of the backing panel. Turn back the ends of the piping at an angle and stitch them down.

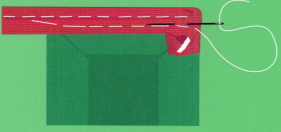

7 Working from the right side, slip stitch the piping to folded edge of the backing panel.

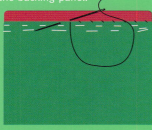

8 With right sides together, pin the backing to the front along the side and lower edges. Hand sew them together securely using a stabbing action, passing the needle from front to back just below the piping cord.

9 Cut a 17 x 18cm rectangle from the remaining pink fabric. Iron the wadding to the wrong side, matching the lower edges. Press back a 2cm turning along the top edge to cover the wadding.

10 Machine stitch the side edges together, leaving an 8mm seam allowance. Trim the seam allowance back to 5mm. Press the resulting tube flat, so that the seam lies centrally on the uppermost side, then press the seam open. Machine stitch the lower edge, leaving a 1cm seam allowance, then trim the seam allowance back to 5mm so the lining will fit neatly inside the case. Press back a 1.5cm turning around the opening of the lining and tack it down.

11 Slip the prepared lining inside the case, with the seam at the centre back. Using a ruler or a chunky knitting needle, push the corners of the lining right down inside the case. Pin and tack the case and the lining together around the opening so that the lining lies just below the piping cord, then stab stitch together.

top tip THE PROPORTIONS OF THIS CASE COULD ALSO BE ADAPTED
TO MAKE A FLORAL VERSION OF THE STRIPE GADGET CASE ON PAGE 86.

Motif Badges

MATERIALS

three 10cm squares 12-count canvas
masking tape
DMC stranded cotton embroidery
  thread in the following colours:
  light pink (151); light green (503);
  turquoise (598); yellow (676);
  mid-brown (841); dark beige (3033);
  dark pink (3731); red (3801);
  mid-green (3848); brown (3857);
  off-white (3865)
tapestry needle
iron
glue stick
sewing needle
canvas bag
thimble

SKILL LEVEL: 1

Embroidering a cushion cover is rewarding but it can take many hours. For the times when you'd prefer a more instant result I came up this fun set of three badges featuring Stanley, a posy of flowers and two luscious cherries. Stitch them in an afternoon to update a canvas bag, your denim jacket... or even a cushion!

1 Mark the centre of the canvas. Bind the edges of the canvas with masking tape. The designs are worked in tent stitch throughout using all six strands of the embroidery thread. Following the charts on page 96, work the central motif, next fill in the background, then finally sew the coloured border.

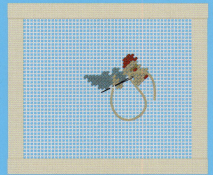

2 Once the design is complete, trim the canvas back to a 1cm margin all round.

3 Place the badge right side down on a clean folded tea towel. Press the corners inwards at a 45 degree angle with the tip of a warm iron. Press the sides of the canvas inwards, folding each one carefully along the edge of the stitching. The corners are now neatly mitred. Keep the turnings in place with a slick of glue.

4 Coat the back of the badge with a thin layer of glue, then position it on your bag. Using two strands of embroidery thread in the same colour as the badge's border, slip stitch the edges to secure it in place. You will need a thimble to protect your finger tip as you push the sewing needle through the thick canvas fabric.

top tip THESE LITTLE BADGES MAKE GREAT PRESENTS FOR FRIENDS AND FAMILY SO MAKE SURE YOU HAVE SOME SPARE CANVAS.

YOU CAN STITCH ALL THREE FROM ELEVEN SKEINS OF THREAD, AND THERE WILL BE PLENTY LEFT OVER FOR A SECOND AND EVEN A THIRD SET.

Motif Badges

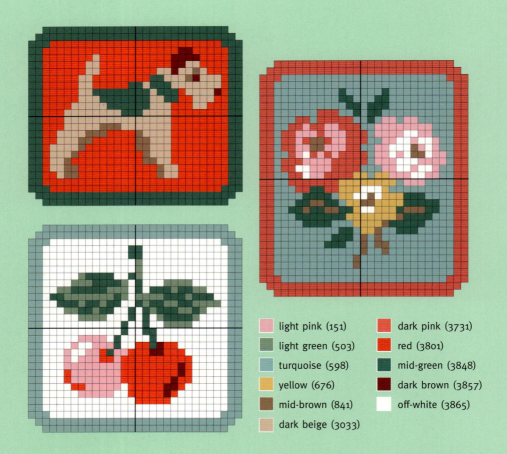

light pink (151)

light green (503)

turquoise (598)

yellow (676)

mid-brown (841)

dark beige (3033)

dark pink (3731)

red (3801)

mid-green (3848)

dark brown (3857)

off-white (3865)

top tip SELF-CONTAINED MOTIFS ARE VERSATILE AND CAN BE ADAPTED IN MANY WAYS. TRY WORKING THEM IN TAPESTRY WOOLS ON

10-COUNT CANVAS TO MAKE PINCUSHIONS, IN CROSS-STITCH FOR A GREETINGS CARD OR DIRECTLY ONTO A GARMENT USING SOLUBLE CANVAS.

Provence Rose Pincushion

MATERIALS

15 x 20cm 10-count canvas
DMC tapestry wool in of the following
  colours:
  white (blanc) – 2 skeins
  light green (7369) – 1 skein
  dark green (7386) – 1 skein
  light pink (7605) – 1 skein
  red (7666) – 1 skein
  light blue (7802) – 1 skein
  mid-pink (7804) – 1 skein
tapestry needle
10.5 x 13cm velvet for backing
small amount of polyester wadding
sewing needle
matching sewing thread

SKILL LEVEL: 1

One of the pleasures of needlework is collecting and making the various bits of equipment that you will need for your future creations. A well-stocked workbox should always hold a needle book, a tape measure, embroidery scissors, a selection of sewing threads, and – very importantly – a well-stuffed pincushion.

1 Mark the centre of the canvas. Bind the edges of the canvas with masking tape. The design is worked in either half cross or tent stitch throughout. Following the chart on page 100, work the central rose. Add the leaves and buds, then work the blue border at the top and bottom. Fill in the white background, not forgetting the dots within the blue border.

2 When the design is complete, block the finished canvas if necessary. Trim the excess canvas down to a 2cm margin all round.

3 Place the pincushion front right side down on a clean folded tea towel. Press the corners inwards at a 45 degree angle with the tip of a warm iron. Press the sides of the canvas inwards, folding each one carefully along the edge of the stitching. The corners are now neatly mitred.

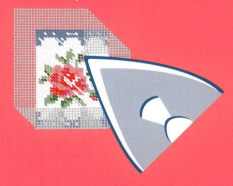

top tip THIS PROJECT IS TOO SMALL TO MOUNT IN A FRAME, SO SIMPLY
BIND THE EDGES OF THE CANVAS WITH MASKING TAPE BEFORE YOU START WORK.

Provence Rose Pincushion

4 Press back a 2cm turning along each edge of the backing panel. Check the size against the pincushion front – they should be exactly the same size, so adjust the turnings if not. Open them out again and press the four corners inwards, lining up the creases. Re-press the turnings and tack them down.

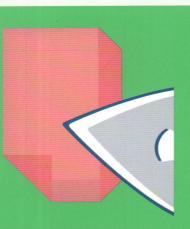

5 Hold the pincushion front and back together, with wrong sides facing. The two layers of fabric will be too thick to pin, so tack them close to the outside edges.

7 Stuff the cushion with the polyester wadding. Pack it down into the corners using the top of a pencil until it is really firm, then oversew the opening to close.

6 Sew the pincushion front to the back by hand. Make small overstitches, picking up one thread of canvas and a small amount of velvet each time. Leave a 4cm opening along one long edge.

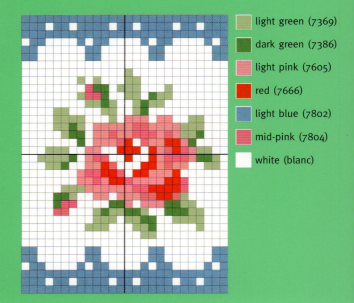

light green (7369)

dark green (7386)

light pink (7605)

red (7666)

light blue (7802)

mid-pink (7804)

white (blanc)

top tip ADD A SPOONFUL OF DRIED LAVENDER FLOWERS TO THE POLYESTER

WADDING: THEIR FRAGRANCE WILL BE RELEASED EACH TIME YOU INSERT A PIN.

100

Little Bunch Dungarees

MATERIALS

pair of denim dungarees
7cm square of soluble canvas
DMC stranded cotton embroidery
   thread – 1 skein in each of the
   following colours:
   blue (322)
   dark pink (602)
   light pink (819)
   brown (840)
   green (912)
   red (3801)
long-eyed embroidery needle
tacking thread

SKILL LEVEL: 1

Dungarees are immensely practical for all small children, but little girls may appreciate some extra embellishment! Soluble canvas enables you to embroider cross-stitch patterns directly onto fabrics like denim, which do not have an even weave, so adding this posy to the pocket is an easily accomplished task.

- ■ blue (322)
- ▨ dark pink (602)
- □ light pink (819)
- ▨ brown (840)
- ■ green (912)
- ■ red (3801)

1 Carefully unpick any labels or badges from the dungaree pocket. Tack the soluble canvas in place, positioning it centrally, 1cm down from the top edge. Work a couple of vertical stitches to indicate the centre of the canvas.

2 To save complicated counting, work the motif from the top downwards. The design is worked in cross stitch throughout using three strands of embroidery thread. Following the chart above, start with the two small leaves, which lie to either side of the centre point and 2cm down from the top edge of the pocket. Continue with the pink and red roses, then the blue flower, the remaining leaves and finally the stalks.

3 When the design is complete, trim away the surplus canvas. To dissolve the soluble canvas, carefully wash the dungarees in warm soapy water following the manufacturer's instructions. Rinse thoroughly, then allow to dry and iron as usual.

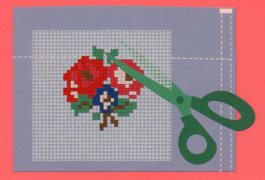

top tip YOU MIGHT FIND IT HELPS TO SLIP YOUR 'NON-SEWING' HAND INTO THE POCKET TO SUPPORT THE FABRIC WHILST YOU ARE SEWING, AND TO WORK THE MOTIF SIDEWAYS RATHER THAN THE CORRECT WAY UP.

Sprig Border Dress

SKILL LEVEL: 1

I was delighted to come across this tiny lace-trimmed petticoat in an antique market. It's hand stitched from the finest cotton lawn with a softly gathered frill at the hem. All it needed as the finishing touch – decades after it was first made – was a scattering of embroidered flowers across the yoke.

MATERIALS

5 x 15cm soluble canvas
DMC stranded cotton embroidery
thread – 1 skein in each of the
following colours:
ecru (ecru)
green (368)
lemon (445)
dark pink (892)
pink (894)
light blue (3753)
embroidery needle
tacking thread

	ecru (ecru)		lemon (445)		pink (894)
	green (368)		dark pink (892)		light blue (3753)

1 Fold the yoke of the dress in half to find the centre. Mark this point with a vertical tacking stitch.

2 Cut a 4 x 5cm piece of soluble canvas and tack it in place centrally on the yoke.

3 The design is worked in cross stitch throughout using two strands of embroidery thread. Following the chart above, work the pink flower of the centre motif, then the green leaves and the remaining flower details.

4 When the centre motif is complete, trim the surplus canvas to make room for the other motifs. Decide on the position of the next sprig, placing it a little higher if preferred to follow the curve of the neckline.

5 Cut a second piece of canvas and tack in place. Work the sprig as before. Repeat on the opposite side, so that each sprig is equidistant from the centre motif. Add the two tiny buds on the outside edges.

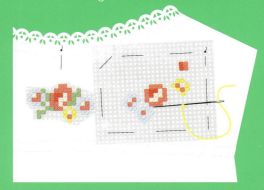

6 To dissolve the soluble canvas, carefully wash the dress in warm soapy water following the manufacturer's instructions. Rinse thoroughly, then allow to dry and iron as usual.

top tip WORK THESE VERSATILE LITTLE MOTIFS IN A CURVE AROUND A NECKLINE OR STITCH THEM SINGLY IN ROWS OR AT RANDOM ACROSS A WIDER AREA.

Lavender Hearts

MATERIALS

15cm square of 14-count cross-stitch
    fabric
DMC stranded cotton embroidery
thread in the following colours:
    ecru (ecru)
    mid-pink (603)
    brown (840)
    green (954)
    lilac (3042)
    dark pink (3804)
cross-stitch needle
10cm square of light-weight iron-on
    interfacing
15cm square of backing fabric
30cm narrow lace edging
tracing paper and pencil
matching sewing thread
dried lavender

SKILL LEVEL: 1

No book of needlework projects is ever complete without a lavender bag! This aromatic posy sachet is a great beginner's project, which introduces some basic hand-sewing skills. It requires only a small amount of thread and fabric, so you'll have enough materials left over to make a few more for your friends.

1 Fold the cross-stitch fabric lightly into quarters to mark the centre point. The design is worked in cross stitch throughout using two strands of embroidery thread.

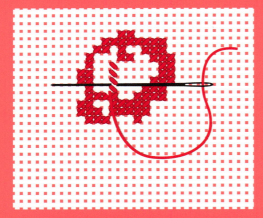

Following the chart on page 108, start with the flowers and work out to the leaves.

2 Trace or photocopy the heart template, and cut it out. Place the template on to the interfacing and draw around the outside edge with a sharp pencil. Cut along the outline.

3 Position the heart centrally over the back of the completed embroidery, with the adhesive side downwards. Following the manufacturer's guidelines, iron it in place. (This will prevent the lavender working through the holes in the fabric).

4 Now tack the template directly over the interfacing and trim the cross-stitch fabric down to an 8mm margin all round. Snip into the fabric at top of the heart.

top tip CROSS-STITCH FABRIC COMES IN A RANGE OF SUBTLE PASTEL COLOURS. THIS TIME I PICKED A SOFT SKY BLUE, BUT THE FLOWERS WOULD WORK EQUALLY WELL AGAINST A BACKGROUND OF PALEST GREEN, POWDER PINK, LEMON OR IVORY.

Lavender Hearts

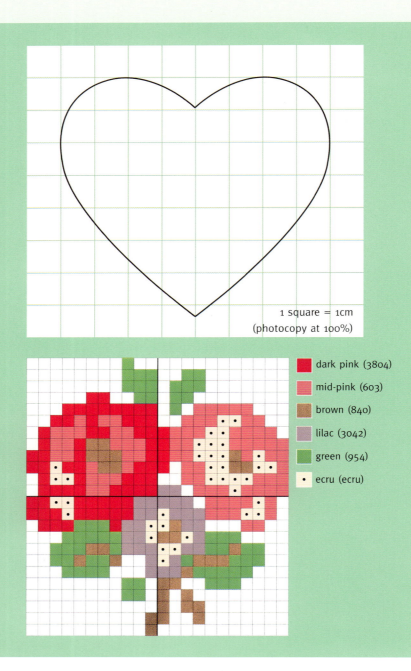

1 square = 1cm
(photocopy at 100%)

■ dark pink (3804)

■ mid-pink (603)

■ brown (840)

■ lilac (3042)

■ green (954)

· ecru (ecru)

5 Turn back the margin and tack it to the template, easing it round the curves. Press from the wrong side and remove the template.

6 Fold the lace in half to find the centre. Starting with this point tucked behind the tip of the heart, slip stitch the lace along the right edge of the heart. Tuck the loose end down between the two curves at the top and stitch in place. Sew the other edge in the same way.

9 Stitch together around the end, passing the needle from front to back and through the lace. Leave a 3cm opening along one edge.

10 Fill the bag with lavender, a teaspoon full at a time, pushing the dried buds right into the curves. Close the gap with neat slip stitches.

7 Tack the template to the backing fabric, then trim and tack the edges as you did before to make a neatened heart.

8 With wrong sides facing, pin and tack the front to the back.

top tip THIS LAVENDER BAG IS ALMOST TOO PRETTY TO HIDE AWAY BETWEEN YOUR LINENS, BUT YOU CAN EASILY TURN IT INTO A HANGING HEART. SEW A LENGTH OF RIBBON TO THE CENTRE TOP, TIE THE ENDS TO MAKE A LOOP AND SLIP IT OVER A HOOK OR DOOR HANDLE.

Stripe Rug

SKILL LEVEL: 2

This fabulous rug is a real showstopper! After the subtle stripes of the gadget case, I wanted to try something similar but on a much larger scale – so here it is. It's not the sort of project that you'll finish in a month: you'll come back to this rug again and again, and learn some interesting new textured stitches as you go.

MATERIALS

70 x 100cm 5-count rug canvas
masking tape
DMC tapestry wool in the following
  colours:
  ecru (7271) – 30 skeins
  mid-green (7384) – 10 skeins
  yellow (7422) – 6 skeins
  black (7538) – 5 skeins
  mid-blue (7592) – 20 skeins
  dark pink (7640) – 27 skeins
  light pink (7804) – 7 skeins
extra large tapestry needle
60 x 95cm linen or hessian for
  backing fabric
dressmaker's pins
quilting thread
large sewing needle

The chart on page 113 shows just one block of the repeating stripe design. Extend the length of the stripes and repeat the design as many times as necessary to cover your canvas. My rug measures approximately 50 x 92cm: I used the quantities of tapestry wool given above and repeated the block of stripes twice. You don't need to buy all the yarn at once, as any difference in the dye lots won't affect the finished appearance, so you can just get few skeins at a time and add in any extra wools you already have.

1 Bind the edges of the canvas with masking tape.

2 Thread a large tapestry needle with a 120cm length of dark blue yarn and knot the ends together so that you are working with a double thickness to cover the canvas completely. Start stitching about 13cm diagonally in from the bottom left corner, with the short edge of the canvas facing towards you.

3 The first row of stitches, represented by the first two rows of squares on the far right-hand side of the chart, consists of 46 double cross stitches. (Instructions for double cross stitch and all the other decorative stitches used to make this rug can be found on pages 18–19 at the front of this book). The second row, represented by a single line of squares, is a line of long-armed cross stitches (see page 18) worked with a double length of ecru yarn.

4 The third row, again represented by two rows of squares, is another row of double cross stitches, this time in dark pink.

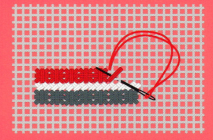

5 Work two rows of yellow cross stitch and another row of double cross stitch in dark pink. The next row, in sloping gobelin stitch (see page 19), is worked over two threads of the canvas using three lengths of ecru yarn. This is necessary to cover the canvas for sloping gobelin stitch only, so use three lengths each time.

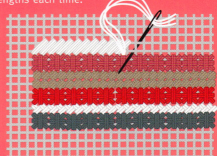

top tip WORK EACH STRIPE EITHER IN A SINGLE COLOUR OR, AS I DID, BLEND IN A FEW SKEINS OF DARKER OR LIGHTER SHADES LEFT OVER FROM OTHER PROJECTS TO GIVE THE STITCHES A RICHNESS AND DEPTH OF COLOUR: THE CLOSE-UP ON PAGES 114–15 SHOWS THIS IN DETAIL.

Stripe Rug

6 Continue following the chart to the end of the repeat, then start again with the first row of dark pink double cross stitch. You can copy the stitches I used as shown in the photograph on pages 114–15 or devise some variations of your own. As a guide, cross and long-armed cross stitches are worked over one canvas thread (one row of squares), double cross, sloping gobelin and plait stitches are worked over two canvas threads (two rows of squares), while a wider version of plait stitch is worked over three threads (three rows of squares).

7 Once the design is finally complete, block the canvas if necessary. Trim the excess canvas down to a 3cm margin all round. Press the corners in at 45 degress to mitre them, then press back the edges of the canvas.

8 Press a 5cm turning all round the backing fabric. To reduce bulk, mitre the corners neatly by pressing the corners inwards, lining up the creases. Trim the tips from each of the corner triangles and then re-press the creases.

9 With wrong sides together, pin the backing fabric to the canvas, making sure that it lies flat.

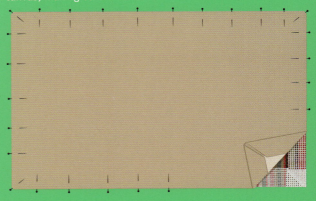

10 Stitch the canvas and backing fabric together by hand using a strong quilting thread. Work a round of slip stitches, each time taking up a single canvas thread and a few threads of the folded edge of the backing fabric.

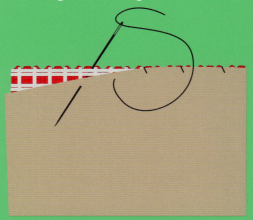

top tip SAFETY ALERT! ALWAYS PLACE A NON-SLIP UNDERLAY BENEATH YOUR RUG TO PREVENT IT SLIDING OVER A HARD SURFACE OR OUT OF PLACE ACROSS CARPETED FLOOR. AN ALTERNATIVE IS ANTI-SLIP SPRAY FINISH, WHICH IS APPLIED TO THE BACK OF THE FINISHED RUG.

ecru (7271)

mid-blue (7592)

mid-green (7384)

dark pink (7640)

yellow (7422)

light pink (7804)

black (7538)

Spot Doorstop

MATERIALS

1 standard UK house brick or
  30 x 50cm mount board or similar
  weight cardboard;
  roll of parcel tape;
  plastic pellet toy filling
50 x 100cm cotton or polyester wadding
matching sewing threads
sewing needle
40 x 50cm 10-count Penelope canvas
  in antique
tapestry frame
DMC tapestry wools in the following
  colours:
  pink (7804) – 3 skeins
  green (7911) – 14 skeins
tapestry needle
fine string
13 x 25cm pink cotton for base
iron
dressmaker's pins

SKILL LEVEL: 1

This practical doorstop is made from a humble house brick that has been transformed with a layer of padding and a vibrant needlepoint cover. The chart is designed to fit a standard UK brick, but if you don't have one to hand, you can make an alternative version from cardboard and fill it!

1 To make a 'brick' cut six pieces of card: two 6.5 x 21.5cm sides, two 10 x 6.5cm ends, and the 10 x 21.5cm lid and base. Fix the sides and ends to the base with parcel tape, then join the edges to make a box. Fill to just below the rim with the plastic pellet toy filling before adding the lid. Bind the completed 'brick' with two layers of parcel tape.

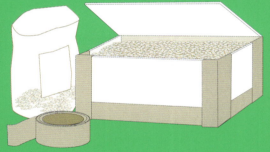

2 Wrap the wadding twice around the brick and tack down the short edge. Make four cuts into the overlap at each end, in line with the corners, so you have four flaps. Fold the lower one up and the side ones inwards. Tack down the side and bottom edges of the top flap.

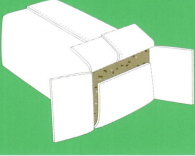

3 Mark the centre of the canvas. Bind the edges of the canvas with masking tape or mount it in a frame, if you wish.

4 The design is worked in a combination tent stitch and mosaic stitch. Following the chart on page 118, counting the squares on the chart carefully to make sure that the spots are spaced regularly, work the pink spots in tent stitch.

5 Fill in the background with mosaic stitch (see page 19) using the green yarn. This stitch consists of small squares made up of two short and one long diagonal stitch: keep the pattern consistent by working part stitches around the dots.

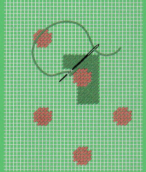

top tip TO GIVE YOUR DOORSTOP A BETTER GRIP ON THE FLOOR IN A CARPETED ROOM, ADD TWO 20CM LENGTHS OF VELCRO TO THE BASE. USE THE HOOKED SIDE AND FIX ONE STRIP TO EACH LONG EDGE OF THE BACKING BEFORE SEWING IT IN PLACE.

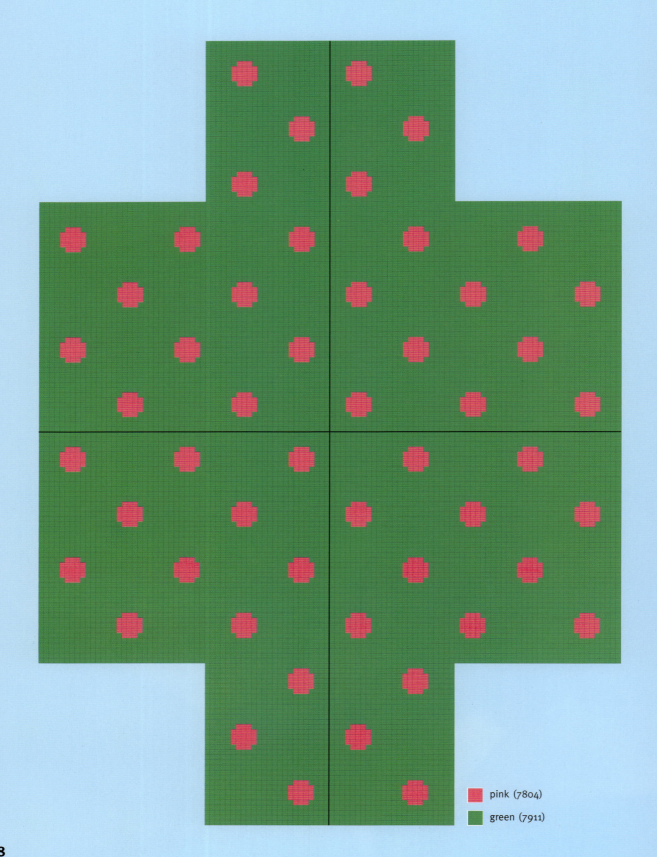

pink (7804)

green (7911)

6 When the design is complete, remove the canvas from the frame and block if necessary. Trim the excess canvas down to a 2cm margin all around the cross shape.

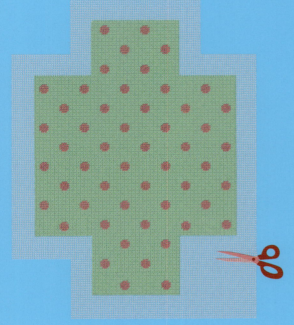

8 To create a tight, upholstered look, lace the cover in place. Thread the tapestry needle with fine string and work a series of long stitches between the two short ends. Draw them up so that the last two rows of mosaic stitch are pulled over the side to the base. Lace the two long ends together in exactly the same way.

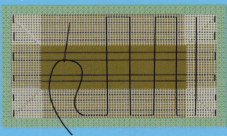

7 Turn under the canvas at one short edge, then take it across to meet the adjacent edge. Starting at the inside corner, slip stitch the two together using a double length of sewing thread. Sew to the end of the green stitching. Do the same on the other three corners and slip the cover over the brick.

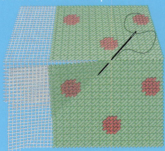

9 Press under a 2cm turning along each edge of the fabric for the base. Pin to the underside of the doorstop, making sure that it lies centrally. Sew in place by hand using small slip stitches worked in matching sewing thread.

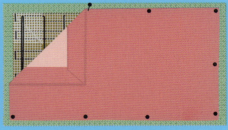

top tip I SOURCED A VIBRANT PINK COTTON FABRIC – THE PERFECT MATCH FOR THE SPOTS – TO COVER THE BASE OF THE DOORSTOP. ALTHOUGH FEW PEOPLE WILL LIFT IT UP AND LOOK UNDERNEATH, IT'S DETAILS LIKE THIS THAT GIVE YOUR WORK A UNIQUE FINISHING TOUCH.

Sail Boat Candleshade

MATERIALS

linen
11cm square soluble canvas
DMC stranded cotton embroidery
   thread – 1 skein in each of the
   following colours:
   white (blanc); green (320); dark blue
   (334); red (666); light blue (775);
   mid-blue (932); yellow (3822)
embroidery needle
length of ricrac equal to the bottom
   circumference of the shade plus 5cm
pencil
sewing machine
matching sewing thread

Cutting out the linen
length: Add 10cm to the bottom
   circumference of the shade
width: Add 5cm to the depth of
   the shade

SKILL LEVEL: 1

This jaunty cross-stitch yacht, surrounded by clouds, gulls and waves, gives a nautical look to a linen candleshade. Designed to slip over either a paper or metal base, this embroidered candleshade will flood your home with a flattering warm light. It almost goes without saying, but never leave a lighted candle unattended.

1 Fold the linen in half lengthways to mark the middle. Tack an 11cm square of soluble canvas centrally over this point, 2cm above the lower edge. Work two lines of tacking stitches diagonally across the canvas to make a large cross: this will give you a centre point from which to start stitching.

2 The design is worked in cross stitch throughout using two strands of the embroidery thread. Following the chart on page 123, and starting in the centre of the fabric, work the yacht's dark blue masts and then the two red and yellow sails.

3 Continue with the green boat, then the waves in mid and light blue. Finally stitch the clouds and pennant in light blue and the gulls in dark blue.

4 Machine stitch the two short edges of the linen together with a 1.5cm seam. Trim the seam allowance back to 5mm and carefully press the seam open. Press back a 1cm turning all round the lower edge.

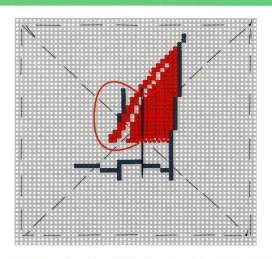

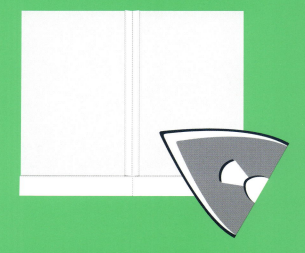

top tip MY SAIL BOAT WORKS VERY WELL AS A SINGLE MOTIF ON THIS SMALL SCALE, BUT IF YOU WISH TO COVER A TABLE LAMPSHADE, SIMPLY ENLARGE THE BACKGROUND FABRIC AND STITCH A WHOLE FLOTILLA OF YACHTS AROUND THE LOWER EDGE.

Sail Boat Candleshade

5 Starting at the back seam, slip stitch the ricrac to the wrong side of the lower edge. Position it so that a series of little scallops just peep out from below the edge, echoing the cross-stitch waves. Neaten the ends as shown on page 30.

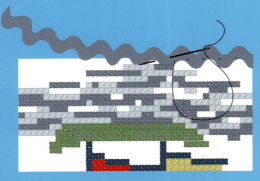

6 Press a 4cm hem all round the upper edge. With a sharp pencil, mark a light line all the way round, 2cm down from the fold. Thread a needle with a double length of sewing thread. Starting at the back seam, work a round of running stitches along the guideline. Work a second line of stitches, directly below the first. Leave both ends of the thread loose.

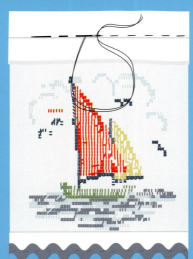

7 Draw the two loose threads up gently until the gathered linen snugly fits the top of the paper shade. Sew in both ends of the thread securely to finish.

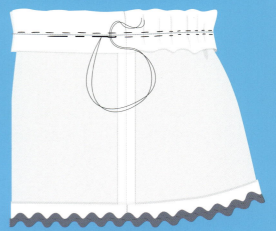

8 Turn the candleshade right side out and press lightly. Slip in place over the paper shade.

top tip FINISH OFF ALL YOUR THREADS NEATLY SO THAT NO STRAY SHADOWS SHOW THROUGH WHEN THE SHADE IS ILLUMINATED.

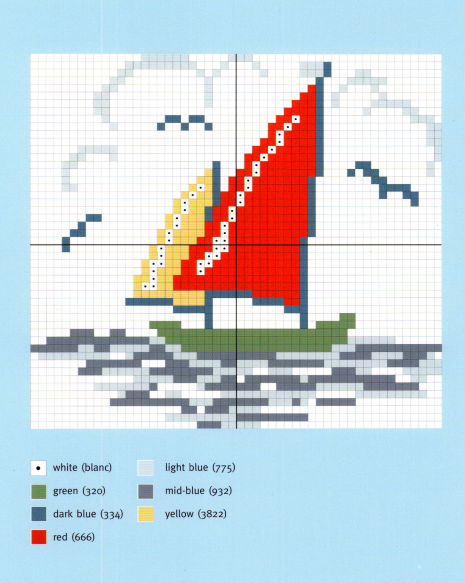

- ⊡ white (blanc)
- ⬛ green (320)
- ⬛ dark blue (334)
- 🟥 red (666)
- ⬜ light blue (775)
- ⬛ mid-blue (932)
- 🟨 yellow (3822)

Spot Tea Cosy

MATERIALS

35 x 90cm 11-count cross-stitch fabric in ecru

DMC stranded cotton embroidery thread – 1 skein in each of the following colours:

   lemon (165); pink (603); blue (813); green (954); coral (3705)

large cross-stitch needle

squared pattern paper or tracing paper

dressmaker's pins

sewing machine

matching sewing thread

sewing needle

30 x 80cm heavy-weight wadding

30 x 80cm lining fabric

75cm matching braid

15 x 8cm thin cardboard

pair of compasses and pencil

one 50g ball of coral cotton yarn

large tapestry needle

SKILL LEVEL: 1

The dotty design looks particularly cheerful in primary colours, so this generously sized cosy is guaranteed to brighten up your breakfast table or an afternoon tea tray. The spots are worked in all six strands of embroidery thread to create a raised appearance and the cosy is topped off with an easy-to-make pompon.

1 Cut the cross-stitch fabric in half lengthways to give two matching pieces measuring 35cm high x 45cm wide. The front and back of the tea cosy are made in exactly the same way.

2 Fold one piece of the cross-stitch fabric lightly into quarters to find the centre point. The design is worked in cross stitch throughout using all six strands of the embroidery thread. Work the cross stitches either in rows or individually, for a slightly plumper look. Following the chart on page 128, and starting in the centre of the fabric, work the central

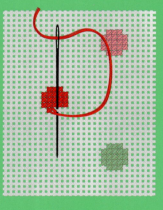

green spot. Continue to work the design outwards, carefully counting the squares between each coloured spot. Finish each spot off neatly so that no threads show through the fabric.

3 Copy the template on page 129 on to squared pattern paper. Pin the template centrally to the embroidered fabric so that the centre line runs through the middle row of spots and the bottom edge lies 3cm below the lowest spots. Cut out the front and back pieces in exactly the same way.

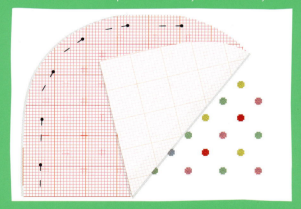

---

top tip TO SAVE TIME, YOU COULD USE A CO-ORDINATING FABRIC TO BACK THE TEA COSY.

REMEMBER TO HALVE YOUR QUANTITIES OF CROSS-STITCH AND BACKING FABRICS IF YOU DO.

Spot
Tea Cosy

4 With right sides facing, place the front on top of the back. Pin and tack the two together all round the curved edge, leaving the lower edge open. Stitch the edges together with a 1.5cm seam. Trim the seam allowance back to 5mm. Turn the tea cosy right side out and press lightly, using a cloth to protect the raised cross stitches. Press under a 1.5cm hem around the opening.

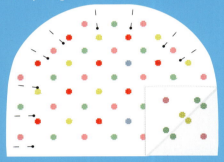

5 Using the template, cut two shapes from the wadding. Trim 2cm from the lower edge of both pieces. Pin the two together all round the curved edge. Stitch the edges together with a 2cm seam. Trim the seam allowance back to 5mm.

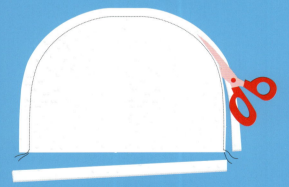

6 The final stage is to make the inner lining. Using the template, cut two shapes from the lining fabric. Pin the two together all round the curved edge. Stitch the edges together with a 2cm seam. Trim the seam allowance back to 5mm.

7 Press back a 2cm hem around the opening of the lining. Slip the lining inside the wadding. Tuck the lower edge of the wadding inside the hem and pin.

8 Slide the wadding and lining inside the main cosy, matching the side seams. Pin the lower edges together so that the lining sits 5mm above the lower edge of the main cosy. Stitch the lining to the cosy either by hand or by machine.

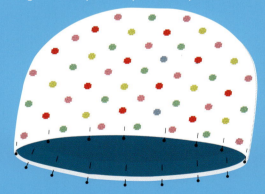

9 Sew the braid to the bottom edge of the cosy, so that the join lies along a seam line. Neaten the ends as shown on page 30.

top tip POLYESTER WADDING MAKES A GOOD LIGHTWEIGHT FILLING FOR THE COSY, BUT YOU COULD BE MORE ECO-CONSCIOUS AND RECYCLE AN OLD WOOLLY JUMPER OR BLANKET INSTEAD.

10 To make the foundation for the pompon, cut two 6cm discs of card, each with a 2cm hole in the centre. Thread a large tapestry needle with three or four lengths of yarn, about 80cm long. Hold the two discs together and pass the needle through the hole, across the back and down through the hole once again. Repeat until the card is covered evenly and the centre hole filled in. Add extra lengths of yarn as you go, leaving the loose ends on the outer edge of the disc.

11 Gently push the point of your scissors under a few layers of yarn at the outer edge and snip through them. Once you have done this, you will be able to slip one blade between the two cardboard discs. Cut through the strands of yarn, all the way round the discs. The discs will keep them together.

12 Cut a length of yarn and slide it between the two discs. Pull the ends up tightly and knot securely. Remove the discs, tearing them if necessary. Trim off the long yarn ends. Roll the pompon between the palms of your hands to give it a nice round shape. Sew the pompon securely to the top of the cosy as the perfect finishing touch.

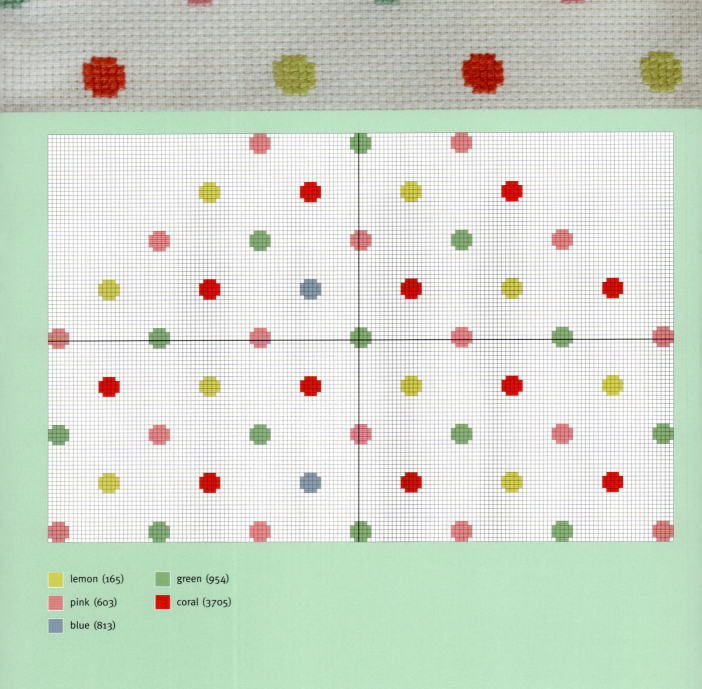

■ lemon (165)	■ green (954)
■ pink (603)	■ coral (3705)
■ blue (813)	

top tip A QUICK WAY TO REPRODUCE THE PATTERN TEMPLATE OPPOSITE IS TO PHOTOCOPY IT TWICE AT THE SAME TIME AS ENLARGING IT BY 125%, THEN CUT OUT THE TWO PIECES AND TAPE THEM TOGETHER ALONG THE CENTRE FOLD.

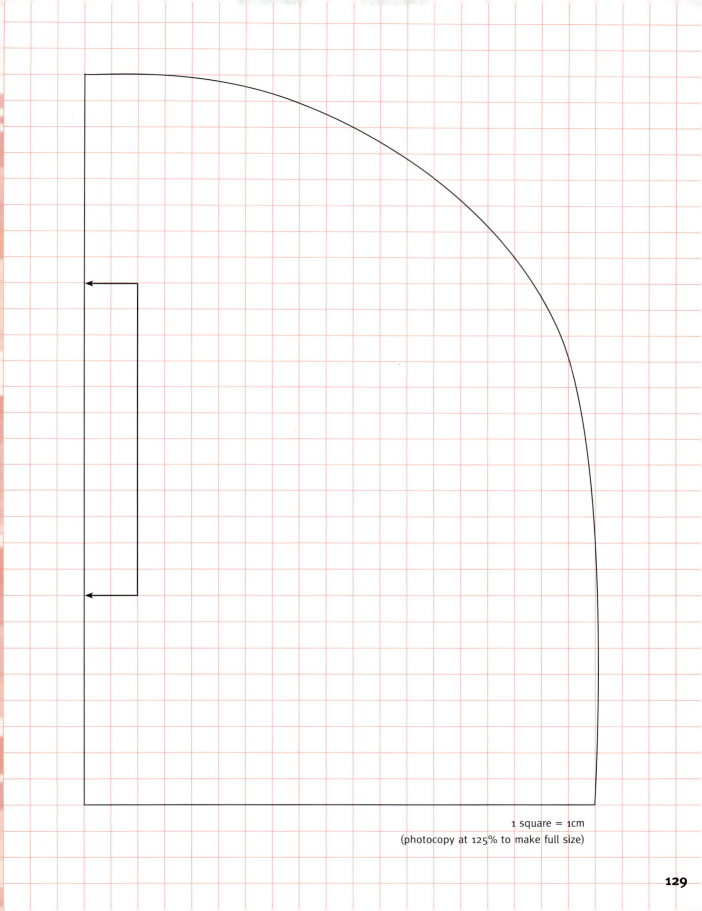

1 square = 1cm
(photocopy at 125% to make full size)

Cherry Border

MATERIALS

length of scalloped edging or hemmed
  fabric strip cut to length of shelf
  plus 5cm
soluble canvas
DMC stranded cotton embroidery
  thread – 1 skein in each of the
  following colours:
  ecru (ecru); light green (320);
  dark red (355); dark green (520);
  red (817); pink (962)
embroidery needle
tacking thread

SKILL LEVEL: 1

This vintage border was a lucky flea market find that just needed a bit of extra embellishment… and fortunately the delectable cross-stitch cherries fitted perfectly on to the embroidered scallops. I used simple metal upholstery tacks to fix the edging onto my shelf, spacing them evenly along the top edge.

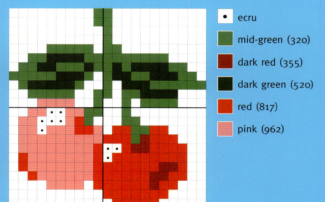

- • ecru
- mid-green (320)
- dark red (355)
- dark green (520)
- red (817)
- pink (962)

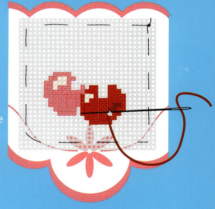

2 The design is worked in cross stitch throughout using two strands of embroidery thread. Following the chart, work the pink and red fruits, then the white highlights and the dark red lowlights. Add the stalks and leaves in two shades of green.

3 When the design is complete, trim away any excess soluble canvas. To dissolve the soluble canvas, carefully wash the border in warm soapy water following the manufacturer's instructions. Rinse thoroughly, then allow to dry. Once dry, press well, adding a little starch or fabric stiffener if you like. Press under the side edges and tack in place along your shelf.

1 For each cherry motif, cut a 5cm square of soluble canvas and tack it centrally to a scallop or along the width of the fabric. If using a ready-made edging, work the motifs in the centre of the scallops. On a plain fabric, measure 8cm evenly between each cherry motif.

top tip IF YOU AREN'T LUCKY ENOUGH TO FIND A SIMILAR SCALLOPED EDGING,

THESE CHERRIES LOOK JUST AS TASTY STITCHED ON TO A NARROW BAND OF PLAIN LINEN.

Bouquet Seat Cover

MATERIALS

60cm square 10-count canvas

tapestry frame

DMC tapestry wools in the following colours:

pale green (7322) – approx 24 skeins, depending on size of seat; mid-pink (7135); off-white (7141); sage green (7392) – 3 skeins each dark blue (7306); light sage (7331); brown (7938) – 1 skein each mustard yellow (7473); dark pink (7640) – 2 skeins each

tapestry needle

large sheet of paper or newspaper

pencil

tapestry needle

scissors

heavy-duty staple gun or small hammer and a box of 13mm tacks

SKILL LEVEL: 3

When you think of traditional needlepoint, a chair seat is one of the first projects that comes to mind... and quite rightly so. It is a valued investment of your time and skill, which will be enjoyed for many years. Start off with a single chair and one day you might end up with a matching set of six around your dining table!

1 To make the template, lift the seat out of the chair and place it on a large sheet of paper. Draw around the outline to give you the actual shape of the chair seat; to allow for the depth of the seat, draw a second line 3mm away from the first. If the seat is deeply padded, you may need to make this margin a little wider.

2 Cut out the template and position it centrally on the canvas. Draw all round the edge of the template on to the canvas to give the outline for your stitching.

3 The design is worked in half-cross stitch throughout. Mark the centre of the canvas. Following the chart on page 134, starting from the centre of the canvas, work the three large roses. Continue to work the design outwards with the smaller flowers, leaves and buds. Fill in the background using the pale green yarn, stitching as far as the pencil line.

top tip | RE-PAINTED MY CHAIR WITH TWO COATS OF LUSTROUS GLOSS PAINT, WHICH WAS SPECIALLY MIXED TO THE SAME SHADE AS THE BRIGHTEST PINK YARN.

■ pale green (7322)	■ sage green (7392)	■ brown (7938)
■ mid-pink (7135)	■ dark blue (7306)	■ mustard yellow (7473)
■ off-white (7141)	■ light sage (7331)	■ dark pink (7640)

Bouquet
Seat Cover

4 When the design is complete, block the work if necessary. Trim the excess canvas down to a 4cm margin all round. With right sides facing, fold the canvas in half lengthways and mark the centre along each margin. Fold in half widthways and do the same.

5 Turn the chair seat upside down. Mark the centre of the top and bottom edges and rule a line between the two. Measure and mark the centre of this line and draw a line across the seat at this point.

6 Place the canvas on the floor with the right side facing downwards. Position the chair seat on top, so that the pencil lines match up on each side.

7 Fold the canvas margin along the bottom edge so that 5–10mm of the stitching lies at the back. Line up the pencil marks, then hammer a tack through the canvas and into the seat. If you prefer, use a staple gun.

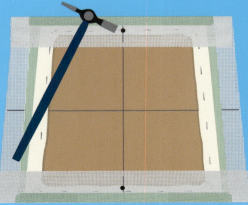

8 Fold back the canvas at the top, pulling it gently and tack it down. Do the same with the side edges, again pulling the canvas gently to maintain the tension.

9 Turn in the corners at 45 degree angles and tack down the canvas. Make sure that the pencil marks remain aligned.

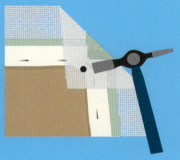

10 Fold over the canvas to one side of the corner and tack down, pulling it gently. Fix down the other side, taking care avoid the previous tack or staple.

11 Continue adding tacks at 3cm intervals in the spaces between the existing tacks. Try not to pull the canvas too tightly or the edges of the seat will become uneven, but keep an even tension all the way across.

12 For a professionally neat finish, cut a piece of calico using the paper template as a guide. Press under a 3cm turning all the way round and tack or staple to the base of the seat to cover the canvas.

13 Drop the seat back in the chair when you have finished.

top tip DO TAKE CARE WHEN HAMMERING IN TACKS OR USING STAPLES,

AS THEY ARE VERY SMALL, VERY SHARP AND VERY CLOSE TO YOUR FINGERTIPS!

Cowboy Seat Cushion

SKILL LEVEL: 2

My cowboy print is a perennial favourite with both children and their parents, so the exuberant Wild West horse and rider motif was a natural choice for this needlepoint kid's cushion. The finished size is 29cm wide and 31cm deep: for a smaller chair you could use a 12-count canvas to reduce the size of the design.

MATERIALS

50cm square 10-count canvas
DMC tapestry wool in the following colours:
  red (7758) – approx 18 skeins, depending on size of seat;
  blue (7029); mid-green (7384); mid-brown (7415); beige (7509); dark brown (7515) – 2 skeins each
  dark cream (7141); light green (7772) – 1 skein each
sheet of paper and pencil
adhesive tape
40cm square backing fabric
40 x 80cm calico
polyester cushion filling
pair of brown shoelaces
sewing machine
dressmaker's pins

1 Start by making a template to fit your chair. Tape a piece of paper to the seat, at front and back, then fold it down over the edges. Draw over the crease and cut along this line. Fold the paper in half widthways and trim as necessary to make sure it is symmetrical. Double check the finished template against the seat just to be sure!

2 Fold the template in half lengthways to find the centre point. Pin the template to canvas, ensuring that it lies squarely on the weave. Draw round the outline with a pencil, then mark the middle.

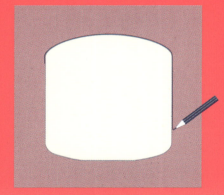

3 The design is worked in half cross stitch throughout. Following the chart on page 138, work the central cowboy. The cowboy's leg is a good starting point, next work the rest of him, followed by the horse. Count the spaces carefully to position the cactuses, lasso, clouds and other details correctly.

4 Fill in the red background, working as far as the pencil line in each direction.

5 Once the design is complete, block the canvas if necessary. Trim the excess canvas down to a 2cm margin (the seam allowance) all round the design.

top tip I COULDN'T RESIST ADDING A PAIR OF OLD-FASHIONED SHOELACES TO SECURE THE CUSHION TO THE CHAIR, INSTEAD OF CONVENTIONAL FABRIC TIES.

red (7758)

beige (7509)

blue (7029)

dark brown (7515)

mid-green (7384)

dark cream (7141)

mid-brown (7415)

light green (7772)

Cowboy Seat Cushion

6 Pin the cushion front, right sides facing, to the backing panel. Cut along the outside edge of the canvas so that both pieces are the same size. Machine stitch the two together, leaving a 15cm opening along the top edge.

7 Press back the seam allowance (including the parts that run along the opening) at front and back. Ease it gently around the corners using a small burst of steam from the iron to set the curve. Turn the cushion right side out through the opening.

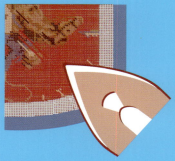

8 Make a specially shaped filling pad for the cushion, following the directions on page 28. Use the paper template as your guide, and add an extra 1cm all round when cutting out the two pieces of calico.

9 Insert the pad through the opening at the top edge. Pin the two sides of the opening together and hand stitch to close.

10 Place the finished cushion on the chair seat and mark the two points where it touches the back struts with pins. Fold one of the shoelaces in half and make an overhand knot at the centre. Stitch this knot securely to one of the marked points, then add the other lace in the same way.

11 Sew your braid to the cushion by hand with matching sewing thread. Use small slip stitches and line the bottom edge up along the seam line as you go. Gather the braid slightly at the corners and finish off the ends as shown on page 30. Here you will also find instructions for machine stitching the braid to the cushion.

top tip THE CUSHION IS BACKED WITH A BLUE FURNISHING WEIGHT COTTON: SALVAGED DENIM FROM AN OLD PAIR OF JEANS WOULD BE A GOOD ALTERNATIVE.

House Picture

MATERIALS

35cm square 14-count cross-stitch fabric
in oatmeal
DMC stranded cotton embroidery thread
in the following colours:
red (309) – 2 skeins
off-white (543); green (562);
shell pink (758); blue (826);
coral (3705); mid-pink (3731);
brown (3858) – 1 skein each
cross-stitch needle
20cm square mount board
picture frame with 20cm square opening
strong sewing thread
sewing needle

SKILL LEVEL: 2

Home Sweet Home! This appealing little house is reminiscent of traditional samplers, but the bright red roof and spotty curtains at the windows give it an unmistakably contemporary look. It is worked on unbleached cross-stitch fabric, which adds colour to the wall – and saves a lot of extra sewing!

1 Mark the centre of the cross-stitch fabric and mount it in a frame. The design is worked in cross stitch throughout using two strands of the embroidery thread. Following the chart on page 143, and starting in the centre of the fabric, first work the brown outline of the door and portico, the step, studs and door handle.

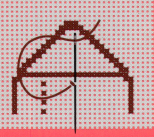

2 Using the coral thread, stitch the letterbox within the door, then fill in the triangle within the portico and the stitches between the steps and the path. Using the blue thread, fill in the door, working carefully around the brown stitches.

3 Count outwards from the door to find the correct position for the frames and sills of the two downstairs windows, which are worked in brown. Add the stitches for the glazing bars. Work the flower petals in coral and shell pink, then the leaves in green. Work the both dots of the curtains and the window panes in off-white.

4 Using mid-pink thread, work the curtains and the centres of the flowers, again, stitching carefully around the dots and the plants so that you don't split the thread.

5 Count upwards from the downstairs windows to find the correct position for the upstairs windows. Work in the same way as the downstairs windows.

6 Count upwards from the top windows and stitch the brown edging to the roof. Then work the roof in dark red – this may take some time! – and the narrow triangles of sky in blue. Finish off by sewing the red flowers in the bushes at the front and then the green bushes themselves.

top tip REMEMBER TO KEEP ALL YOUR STITCHES IN THE SAME DIRECTION WHEN WORKING LARGE EXPANSES OF CROSS STITCH LIKE THE ROOF.

House
Picture

7 When the design is complete, remove the finished piece from the frame and press lightly from the wrong side. Trim the fabric down to a 3cm margin all round.

8 The best way to mount your completed embroidery is to stitch it over a piece of board. Draw two centre lines across the back of the mount board to divide it into equal quarters. Lay the finished picture face downwards on a flat surface and position the mount board centrally on the back, so that the tacking lines match up with the pencil marks.

9 Thread a needle with a long length of strong thread. Fold the edges of the fabric inwards. Fasten the thread the centre point of one edge of the fabric, then make a long stitch across the card to the opposite edge. Continue lacing outwards, as far as the edge of the mount board, then lace from the centre to the other side.

10 Check that the sides are parallel by making sure that the lines of holes in the cross-stitch fabric lie along the edges of the board: adjust the lacing if not. Lace the other two sides in the same way. Finally fix your mounted picture in the frame.

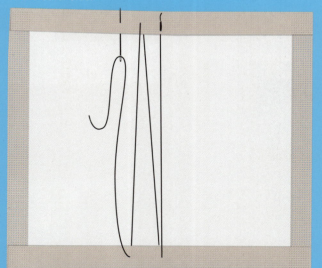

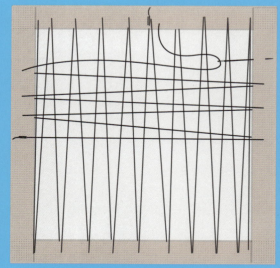

top tip THE MOUNTING BOARD SHOULD BE THE SAME COLOUR AS THE CROSS STITCH FABRIC TO PREVENT ANY COLOUR SHOWING THROUGH THE HOLES.

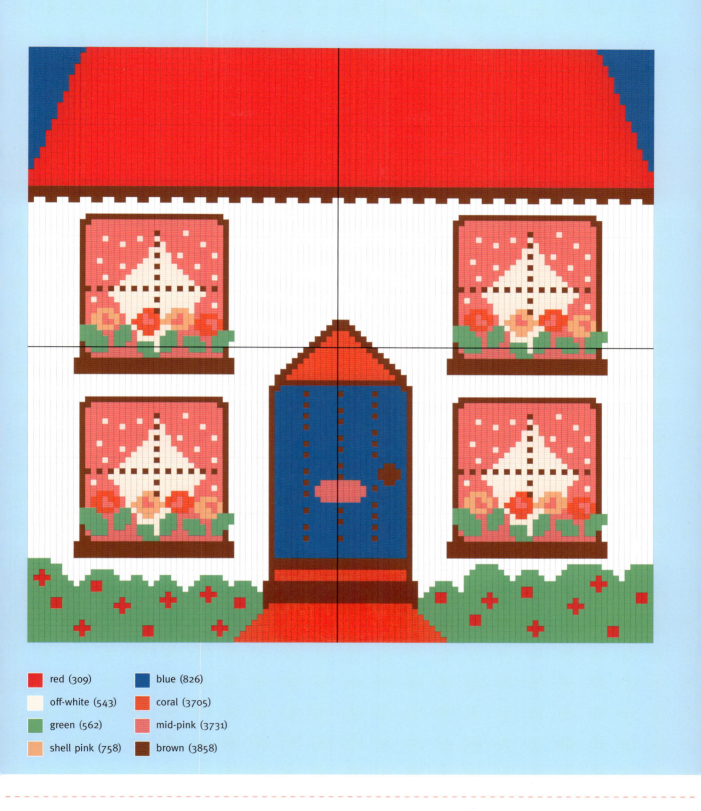

red (309)

blue (826)

off-white (543)

coral (3705)

green (562)

mid-pink (3731)

shell pink (758)

brown (3858)

Cowboy Picture

MATERIALS

embroidery frame
40 x 45cm 11-count cross-stitch fabric
  in ecru
DMC stranded cotton embroidery
  thread in the following colours:
  red (321); blue (334); dark brown (838);
  light brown (841); dark green (986);
  light green (3364); mid-brown (3772)
  – 2 skeins each
  off-white (3866) – 1 skein
small tapestry needle
graph paper and pencil
picture frame
mount board, cut to fit aperture in frame
sewing needle
strong thread

SKILL LEVEL: 2

Generations of children learnt to sew by working fine cross-stitch samplers, complete with an improving motto. Nowadays samplers are usually made to commemorate a birth or other family event: you'll find an alphabet overleaf so that you can personalise your own version of this timeless cowboy picture.

1 Mark the centre of the cross-stitch fabric and mount it in a frame. The design is worked in cross stitch throughout using all six strands of the embroidery thread, which gives the stitches a raised appearance. Following the chart on page 146, and starting in the centre of the fabric, work the cowboy's leg in blue.

2 Stitching outwards, work the cowboy and horse. Counting carefully, work the lasso, clouds, buildings and cactuses.

3 Draw up your monogram and date on graph paper, leaving a one-square gap between the characters and adding a single stitch as a full-stop after any initials. Fold the paper in half to find the centre: this corresponds with the marks on the fabric. Embroider the letters and numbers either side of this point.

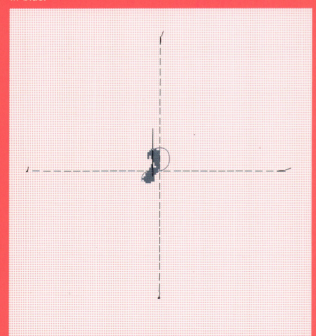

top tip IF YOU WANT TO INCLUDE A COMPLETE NAME OR A SHORT MESSAGE, ADD AN EXTRA 10CM OR MORE TO THE DEPTH OF THE FABRIC.

🟥 red (321)	🟩 dark green (986)	🟫 light brown (841)	🟧 mid-brown (3772)
🟦 blue (334)	🟥 dark brown (838)	🟩 light green (3364)	⬜ off-white (3866)

Cowboy Picture

4 When the design is complete, remove the finished piece from the frame and press lightly from the wrong side. Trim the fabric down to a 3cm margin all round.

5 Draw two centre lines across the back of the mount board to divide it into equal quarters. Lay the finished picture face downwards on a flat surface and position the mount board centrally on the back, so that the tacking lines match up with the pencil marks.

6 Thread a needle with a long length of strong thread. Fold the edges of the fabric inwards. Fasten the thread the centre point of one edge of the fabric, then make a long stitch across the card to the opposite edge. Continue lacing outwards, as far as the edge of the mount board, then lace from the centre to the other side.

7 Check that the sides are parallel by making sure that the lines of holes in the cross-stitch fabric lie along the edges of the board: adjust the lacing if not. Lace the other two sides in the same way. Finally fix your mounted picture in the frame.

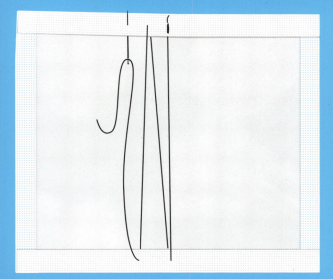

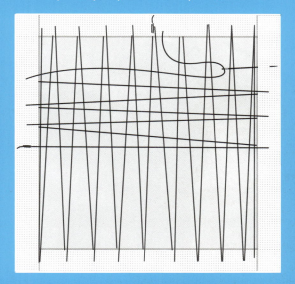

top tip IF YOU'D PREFER A COLOURED BACKGROUND, LIKE THE NEEDLEPOINT COWBOY ON PAGE 137,

USE A RED CROSS-STITCH FABRIC AND CHANGE HIS SHIRT TO A BLUE DENIM SHADE.

Glossary of Terms

Like other crafts, sewing, needlepoint and cross stitch have their own particular technical vocabulary so you may come across a few unfamiliar words. Here are the most common terms, many of which are explained further in the introductory pages.

Aida cloth The threads of this easy-to-use cross stitch fabric are woven in square blocks, separated by holes. This creates a grid pattern that is easy to follow when you are counting the stitches.

Bargello Also known as Byzantine Work, a geometric needlepoint technique worked in upright stitches on mono canvas, following a coloured chart.

Bias grain This is found by drawing a line at a 45 degree angle to the selvedge, or straight woven edge, of the fabric. Because it lies across the straight lengthwise and crosswise grain, a fabric strip cut along the cross, or bias grain, will have a lot of stretch or 'give'.

Blocking Needlepoint stitches can often pull the canvas weave out of shape: this describes the process of restoring the stitched canvas to its original square or rectangle.

Calico Unbleached cotton calico fabric is useful for making cushion pads.

Canvas Available in three types – mono, interlock and duo – and in a range of sizes, this foundation fabric is used for all needlepoint.

Count Count (or mesh) refers to the number of holes per inch, in needlepoint and cross stitch fabrics, which determines size of the stitches. The higher the count the smaller the stitches will be.

Cushion pad Fill your completed cushion cover with a cotton covered pad. These come in various shapes and sizes, filled with polyester or feathers. Hypoallergenic fibres are also available.

Embroidery hoop A lightweight frame for cross stitch, made up of two wooden rings, between which the fabric is held under tension.

Envelope backing A simple way to back a cushion, made up of two overlapping panels. You can add buttons and buttonholes if you wish.

Evenweave Fabric woven from warp and weft threads of similar dimensions.

Grain Fabric consists of two sets of interwoven threads, which go from top to bottom (the warp) and from side to side (the weft). The warp grain runs the length of a piece of fabric, from the top to bottom. Always cut fabric along the grain.

Gusset A narrow piece of fabric used to reinforce or to give depth to a cushion.

Hem A fabric edge that is turned under to the wrong side and stitched in place.

Interfacing Available in sew-in and iron-on versions, this is a soft non-woven fabric used to give strength and body to a light-weight material.

Lengthways As in 'fold lengthways': fold parallel to the longer edge of a piece of fabric.

Linen A natural fabric, woven from flax threads. Vintage linen sheets can be re-used as cushion backings and have wonderfully soft textures.

Masking tape A flexible, easily removed adhesive paper tape used by decorators. Use 2.5cm wide tape to bind the rough edges of needlepoint canvas and to stop it fraying.

Pattern paper Produced in large sheets, printed with a grid of inches or centimetres, this paper is used for drawing up full-size pattern pieces.

Piping cord A fine, loosely twisted cotton 'rope' available in different thicknesses. It is covered with a bias strip of fabric to make piping.

Glossary of Terms

Plush/pile Velvet and carpet both have a pile – a soft surface made up of many short cut threads. The pile causes the colour of the fabric to vary from different angles, so if you are using two pieces of velvet, always make sure the pile lies in the same direction for both.

Ply A ply is an individual strand of thread. There are six plies in embroidery thread, which can be used together or separated out and regrouped for finer stitches. Tapestry wool is made up of four loosely twisted plies that are worked together.

Press seam open Use the tip of the iron to separate the two seam allowances, and press along the seam line so that one seam allowance lies on each side of the stitches.

Rug canvas With a count of just 5 stitches, this is the largest scale canvas available and is used for needlepoint mats.

Scroll frame An adjustable four-sided frame with rotating top and bottom struts, useful for working larger projects.

Seam The line along which two fabric edges are stitched together.

Seam allowance The distance between the cut edge of the fabric and the line of stitching.

Selvedge The woven edges of a fabric. The grain of the fabric lies parallel to the selvedge.

Size A stiffening agent, used to make canvas fibres rigid.

Slip stitch This creates an unobtrusive seam, made by stitching alternately through the edges of two pieces of fabric, either along an opening or a hem.

Soluble canvas A temporary canvas for working counted cross stitch on non-evenweave fabrics.

Stab stitch This is made by passing the needle through the fabric at right angles, making tiny stitches which appear as small dots on the surface. Use it to sew through thick layers.

Stretcher frame A rigid wooden frame on to which canvas or cross stitch fabric is pinned to maintain tension. The frame is the same size as the fabric.

Tacking Also called basting, these are easily-unpicked stitches about 1.5cm long, used to hold two fabric edges together before seaming. Use tacking to mark the centre of your background fabric.

Tapestry needles Blunt, round ended needles with large eyes, which pass easily through the holes in canvas or cross stitch fabric.

Tapestry yarn A soft 4-ply wool used for needlepoint, which is available in a wide spectrum of colours.

Tension Canvas and cross stitch fabric should be stretched tight, or kept under tension, in a frame for the best results. The term also refers to the degree of tightness in the stitches and varies according to how the yarn or thread is pulled – always keep an even tension when stitching.

Ticking A strong, striped cotton fabric with a diagonal weave that is used for pillow pads and mattress covers. Look out for vintage ticking, in unique striped designs.

Turn through The process of turning a finished item right sides out, through an opening in one of the seams. Ease the seams out and push the corners into points with a blunt pencil.

Wadding Also called batting, this is a thick, non-woven cotton or polyester fabric used to give depth and thickness. It is used pad bags and quilts.

Widthways Fold in half widthways: fold parallel to the shorter side of the fabric.

Colour Conversions

Each tapestry yarn or embroidery thread manufacturer has their own palette of colours, and use different dyes to produce each shade. This means that the alternative numbers given below are equivalents rather than exact matches. I recommend using yarn or thread from only one manufacturer for each project, rather than mixing threads from more than one source. Also, remember to check the meterage of the skeins. In this book, the number of skeins given in the materials list for each project is based on a skein containing 8m of yarn or thread.

Bargello Cushion (pages 34–37)

tapestry yarn	DMC	ANCHOR
white	blanc	8002
yellow	7049	8092 or 8112
red	7106	8212 or 8214
pink	7202	8412
green	7386	9006 or 9020
fawn	7411	–
blue	7802	8788 or 8818

Spot Cushion (pages 38–41)

tapestry yarn	DMC	ANCHOR
red	7106	8212 or 8214
off-white	7510	9052
blue	7555	–

Provence Rose Pillow (pages 42–45)

embroidery thread	DMC	ANCHOR	MADEIRA
mid-green	562	205	1213
light green	564	219	1211
light blue	747	158	1104
light pink	963	73	502

coral	3705	28	214
light coral	3706	27	303
light cream	3865	2	2403

Union Jack Cushion (pages 46–49)

tapestry yarn	DMC	ANCHOR
dark red	7108	8218 or 8442
mid-pink	7223	8506
beige	7230	9674
green	7391	8048 or 9332
yellow	7455	9524
grey-blue	7705	8720 or 9766
dark pink	7758	8400

Spray Flower Cushion (pages 50–53)

embroidery thread	DMC	ANCHOR	MADEIRA
light pink	604	50	613
light gold	676	942	2013
light green	772	259	2205
ecru	842	388	2109
mid-pink	899	27	414
green	992	1070	1110
dark pink	3350	896	604
turquoise	3766	161	1106
brown	3857	1050	2008

House Cushions (pages 54–57)

tapestry yarn	DMC	ANCHOR
ecru	ecru	8004, 8006, 8032 or 8292
pink	7004	8394 or 8432
pinky-red	7106	8212 or 8214
dark cream	7141	9482
dark blue	7306	8792
mid-green	7386	9006 or 9020
yellow	7472	8018
dark green	7541	–

dark red	7544	8216
brown	7622	9796
red	7666	8200
light green	7771	9096, 9098 or 9164
mid-blue	7802	8788 or 8818

Electric Flower Cushion (pages 58–61)

tapestry yarn	DMC	ANCHOR
mid-pink	7135	–
dark pink	7136	–
dark blue	7287	–
green	7406	9078
yellow	7470	8016
off-white	7510	9052
light blue	7594	8734 or 8832

Bargello Hippie Bag (pages 62–65)

tapestry yarn	DMC	ANCHOR
light blue	7294	8834
orange	7303	–
off-white	7331	9056 or 9064
dark blue	7336	8794
yellow	7485	8024, 8044 or 8102
brown	7515	9662
green	7541	–

Spray Clutch Bag (pages 66–69)

tapestry yarn	DMC	ANCHOR
mid-pink	7195	8368
light pink	7221	8504
dark blue	7296	–
light green	7376	9174, 9176 or 9262
dark green	7396	–
dark cream	7411	–

Colour Conversions

dark brown	7432	9624
gold	7494	9404, 9424 or 9426
dark pink	7758	8400
teal green	7927	–

Sail Boat Beach Bag (pages 70–73)

embroidery thread	DMC	ANCHOR	MADEIRA
dark red	498	1005	2502
red	817	39	507
blue-green	926	235	1703
dark blue-green	930	922	1707

Bouquet Knitting Bag (pages 74–77)

embroidery thread	DMC	ANCHOR	MADEIRA
lime green	166	279	1308
olive green	830	889	2112
red	891	35	214
pink	956	33	409
light orange	977	363	2307
brown	3031	905	1904
pale green	3348	254	1501
beige	3782	388	1906

Union Jack Purse (pages 78–81)

tapestry yarn	DMC	ANCHOR
yellow	7504	8020
off-white	7510	9052
dark pink	7603	8454 or 8456
light pink	7605	–
red	7666	8200
blue	7802	8788 or 8818
green	7911	8988 or 9118

Stanley Pencil Case (pages 82–85)

tapestry yarn	DMC	ANCHOR
beige	7520	–
tan	7525	–
black	7624	9768 or 9798
grey	7626	9764
red	7666	8200

Stripe Gadget Case (pages 86–89)

embroidery thread	DMC	ANCHOR	MADEIRA
light blue	164	1042	1210
lemon	677	300	2207
beige	822	1011	1908
coral	893	27	303
light green	927	849	1701
pink	3326	36	2605
dark blue	3768	400	1704

Electric Flower Specs Case (pages 90–93)

embroidery thread	DMC	ANCHOR	MADEIRA
red	349	35	410
green	469	681	1602
off-white	648	900	1709
yellow	733	280	2111
purple	915	65	706
pink	3805	38	413
lilac	3835	99	1808

Motif Badges (pages 94–97)

embroidery thread	DMC	ANCHOR	MADEIRA
light pink	151	73	502
light green	503	875	2604
turquoise	598	1092	1101
yellow	676	942	2013
mid-brown	841	378	1906

dark beige	3033	880	1907
dark pink	3731	1024	610
red	3801	35	410
mid-green	3848	189	1108
brown	3857	1050	2008
off-white	3865	2	2403

Provence Rose Pincushion (pages 98–101)

tapestry yarn	DMC	ANCHOR
white	blanc	8002
light green	7369	9016
dark green	7386	9006 or 9020
light pink	7605	–
red	7666	8200
light blue	7802	8788 or 8818
mid-pink	7804	8452

Little Bunch Dungarees (pages 102–103)

embroidery thread	DMC	ANCHOR	MADEIRA
blue	322	131	1004
dark pink	602	41	506
light pink	819	271	2314
brown	840	393	1913
green	912	205	1212
red	3801	35	410

Sprig Border Dress (pages 104–105)

embroidery thread	DMC	ANCHOR	MADEIRA
ecru	ecru	2	2101
green	368	241	1307
lemon	445	802	2207
dark pink	892	28	214
pink	894	36	504
light blue	3753	1037	2504

Lavender Hearts (pages 106–109)

embroidery thread	DMC	ANCHOR	MADEIRA
ecru	ecru	2	2101
mid-pink	603	62	414
brown	840	393	1913
green	954	203	1201
lilac	3042	676	807
dark pink	3804	54	611

Stripe Rug (pages 110–115)

tapestry yarn	DMC	ANCHOR
ecru	7271	–
mid-green	7384	–
yellow	7422	–
black	7538	–
mid-blue	7592	8836
dark pink	7640	–
light pink	7804	8452

Spot Doorstop (pages 116–119)

tapestry yarn	DMC	ANCHOR
pink	7804	8452
green	7911	8988 or 9118

Sail Boat Candleshade (pages 120–123)

embroidery thread	DMC	ANCHOR	MADEIRA
white	blanc	1037	2504
green	320	215	1212
dark blue	334	977	910
red	666	1098	411
light blue	775	158	1104
mid-blue	932	1033	1710
yellow	3822	288	110

Spot Tea Cosy (pages 124–129)

embroidery thread	DMC	ANCHOR	MADEIRA
lemon	165	293	103
pink	603	62	414
blue	813	140	909
green	954	203	1201
coral	3705	28	214

Cherry Border (pages 130–131)

embroidery thread	DMC	ANCHOR	MADEIRA
ecru	ecru	2	2101
light green	320	215	1212
dark red	355	884	2304
dark green	520	862	1514
red	817	39	507
pink	962	27	414

Bouquet Seat Cover (pages 132–135)

tapestry yarn	DMC	ANCHOR
mid-pink	7135	–
off-white	7141	9482
dark blue	7306	8792
light green	7322	8874 or 8894
grey	7331	9056 or 9064
green	7392	–
yellow	7473	8042
dark pink	7640	–
brown	7938	–

Cowboy Seat Cushion (pages 136–139)

tapestry yarn	DMC	ANCHOR
blue	7029	–
dark cream	7141	9482
mid-green	7384	–

mid-brown	7415	9368 or 9392	
beige	7509	9654 or 9656	
dark brown	7515	9662	
red	7758	8400	
light green	7772	9172	

House Picture (pages 140–143)

embroidery thread	DMC	ANCHOR	MADEIRA
red	309	42	507
off-white	543	933	305
green	562	205	1213
shell pink	758	336	2313
blue	826	176	910
coral	3705	28	214
mid-pink	3731	1024	610
brown	3858	936	2311

Cowboy Picture (pages 144–147)

embroidery thread	DMC	ANCHOR	MADEIRA
red	321	42	507
blue	334	977	910
dark brown	838	905	1904
light brown	841	378	1906
dark green	986	878	1514
light green	3364	859	1401
mid-brown	3772	679	402
off-white	3866	2	2403

Useful Addresses

Needlecraft shops

Burford Needlecraft
150 High Street
Burford
Oxfordshire OX18 4QU
01993 822 136
www.needlework.co.uk

Cross Stitch Centre
16 Fenkle Street
Alnwick
Northumberland NE66 1HR
01670 511 241
www.cross-stitch-centre.co.uk

Sew and So
Unit 8a
Chalford Industrial Estate
Chalford
Stroud
Gloucestershire GL6 8NT
01453 889 988
www.sewandso.co.uk

The Needlecraft Shop
225 Mellis Road
Thornham Parva
Eye
Suffolk IP23 8ET
01379 679 486
www.theneedlecraftshop.co.uk

Haberdasheries and fabric shops

Bedecked
5 Castle Street
Hay-on-Wye
Hereford HR3 5DF
01497 822769
www.bedecked.co.uk

The Bramble Patch
West Street
Weedon
Northamptonshire NN7 4QU
01327 342212
www.thebramblepatch.co.uk

Christie Bears
2 Mill Barn
Mill Road
Boverton
Llantwit Major
South Glamorgan CF61 1UB
01446 790 090
www.christiebears.com

Cloth House
47 Berwick Street
London W1F 8SJ
020 7437 5155 and
98 Berwick Street
London W1F 0JQ
020 7287 1555
www.clothhouse.net

Coast & Country Crafts & Quilts
Barras Moor Farm
Perranarworthal, Truro
Cornwall TR3 7PE
01872 870478
www.coastandcountrycrafts.co.uk

The Cotton Patch
1283–1285 Stratford Road
Hall Green
Birmingham B28 9AJ
0121 7022840
www.cottonpatch.net

Creative Quilting
32 Bridge Road
Hampton Court Village
East Molesey
Surrey KT8 9HA
020 8941 7075
www.creativequilting.co.uk

Deckchair Stripes
Unit 4 Waverton Business Park
Waverton
Chester CH3 7PD
01244 336 387
www.deckchairstripes.com

Design-a-Cushions
74 Drum Brae South
Edinburgh EH12 8TH
0131 539 0080
www.design-a-cushions.co.uk

Harts of Hertford
113 Fore Street
Hertford SG14 1AS
01992 558106
www.hartsofhertford.co.uk

The Fat Quarters
5 Chopwell Road
Blackhall Mill
Newcastle Upon Tyne NE17 7TN
01207 565728
www.thefatquarters.co.uk

John Lewis
300 Oxford Street
London W1A 1EX
and branches nationwide
08456 049049
www.johnlewis.com

MacCulloch & Wallis
25–26 Dering Street
London W1S 1AT
020 7629 0311
www.macculloch-wallis.co.uk

The Makery Emporium
16 Northumberland Place
Bath
Avon BA1 5AR
01225 487708
www.themakeryonline.co.uk

Mandors
134 Renfrew Street
Glasgow G3 6ST
0141 332 7716
www.mandors.co.uk

Merrick & Day
Redbourne Road
Redbourne
Lincolnshire DN21 4TG
01652 648 814
www.merrick-day.com

Millie Moon
24–25 Catherine Hill
Frome
Somerset BA11 1BY
01373 464650
www.milliemoonshop.co.uk

Our Patterned Hand
49 Broadway Market
London E8 4PH
020 7812 9912
www.ourpatternedhand.co.uk

Patch – Fabric and Haberdashery
9 Bevan Street East
Lowestoft
Suffolk NR32 2AA
01502 588778
www.patchfabrics.co.uk

Patchwork Direct
Wesleyan House
Dale Road
Darley Dale
Derbyshire DE4 2HX
01629 734100
www.patchworkdirect.com

Patchwork Garden
630 Abbeydale Road
Sheffield
South Yorkshire S7 2BA
0114 258 3763
www.patchworkgarden-shop.co.uk

Peabees Patchwork Bazaar
1 Hare Street
Sheerness
Kent ME12 1AH
01795 669 963

Pelenna Patchworks
5 Bevans Terrace
Pontrhydyfen
Port Talbot
West Glamorgan SA12 9TR
01639 898444
www.pelennapatchworks.co.uk

Useful
Addresses

Quilter's Haven
68 High Street
Wickham Market
Woodbridge
Suffolk IP13 0QU
01728 746275
www.quilters-haven.co.uk

Rags
19 Chapel Walk
Crowngate Shopping Centre
Worcester WR1 3LD
01905 612330

Sew and So's
14 Upper Olland Street
Bungay
Suffolk NR35 1BG
01986 896147
www.sewsos.co.uk

Tikki
293 Sandycombe Road
Kew
Surrey TW9 3LU
020 8948 8462
www.tikkilondon.com

Needlepoint Classes

All Stitched Up
Errington House
Humshaugh
Hexham
Northumberland NE46 4HP
01434 672 389
www.needle-point.co.uk

Royal School of Needlework
020 3166 6938
www.royal-needlework.org.uk

Tapisserie
54 Walton Street
London SW3 1RB
020 7581 2715
www.tapisserie.co.uk

Sewing Classes

Heatherlea Design
01332 661562
www.heatherleadesign.com

Just Between Friends
44 Station Way
Buckhurst Hill
Essex IG9 6LN
020 8502 9191
www.justbetweenfriends.co.uk

Liberty Sewing School
Regent Street
London W1B 5AH
020 7734 1234
www.liberty.co.uk

The Makery
146 Walcott Street
Bath BA1 5BL
01225 421 175
www.themakeryonline.co.uk

Modern Approach Sewing School
Astra Business Centre
Roman Way
Ribbleton
Preston PR2 5AP
07910 740120
www.sewjanetmoville.co.uk

The Papered Parlour
7 Prescott Place
London SW4 6BS
020 7627 8703
www.thepaperedparlour.co.uk

Sew Over It
78 Landor Road
Clapham North
London SW9 9PH
020 7326 0376
www.sewoverit.co.uk

Sue Hazell Sewing Tuition
Southcombe House
Chipping Norton
Oxfordshire OX7 5QH
01608 644877
www.sewing-tuition.co.uk

The Studio London
Studio 1 & 5
Trinity Buoy Wharf
64 Orchard Place
London E14 0JW
020 7987 2421

The Thrifty Stitcher
Unit 21
4–6 Shelford Place
Stoke Newington
London N16 9HS
07779 255087
www.thethriftystitcher.co.uk

A few handy websites:

DMC Creative World
www.dmccreative.co.uk
For stockists of DMC stranded cotton
and tapestry wool.

Elliot Anti-Slip
www.antislip.biz
Anti-slip underlay, tape and spray
to prevent rugs slipping on tiled or
wooden floors.

Etsy
www.etsy.com
An online marketplace for everything
handmade and vintage, including
fabric and other sewing supplies.

Ribbon Moon
www.ribbonmoon.co.uk
For ricrac and bias binding in a
wide range of colours and widths.

Cath Kidston Stores

Aberdeen
Unit GS20, Union Square Centre,
Guild Square, Aberdeen AB11 5PN
01224 591 726

Bath
3 Broad Street, Milsom Place, Bath BA1 5LJ
01225 331 006

Belfast
24–26 Arthur Street, Belfast BT1 4GF
02890 231 581

Bicester Village Outlet Store
Unit 43a, Bicester Village,
Bicester OX26 6WD
01869 247 358

Birmingham – Selfridges
Upper Mall, East Bullring,
Birmingham B5 4BP
0121 600 6967

Bluewater
Unit L003, Rose Gallery,
Bluewater Shopping Centre DA9 9SH
01322 387 454

Bournemouth
5–6 The Arcade, Old Christchurch Road,
Bournemouth BH1 2AF
01202 553 848

Brighton
31a & 32 East Street, Brighton BN1 1HL
01273 227 420

Bristol
79 Park Street, Clifton, Bristol BS1 5PF
0117 930 4722

Cambridge
31–33 Market Hill, Cambridge CB2 3NU
01223 351 810

Canterbury
6 The Parade, Canterbury CT1 2JL
01227 455 639

Cardiff
45 The Hayes, St David's, Cardiff CF10 1GA
02920 225 627

Cheltenham
21 The Promenade, Cheltenham GL50 1LE
01242 245 912

Chichester
24 South Street, Chichester PO19 1EL
01243 850 100

Dublin
Unit CSD 1.3, Dundrum Shopping Centre,
Dublin 16
00 353 1 296 4430

Edinburgh
58 George Street, Edinburgh EH2 2LR
0131 220 1509

Exeter
6 Princesshay, Exeter EX1 1GE
01392 227 835

Glasgow
18 Gordon Street, Glasgow G1 3PB
0141 248 2773

Guildford
14–18 Chertsey Street, Guildford GU1 4HD
01483 564 798

Gunwharf Quays Outlet Store
Gunwharf Quays, Portsmouth PO1 3TU
02392 832 982

Harrogate
2–6 James Street, Harrogate HG1 1RF
01423 531 481

Heathrow Terminal 4
Departure Lounge,
Heathrow Airport TW6 3XA
020 8759 5578

Jersey
11 King Street, St Helier, Jersey JE2 4WF
01534 726 768

Kildare Village Outlet Store
Unit 21c, Kildare Village, Nurney Road,
Kildare Town
00 353 45 535 084

Kingston
10 Thames Street,
Kingston upon Thames KT1 1PE
020 8546 6760

Leeds
26 Lands Lane, Leeds LS1 6LB
0113 391 2692

Liverpool
Compton House, 18 School Lane,
Liverpool L1 3BT
0151 709 2747

London – Battersea
142 Northcote Road,
London SW11 6RD
020 7228 6571

London – Chiswick
125 Chiswick High Road, London W4 2ED
020 8995 8052

London – Covent Garden
28–32 Shelton Street, London WC2H 9JE
020 7836 4803

London – Fulham
668 Fulham Road, London SW6 5RX
020 7731 6531

London – Kings Road
322 Kings Road, London SW3 5UH
020 7351 7335

London – Marylebone
51 Marylebone High Street, London W1U 5HW
020 7935 6555

London – Notting Hill
158 Portobello Road, London W11 2BE
020 7727 0043

London – Selfridges
Oxford Street, London W1A 1AB
020 7318 3312

London – Sloane Square
27 Kings Road, London SW3 4RP
020 7259 9847

London – St Pancras
St Pancras International Station,
London NW1 2QP
020 7837 4125

London – Wimbledon Village
3 High Street, Wimbledon SW19 5DX
020 8944 1001

Manchester
62 King Street, Manchester M2 4ND
0161 834 7936

Manchester – Selfridges
1 Exchange Street, Manchester M3 1BD
0161 629 1184

Marlborough
142–142a High Street, Marlborough SN8 1HN
01672 512 514

Marlow
6 Market Square, Marlow SL7 1DA
01628 484 443

Newcastle – Fenwicks
Northumberland Street,
Newcastle Upon Tyne NE99 1AR
0191 232 5100

Oxford
6 Broad Street, Oxford OX1 3AJ
01865 791 576

Reading
96 Broad Street, Reading RG1 2AP
01189 588 530

St Albans
Unit 4, Christopher Place,
St Albans AL3 5DQ
01727 810 432

St Ives
67 Fore Street, St Ives TR26 1HE
01736 798 001

Tunbridge Wells
59–61 High Street, Tunbridge Wells TN1 1XU
01892 521 197

Winchester
46 High Street, Winchester SO23 9BT
01962 870 620

Windsor
24 High Street, Windsor SL4 1LH
01753 830 591

York
32 Stonegate, York YO1 8AS
01904 733 653

For up-to-date information on all Cath Kidston
stores, please visit www.cathkidston.co.uk

Acknowledgements

Many thanks to Lucinda Ganderton and her team of lady stitchers: Karen Belton, Shirley Cross, Jane Fowler, Lis Gunner, Alison Hadfield, Sandra Hubbard, Phyllis Johnson, Sheila Meen, Lynda Potter, Jen Russell and Janice Spooner for making all of the projects; and to Pia Tryde, Elaine Ashton, Laura Mackay, Elisabeth Lester and Caroline Bell. Thanks also to Helen Lewis, Lisa Pendreigh, Katherine Case and Bridget Bodoano at Quadrille Publishing.

Cath Kidston

Series Creative Coordinator: Elaine Ashton
Design Assistant to Cath Kidston:
Laura Mackay
Stitching Coordinator and Consultant:
Lucinda Ganderton
Stitching Assistants: Karen Belton,
Shirley Cross, Jane Fowler, Lis Gunner,
Alison Hadfield, Sandra Hubbard,
Phyllis Johnson, Sheila Meen, Lynda
Potter, Jen Russell, Janice Spooner

Editorial Director: Anne Furniss
Art Director: Helen Lewis
Project Editor: Lisa Pendreigh
Designer: Katherine Case
Photographer: Pia Tryde
Illustrator: Bridget Bodoano
Production Director: Vincent Smith
Production Controller: Aysun Hughes

If you have any comments or queries regarding the instructions in this book, please contact us at enquiries@quadrille.co.uk.

This edition first published in 2012 by
Quadrille Publishing Limited
Alhambra House
27–31 Charing Cross Road
London WC2H 0LS
www.quadrille.co.uk

Projects, templates and text copyright © Cath Kidston 2010
Photography © Pia Tryde 2010
Design and layout copyright © Quadrille Publishing Limited 2010

Cataloguing-in-Publication Data: a catalogue record for this book is available from the British Library.

ISBN 978 184949 205 8

Printed in China